I0795830

IMAGES
of America

BYRNES DOWNS

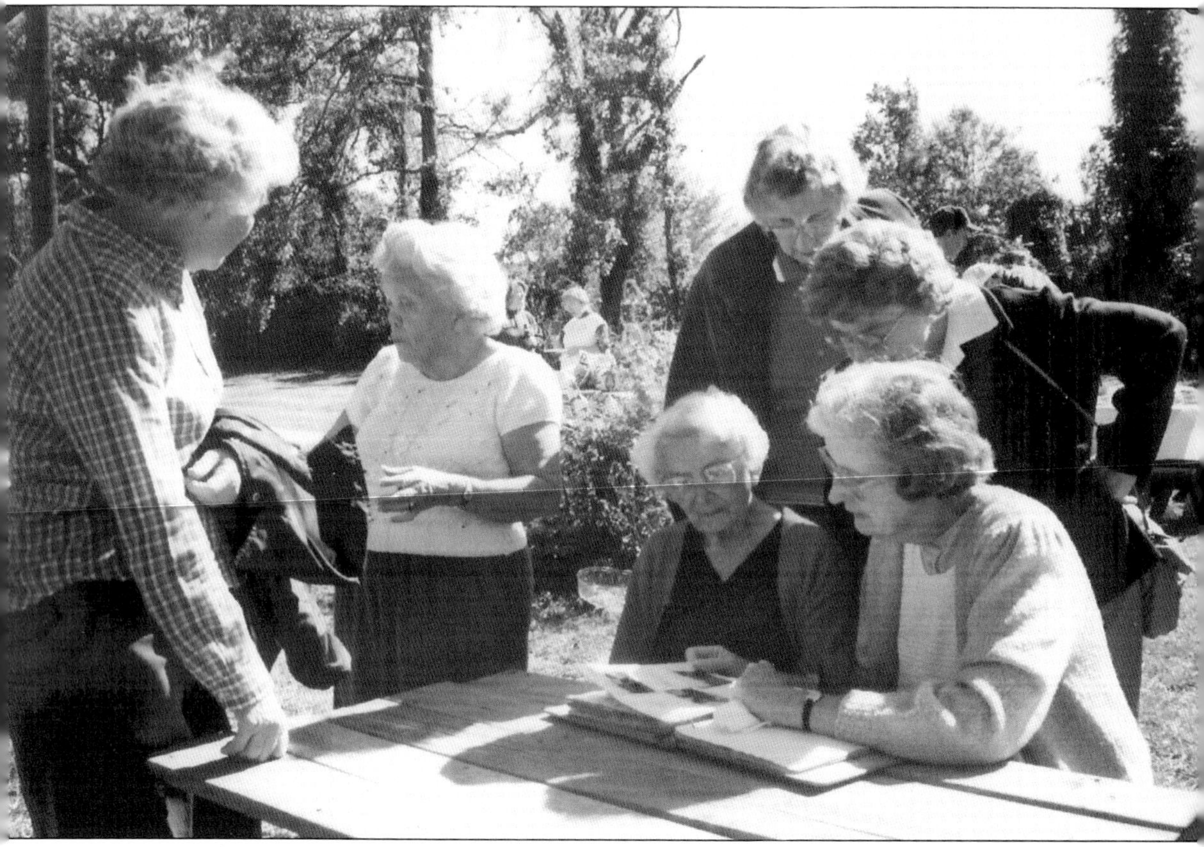

In November 1995, Byrnes Downs held a 50th birthday celebration on the West Ashley Greenway. Margaret Thorne Seidler, who inherited the *History Byrnes Downs Garden Club* from her grandmother Mrs. Thomas J. Thorne Sr. (Anne), loaned it to the neighborhood for the party. Anne lived in Byrnes Downs and had served as temporary chairman for the organizational meeting in January 1948. Several ladies are enjoying *History Byrnes Downs Garden Club,* by May T. Rossiter. Annie Shier (standing, left) and Dorothy Steenken (standing, third from the left) are sisters and longtime residents. Their parents, Henry and Sophie Steenken, purchased 3 Colleton Drive in 1945.

On the Cover: In January 1948, fifteen ladies who were residents of Byrnes Downs met at 7 Craven Avenue, the home of Mrs. W. H. Mikell Jr., to discuss the formation of a Garden Club. Beautification of this new neighborhood was their primary mission. The boys of the neighborhood were organized into "The Little Helpers Club," which assisted in beautification projects and keeping the neighborhood clean. Herbert Koger uses a hoe to level the turf at the sidewalk. From left to right, Jerry Quinn, Sam Diggle, and Charles Bennett clear debris from the brick entrance column. The Strobel family owned the home at the corner of Campbell Drive and Savannah Highway pictured in the background. This photograph illustrated a *News and Courier* article titled "Byrnes Downs Garden Club Ends Year of Usefulness to Community." When Byrnes Downs celebrated its 50th birthday with a party on the West Ashley Greenway, both Charles Bennett and Jerry Quinn came to help the neighborhood celebrate. (Reproduced with permission from the *Post and Courier*, by staff photographer Holcombe.)

IMAGES
of America

BYRNES DOWNS

Donna F. Jacobs

ARCADIA
PUBLISHING

ISBN 978-0-7385-5430-3

Published by Arcadia Publishing
Charleston, South Carolina

Printed in the United States of America

Library of Congress Catalog Card Number: 2008923473

For all general information contact Arcadia Publishing at:
Telephone 843-853-2070
Fax 843-853-0044
E-mail sales@arcadiapublishing.com
For customer service and orders:
Toll-Free 1-888-313-2665

Visit us on the Internet at www.arcadiapublishing.com

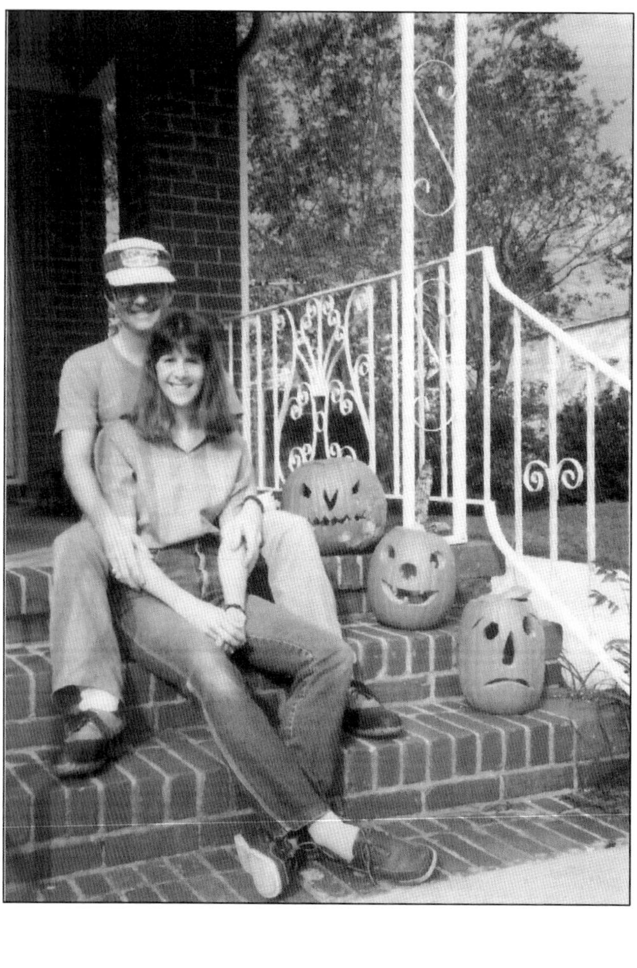

Jeffrey and Donna Jacobs moved into their Byrnes Downs home in September 1985 after a month of renovations. They celebrated the first Halloween with a trio of carved pumpkins. This book is dedicated to Jeff, the pumpkin artist. His perspective was an invaluable resource during the writing of this book.

CONTENTS

ACKNOWLEDGMENTS

The enthusiasm with which May T. Rossiter recorded *History Byrnes Downs Garden Club* is the real inspiration for this book, and I thank her. Margaret Thorne Seidler and her family recognized this historic gem, kept it safe, and honored me by sharing it. I spent wonderful afternoons in Camilla Blanton's dining room listening to the rich stories of her and her husband Red's 63 years in Byrnes Downs. Charlotte Hanckel Hay and her brother Frank Hanckel shared the wonders of growing up on Coburg Dairy Farms. Frank also gave me a delightful tour of the dairy's museum, which is a real treasure. Charlotte spent numerous Wednesday mornings with me in her living room enjoying the gorgeous view of the dairy's marsh, sharing memories, local history, and fun stories. I will always be indebted to her for perspective and assistance. Rutledge Corvette spent hours on the phone telling me stories in great detail of his and his parents' lives in Byrnes Downs and Charleston. The Caldwell family has entertained me for several years with stories of their life in Byrnes Downs. Ethel Nepveux recounted not only the neighborhood life, but also the business life and the life of a community activist. Tom Kwiatkowski, from whom we purchased our home, shared the story of his time in Byrnes Downs with his wife, Francis. Peggy Bohne introduced me to several invaluable resources. Sandra Foxworth and Robert Ball enticed me with stories of growing up on Albemarle Point. Warren Cobb of *West Of* helped get the word out about the upcoming publication. The community responded with photographs and stories that are only the beginning of a greater community story. A November visit with Tom Spain, director of photography at the *Post and Courier*, was filled with stories of old diners, a movie recommendation, and permission to use the great cover photograph. Irene Burk Tezza and Ruth Burk Gay are rich with stories of life with Joe and Mamie Harrison and their farm. To everyone who contributed to the book, I thank you for sharing your photographs, stories, and time so that I could begin to tell the story of life in Byrnes Downs and West Ashley. Unless otherwise noted, all images are courtesy of the author.

INTRODUCTION

The charm of Byrnes Downs was cast in the first brick, sealed with mortar, decorated with trees and gardens, and nurtured by the people who lived, loved, raised families, and passed away in these brick bungalows called home. Blanton, Cacioppo, Caldwell, Carroll, Corvette, Hartnett, Harvey, Melfi, Strobel, Steenken, Thorne, Wilson, and Webb are just a few of the names of families who began their lives together in these 850-square-foot cottages in the mid-1940s. They laid the groundwork for a neighborhood that in the 21st century retains all the charm and magic placed in that very first brick.

As the story goes, once upon a time, there was a cabbage patch until the V-Housing Corporation decided to purchase the farmland and develop a neighborhood to fill a housing shortage. The Charleston Navy Yard was teeming with workers, young soldiers were coming home to families, World War II was ending, and many people wanted to begin their life in their own home in a new community. Byrnes Downs was one such community being developed by the V-Housing Corporation in St. Andrew's Parish.

The area of West Ashley known as St. Andrew's Parish has a history that dates back to plans laid down by King Charles I of England. In 1663, he granted the charter of Carolina to eight Lords Proprietors, whose names decorate the rivers, counties, towns, and streets of the area. Byrnes Downs is no exception, with the streets bearing the names of governors of the state whose heritage dates back to some of these original Lords Proprietors. Campbell, Yeamans, Lyttleton, Nicholson, Craven, Sothel, Broughton, Ludwell, Colleton, and Tynte were the names of governors from 1672 to 1775. This information was presented to the community in both the *Byrnes Downs News*, which cost 5¢ when published in the mid-1950s, and repeated again in the *West Ashley Journal*, which cost 10¢ when published in the 1960s. The *Byrnes Downs News* was published from Jimmy McElveen's home at 28 Yeamans Avenue. The *West Ashley Journal* had its office at 1 Daniel Street in Byrnes Downs. The neighborhood proper was named in honor of James F. Byrnes, who was a native Charlestonian with an extensive political history serving at various levels of government. Byrnes served as the secretary of state under President Truman, taking the oath of office during the turbulent wartime of 1945. He was a good friend of the Long family, and J. C. Long supported him in his successful bid for governor in 1951. His term ran until 1955.

In 1943, the Exchange Club of St. Andrew's Parish prepared a *Celebration of Progress—St. Andrew's Parish*. The publication contained an article titled "St. Andrews Parish: Its Historic Past—Its Progressive Present—Its Glorious Future." The introduction to the article read, "In almost every land there is some hallowed spot, some area bounded by the glories and traditions of a primitive past that crystallized into a bountiful present, which is cherished by the people around it as the birthplace of their culture. Rome had its seven hills, Greece its Aeolian Isles and many Carolinians have looked back with comparable pride to Saint Andrew's Parish." What a perfect description of a community's pride that has prevailed into the 21st century. By 1960, residents and businesses were interested in receiving municipal services from the City of Charleston. Special elections were held, and on May 16, 1960, Wards 13 and 14, which included

Byrnes Downs, were annexed into the city of Charleston. Residents of this area were passionate about their community, and this passion flowed into developing this part of the city into an enviable place to live, work, play, and worship.

The concept of six degrees of separation states people are only six steps away from being connected to anyone else on earth. In St. Andrew's Parish, it might be two steps. In 1703, St. Andrew's Parish was one of 10 Colonial parishes established by an act of Parliament in England. The population of the 147-square-mile area was approximately 100 families. By 1947, the parish's census was approximately 11,000, and by 1960, the census recorded 25,887 persons. Generations of families were establishing their lives and memories. The connected community stories that have revealed themselves evidence the very close-knit fabric of the parish. There is such a beautiful resonance created in storytelling, both in the listening and in the telling, that the voices of generations can be magnified by this effort. One such story is about bathroom tile and the houses of Byrnes Downs. Tezza Tile was awarded the contract to lay the tile in the houses of Byrnes Downs. It was Mickey Tezza's Saturday job to place the proper color tile on the houses' front porches—blue and white tile if the back door was located on the back of the house and black and white tile if the back door was located on the side of the house. This difference in tile color also denotes the difference between two-bedroom and three-bedroom houses, respectively. Mickey Tezza is married to Irene Burk Tezza. Irene's aunt Mamie Harrison, on her mother's side, was the second wife of Joe Harrison, the prominent planter who owned the land that would become the site for Byrnes Downs. Irene and her sister Ruth tell remarkable stories of time spent visiting with their Uncle Joe and Aunt Mamie.

Discover your steps of separation, and may these photographs and stories be precious reminders of the beginning of suburban life in Byrnes Downs and the greater St. Andrew's Parish area.

One

V-Housing Corporation Develops Byrnes Downs

On January 12, 1942, the V-Housing Corporation filed with the secretary of state of South Carolina a charter with the following persons listed as officers: Vincent Chicco, president; W. K. Prause, vice president; L. L. Long, secretary; and C. Fletcher Carter Jr., treasurer. In addition, nine items were listed in the charter declaration. The fourth item set forth "that the general nature of the business which it is proposed to do is to own and deal in the sale and transfer of real estate and real estate mortgages." With this mission in mind, V-Housing Corporation began buying land and designing subdivisions. Byrnes Downs is one of the successful war housing projects financed by V-Housing Corporation. The corporation was responsible for installing electricity, water, sewerage systems, streets, and sidewalks in the area. Many of the residents of Byrnes Downs have recounted that J. C. Long built these homes. This story may have originated from the wording on the plat: "Recorded by filing in Plat Book 7 page 128 at 9:25 o'clock February 3, 1944. This tracing furnished by J. C. Long." But in fact, it was L. D. Long of the Long Construction Company who built the two- and three-bedroom bungalows. One intriguing side note to this story is that the plat for Byrnes Downs is divided into blocks and lots. Blocks are identified with letters of the alphabet, and lots are identified with numbers. Blocks on the south side of Savannah Highway begin with the letter "G." It has been discovered that the A–F blocks of Byrnes Downs were platted on the north side of the highway. This neighborhood is now known as Westwood. To date, there is no explanation for why the V-Housing Corporation did not pursue the development on the north side. In the late 1940s, the *Post and Courier* ran an article, "Do You Know Your Charleston?" featuring Byrnes Downs and the success of this thriving community. This success is a tribute to all the people who first moved into these homes and began planting gardens, building garages, raising families, and enjoying life in the neighborhood.

THE V-HOUSING CORPORATION

Presents to the St. Andrew's Parish

THE

BYRNES DOWN SUBDIVISION

374 Modern, permanent homes inspired by the desire to contribute to winning of the War. Designed as permanent homes for our permanent Citizens

Without Victory We Will Be Without Homes

V-HOUSING CORPORATION

This advertisement appeared in the October 22, 1943, edition of the *Celebration of Progress—St. Andrew's Parish South Carolina*, sponsored by the Exchange Club of St. Andrew's Parish. The subdivision is named as "Byrnes Down," although all further reference to the neighborhood is with the name "Byrnes Downs." In this edition, Westwood is not among the residential developments listed in St. Andrew's Parish. (Courtesy of Bill Wallace.)

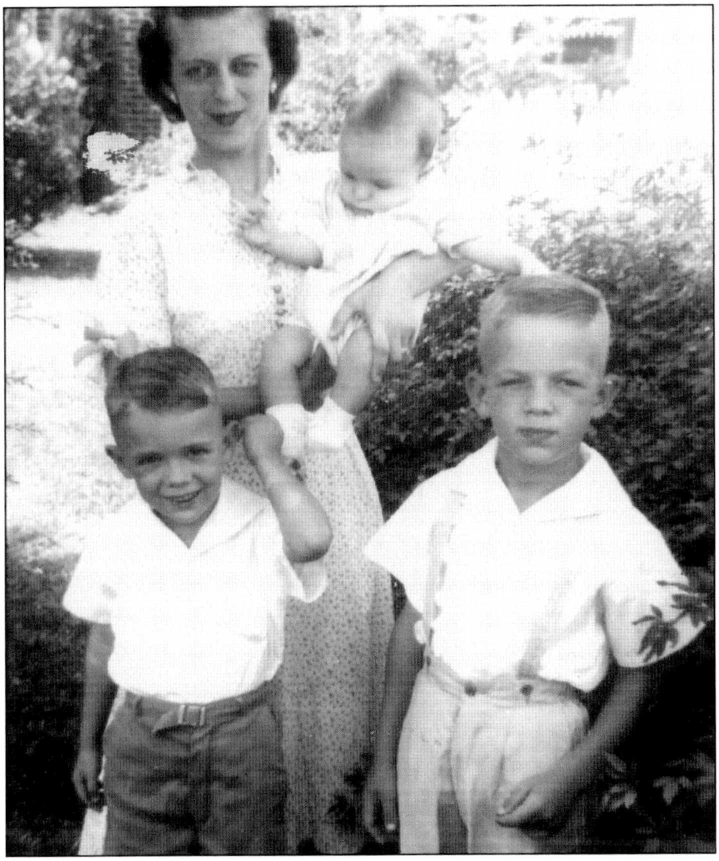

Mendel and Virginia Caldwell were married while Mendel was serving in the U.S. Navy. They moved back to the Charleston area after his tour of duty was completed. When they went looking for a place to live, he was told, "Son, don't rent, go buy a home in Byrnes Downs." According to Mendel, "That was the best decision I ever made." In October 1945, they purchased their home on Colleton Drive and became one of the original residents of Byrnes Downs. Virginia and Mendel raised their three sons—Ronnie, Gary (center), Mendel Jr.—at their home on Colleton Drive. (Both courtesy of the Caldwell family.)

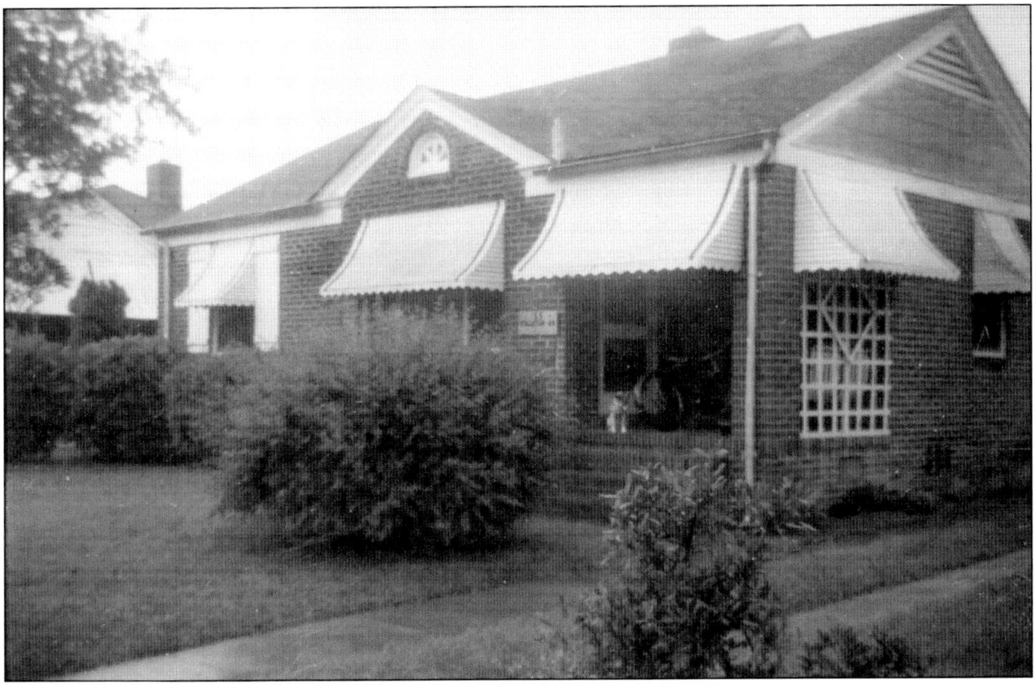

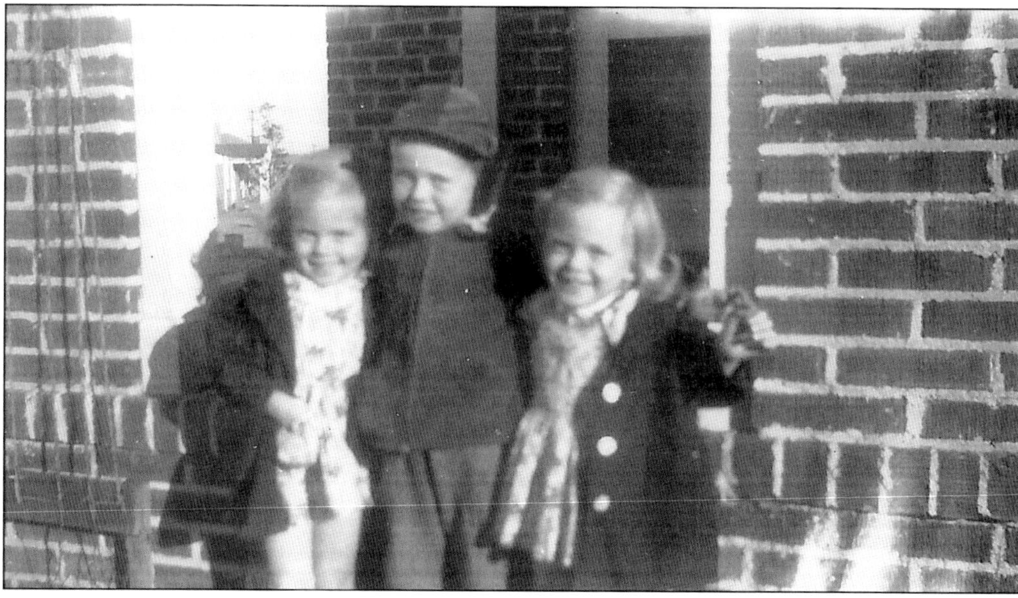

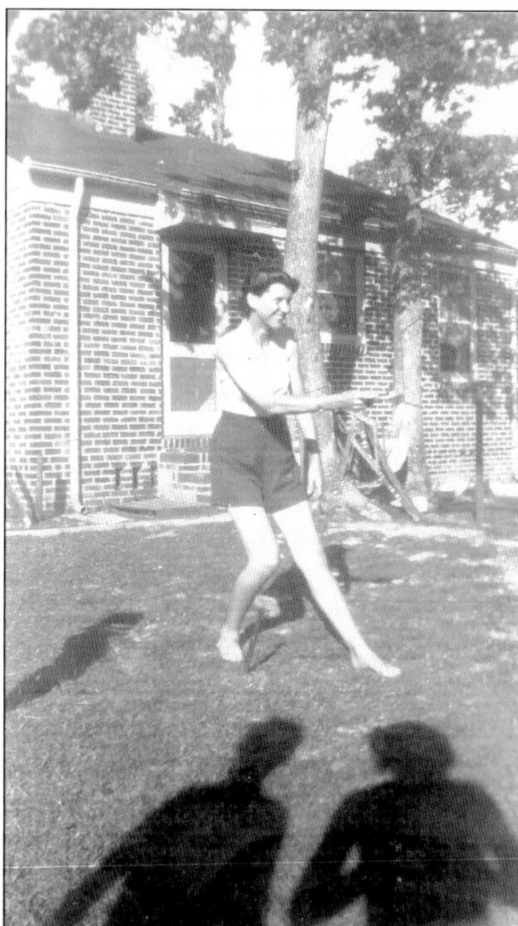

Camilla and Sam ("Red") Blanton moved to California from Charleston during the war so Red could work for Douglas Aircraft. When they returned to Charleston, housing was in very short supply, and they lived in several locations until they found a house to rent at 13 Sothel Drive in the new subdivision of Byrnes Downs. In the upper photograph, dated January 4, 1945, Russell, Camilla's sister's son, is flanked by the Blantons' twin daughters, Susan (left) and Judi (right), at their Sothel home. In April 1946, they decided to buy their lifelong home at 42 Colleton Drive. The Blantons loved to have fun and immediately began organizing parties, outings, and backyard games. June 1946 finds Red's sister Dot (at left) pitching horseshoes in the Blantons' backyard. (Both courtesy of Camilla Blanton.)

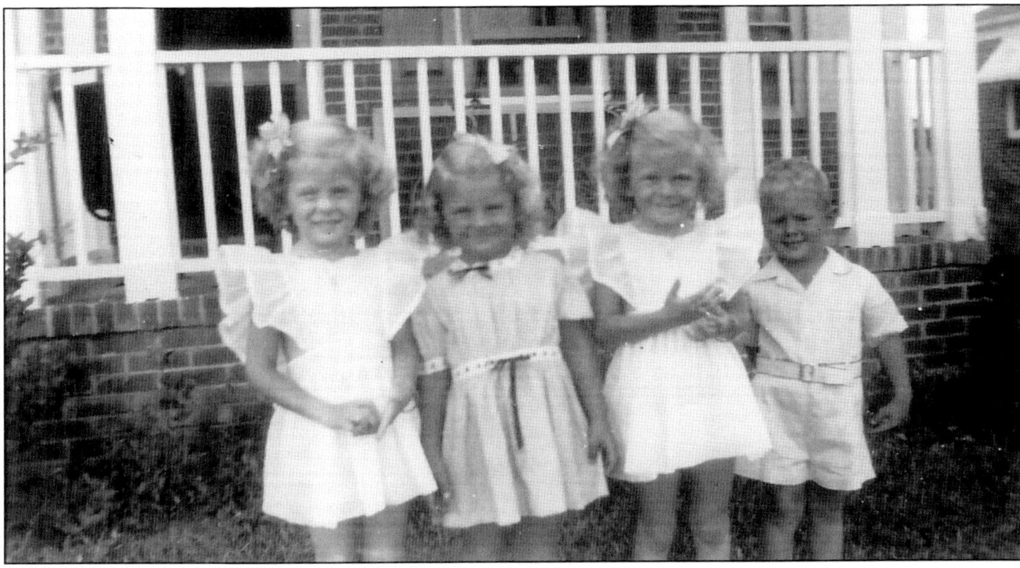

Camilla recalls taking her daughters as well as the neighborhood children to Sunday school, to church, to the beach, and on picnics to the park. "Just having fun," Camilla says with a smile and a twinkle in her eye. From left to right in the top photograph, Susan Blanton, Cynthia Vann, Judi Blanton, and Joel Vann are dressed up for church in July 1947. In the bottom photograph, dated August 1948, Judi (left) and Susan (right) pose with Jerry Tumbleston, who lived across the street on Colleton Drive. (Both courtesy of Camilla Blanton.)

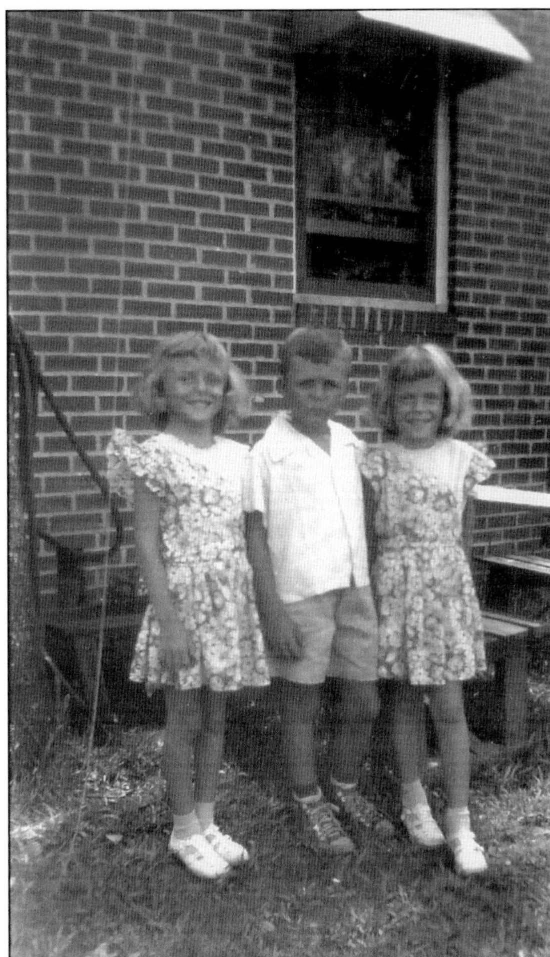

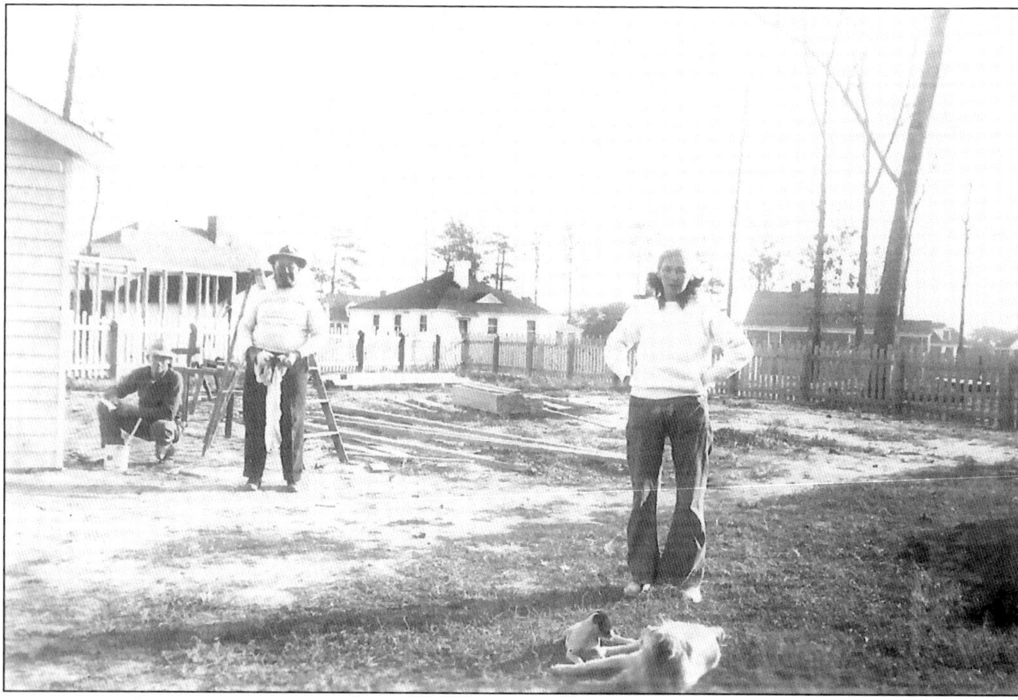

In 1945, Sophie T. Steenken purchased Lot 4, Block R on Colleton Drive. She and her husband, Henry, were among the first homeowners listed in the tax records at the Register Mesne Conveyance (RMC) office. Henry began work on the garage in 1945 so he could have a place for his car and to store his tools. Charlie Andrews (kneeling, left), who lived next door; Henry (standing, center); his daughter Annie; and their dogs, Lady and Skippy, pose with the newly completed garage. Below is the Steenken home on Colleton Drive as it appeared in 1946. Annie Steenken Shier moved to Ludwell Drive in 1956, raised her children in Byrnes Downs, and resides there today. (Both courtesy of Annie Steenken Shier.)

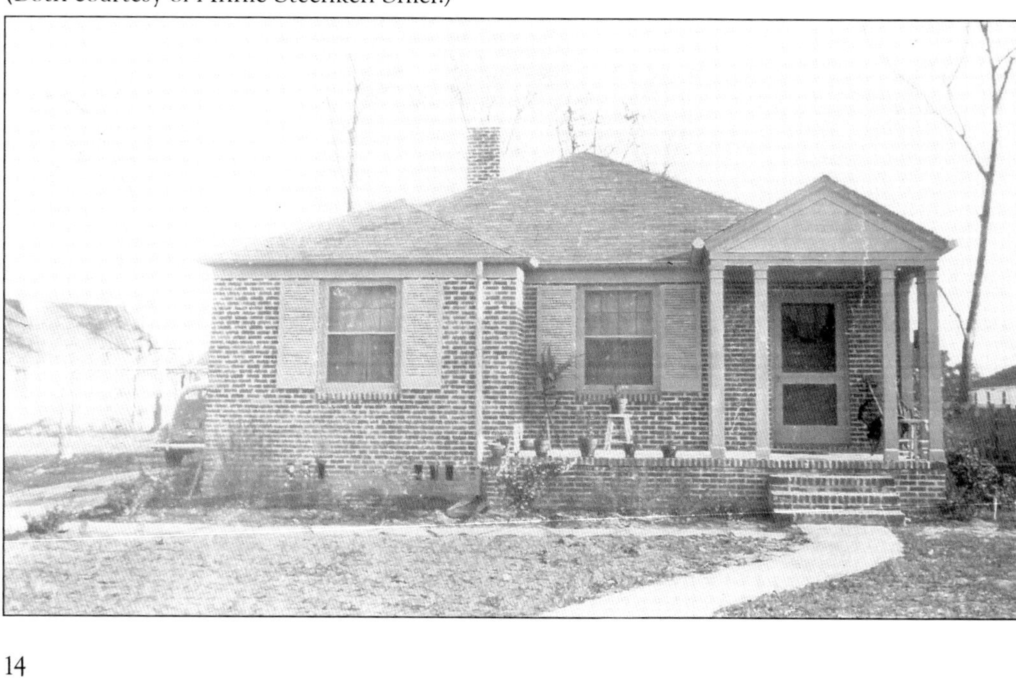

Rutledge Corvette's parents, John Emiel and Ruth Fariey Corvette, purchased Lot 15, Block J on Campbell Drive in March 1945. When Rutledge returned from his tour of work duty at Pearl Harbor, he lived with his parents at 28 Campbell Drive before being drafted into the army. In September 1946, Rutledge and his wife, Margaret, purchased 27 Campbell Drive and raised four children in their home. Beth Corvette is seen celebrating her first birthday. (Courtesy of Rutledge and Margaret Corvette.)

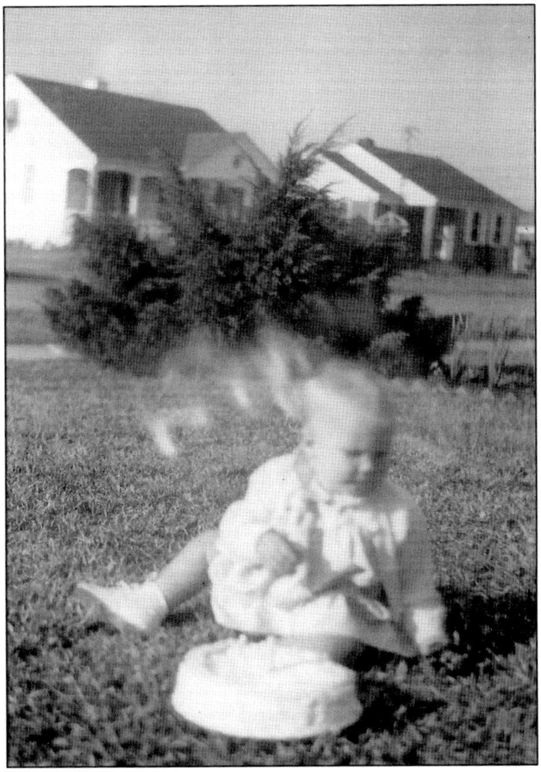

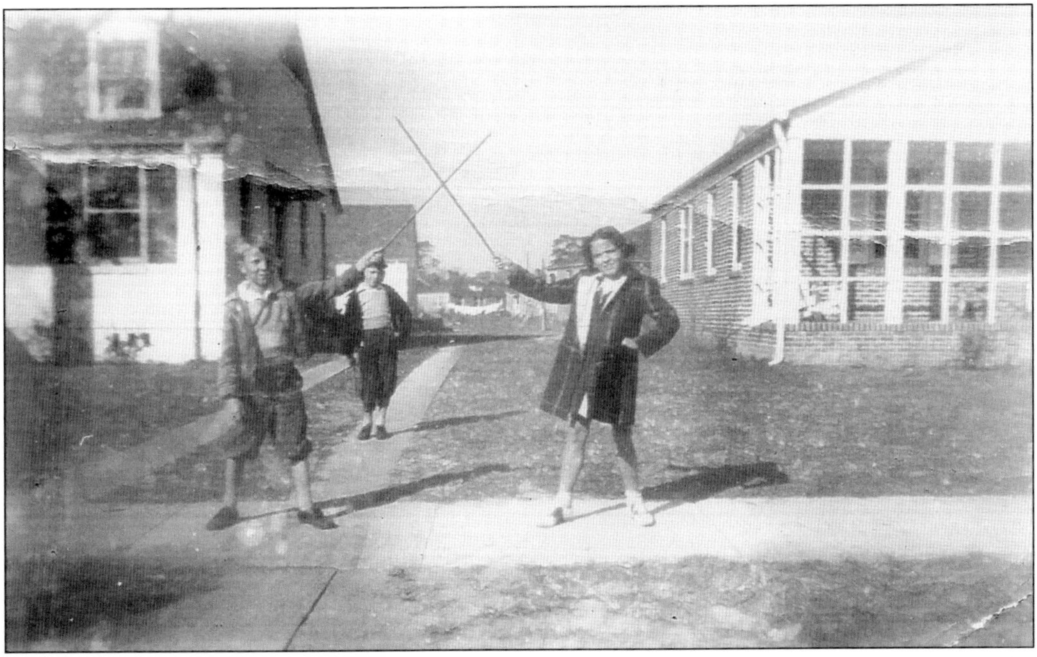

"No trees and very little shrubbery in the yard" was a popular description residents gave for the early yards in Byrnes Downs. This is quite evident in this early photograph depicting children playing along Campbell Drive. The Garden Club that formed in January 1948 would soon correct this situation. (Courtesy of Frances and Joe Roy.)

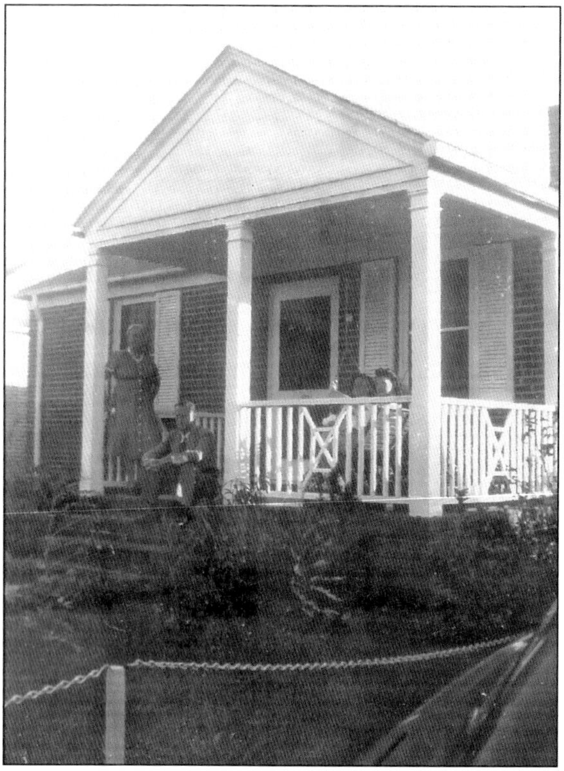

J. B. Weathers was a mechanic for Associated Petroleum Carriers when he was offered a job as maintenance foreman for SCE&G's bus service in Charleston. He and his wife, Carrie, purchased their home at 119 (later renumbered to 651) Savannah Highway in 1945. They were encouraged to purchase the house next door as an investment, but J. B. was not known for being a risk taker. J. B. enjoyed several hobbies, including gardening. The back lawn soon succumbed to the vegetable garden, and J. B. proudly poses with the "fruit" or rather "vegetable" of his labor in the 1948 photograph below. (Both courtesy of William H. Barron Jr.)

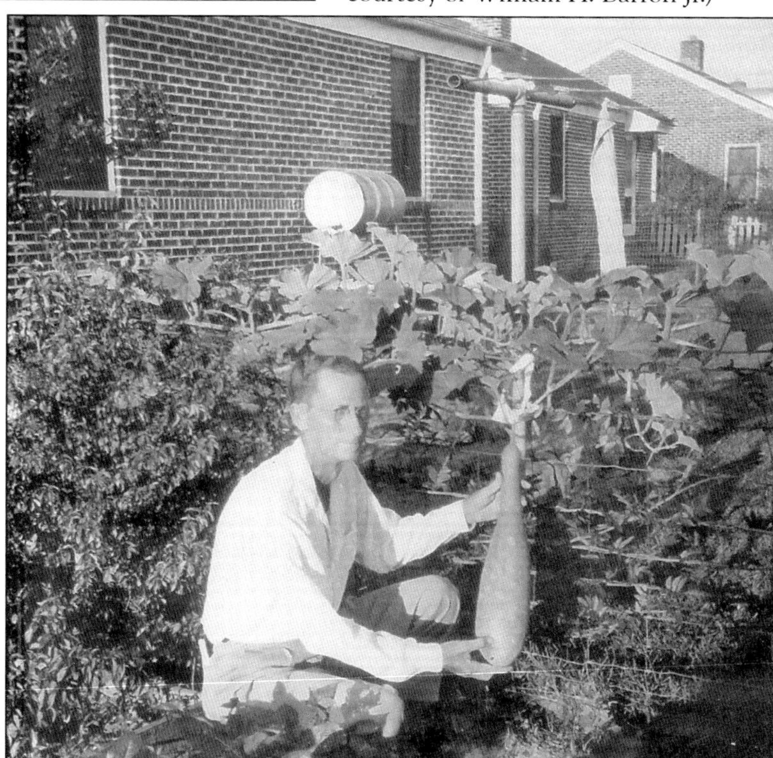

Gus and Cornelia Cacioppo married in 1947 and are pictured here cutting their wedding cake. They initially lived in the second story of his family's home on Alexander Street in downtown Charleston. Like many young married couples, they wanted a home of their own. Cornelia went house hunting and found their future home at 6 Lyttleton Avenue. With a $1,000 down payment, they were able to move in and set up housekeeping. Gus is an accomplished musician; during their early years together, he worked at Charleston Office Supply by day and played saxophone at night. He is seen below (second from right) with his band. On August 25, 2007, at the age of 93, Gus was featured in the "High Profile" section of the Saturday edition of the *Post and Courier.* The featured photograph showed him proudly holding his saxophone in this home at 6 Lyttleton Avenue, Byrnes Downs. (Both courtesy of Gus Cacioppo.)

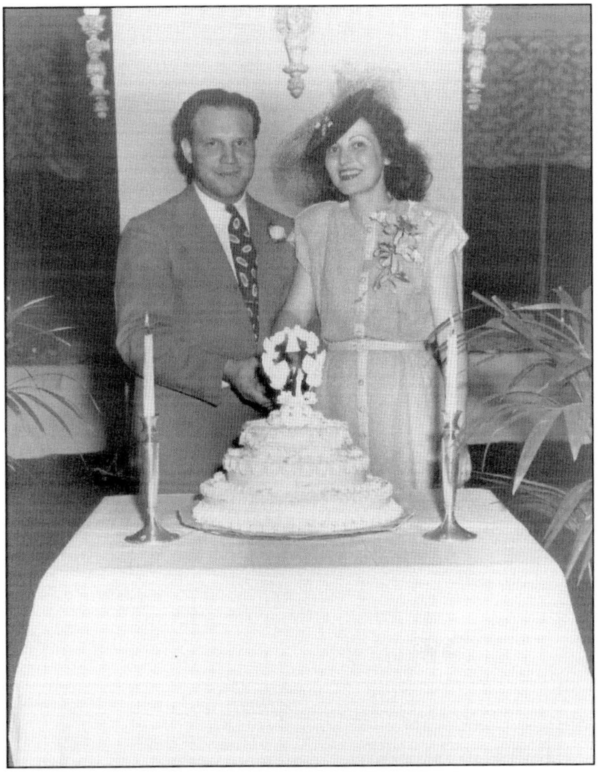

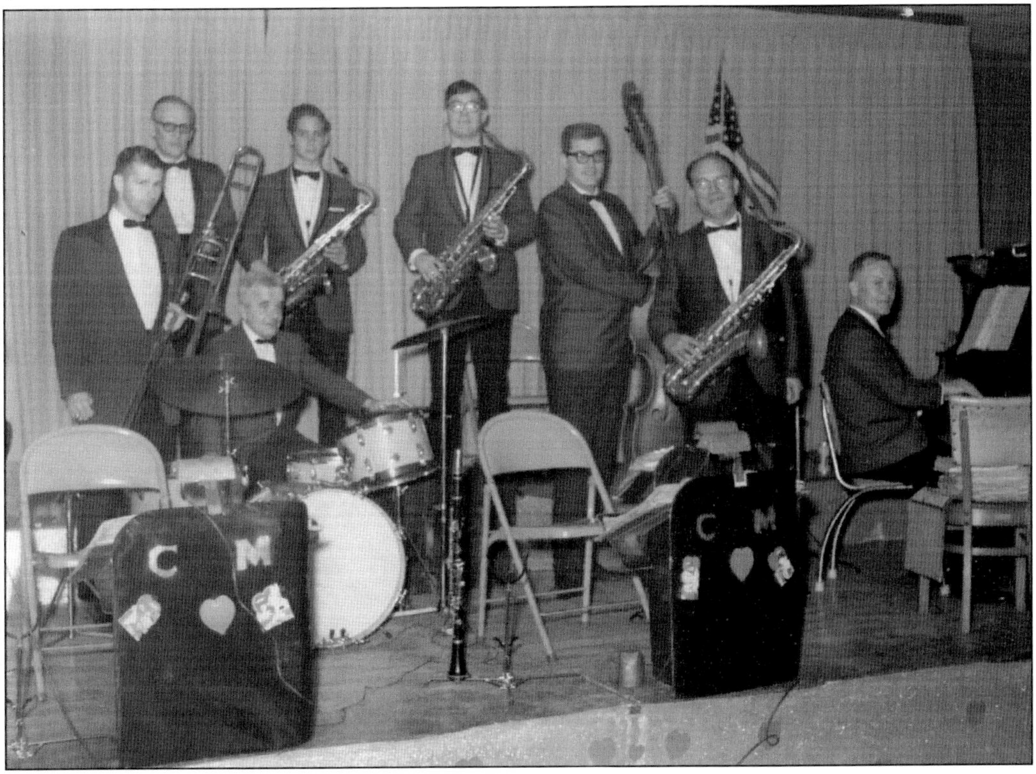

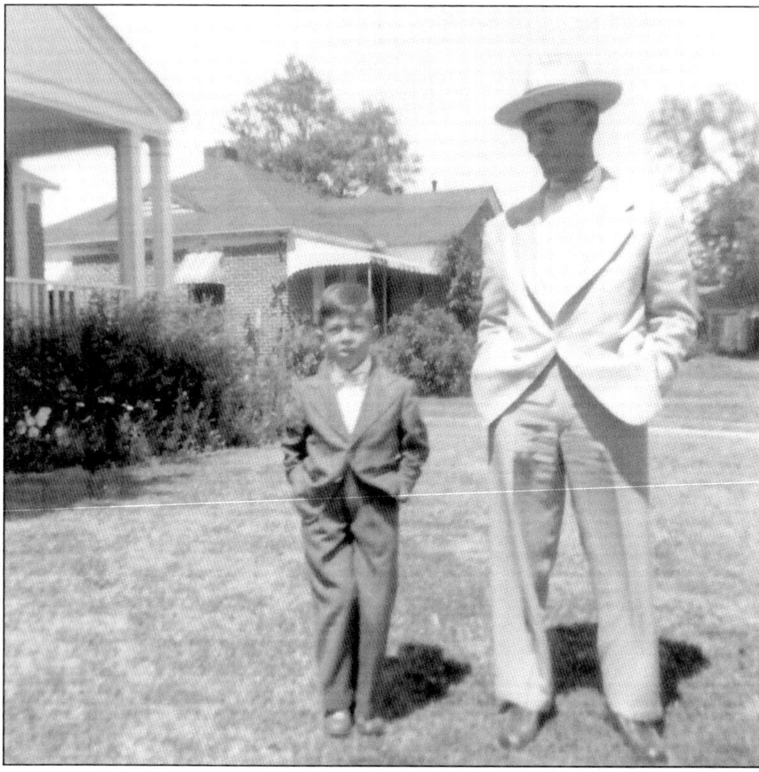

George and Sara Calas lived on Colleton Drive just down the street from Camilla and Red Blanton. George and his son, Charlie Bob, posed for the photographer in their front yard. Written on the back of this photograph is "Tel pere, tel fils!" which loosely translates from French as "Like Father, Like Son." (Courtesy of Camilla Blanton.)

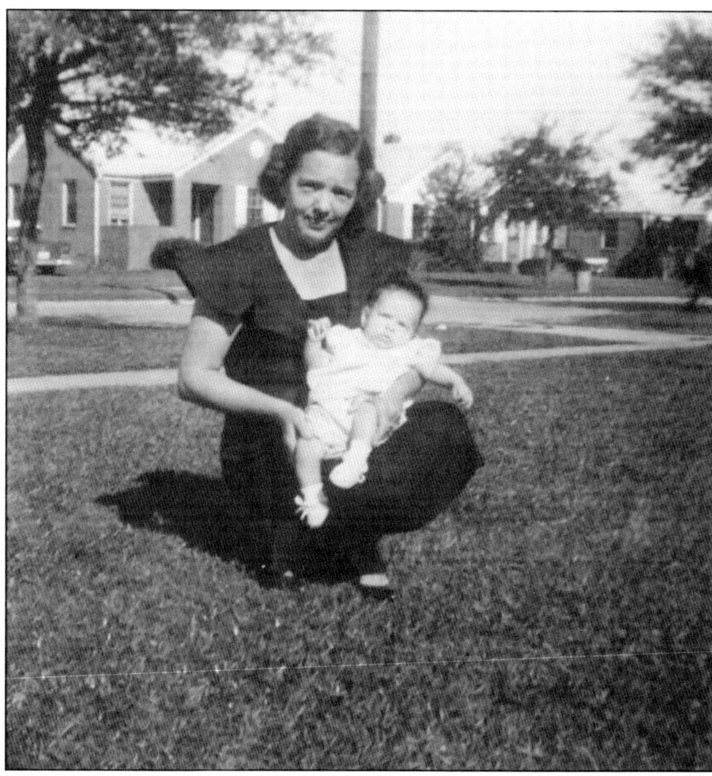

Doris and Lawrence Hartnett, with their two children Nancy and Jeanne, moved into 11 Yeadon Avenue in 1949. Their family continued to grow with the addition of a son, Larry, and daughter Joyce. Joyce, pictured in her mother's arms, was born in 1949. Today Joyce and her husband, Marvin, own the family home on Yeadon Avenue. Jeanne liked the neighborhood so much that she moved just a few houses down on Yeadon Avenue. (Courtesy of the Hartnett family.)

T. J. Thorne Jr. ("Tommy") married June Dandridge in December 1947. At the time, he worked in his family business, Woodstock Manufacturing Company, and served as a lieutenant colonel in the Army Reserves, having completed his tour of active duty. Like many men returning from the war, he wanted to start his family life in his own home. In January 1949, June holds her newborn daughter Lynda on the front porch of her and Tommy's home on Nicholson Street (at right). A few months later, Tommy holds Lynda in his arms (below). Gracing the background in this photograph are some of the newly built homes. June was one of the charter members of the Garden Club that would soon begin beautifying the neighborhood. (Both courtesy of Margaret Thorne Seidler.)

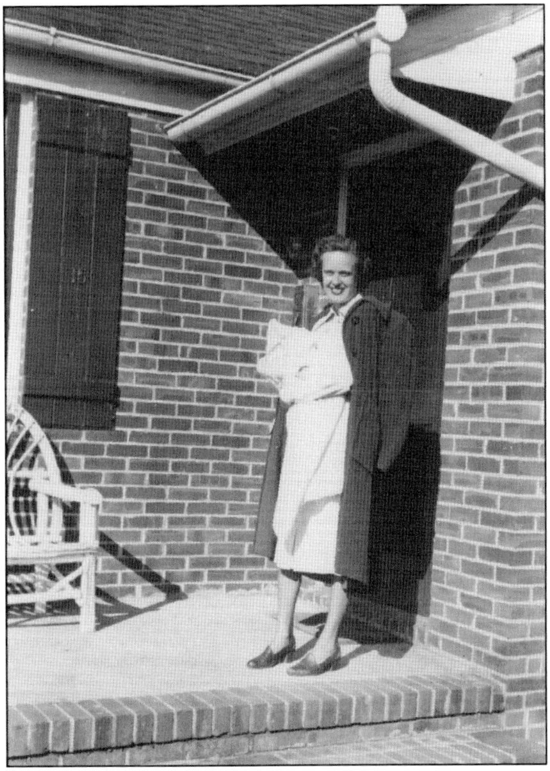

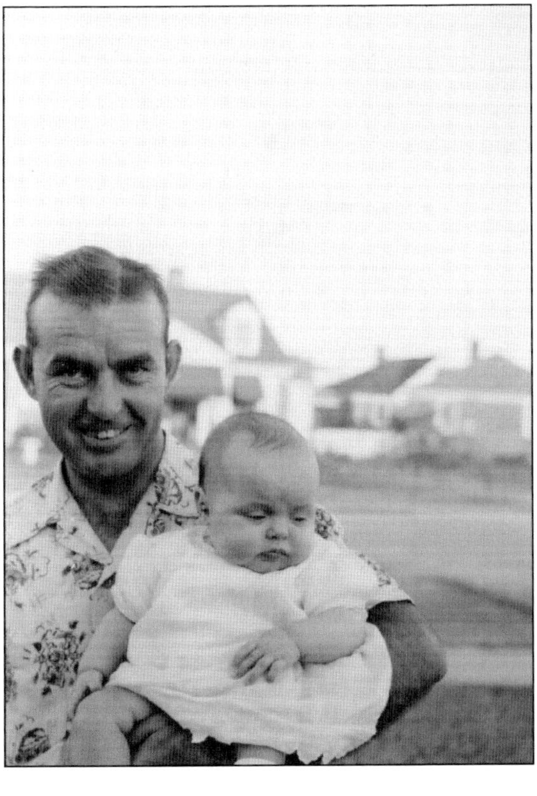

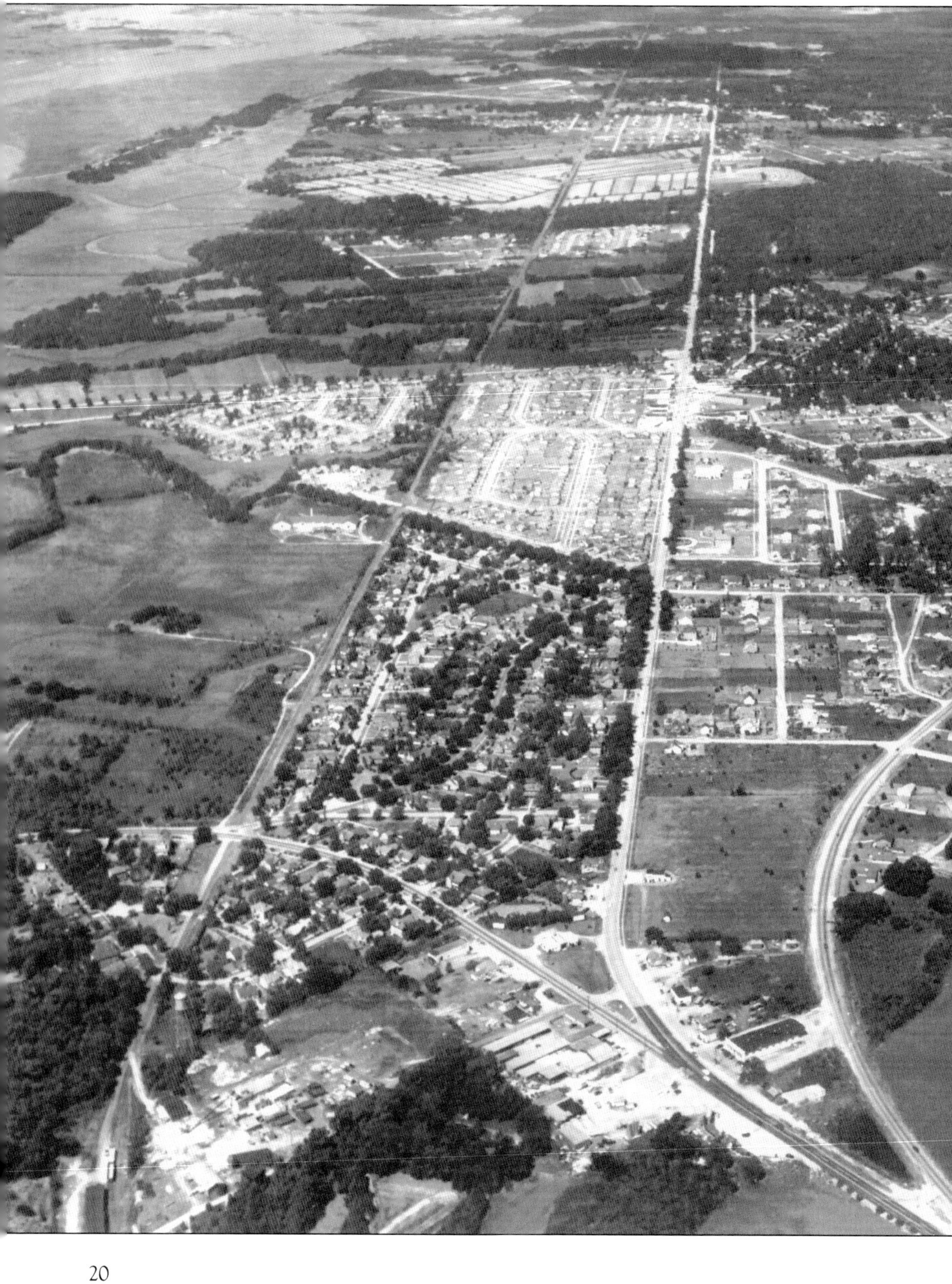

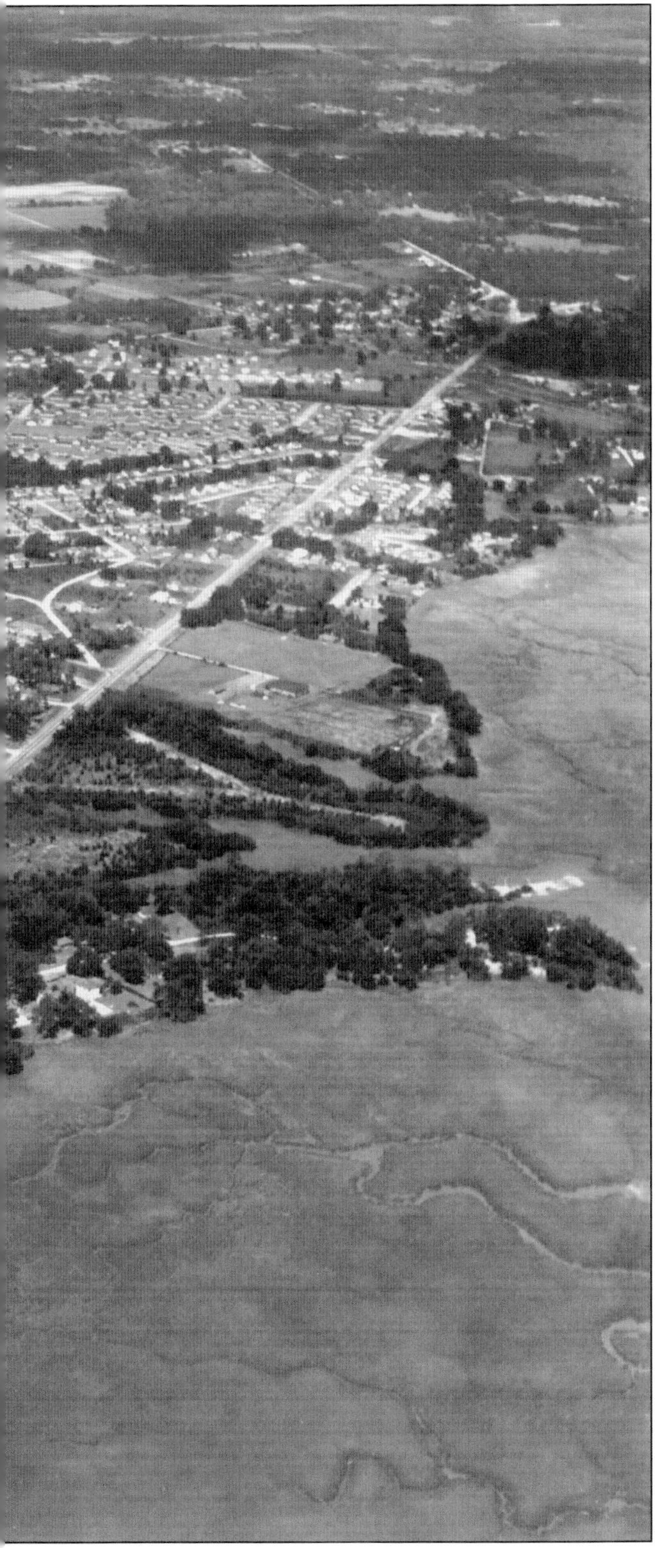

J. C. Hare hated to fly, but his good friend Roland Wooten, the postmaster for Charleston, had a passion for flight. This spectacular aerial photograph was found among the papers of J. C. Hare. The speculation is that Roland took this photograph one day while flying and shared it with J. C. because J. C. and his wife, Connie, wanted to move from their home on Tradd Street to the "country." The presence and absence of certain landmarks date this photograph to late 1950 or early 1951. Byrnes Downs is easily located in the middle left-hand side of the photograph as the newly planted trees are not predominant enough to create a canopy. Some landmarks are St. Andrew's Elementary School (left, below Byrnes Downs) with its original white facade, the tree-lined road to Coburg Dairy Farms (far left), Windermere (center, left), Avondale (center), the undeveloped land of the future Westwood (below Avondale), the house on the property that would soon become South Windermere, and homes in Moreland (lower center and right). (Courtesy of Cantey Hare.)

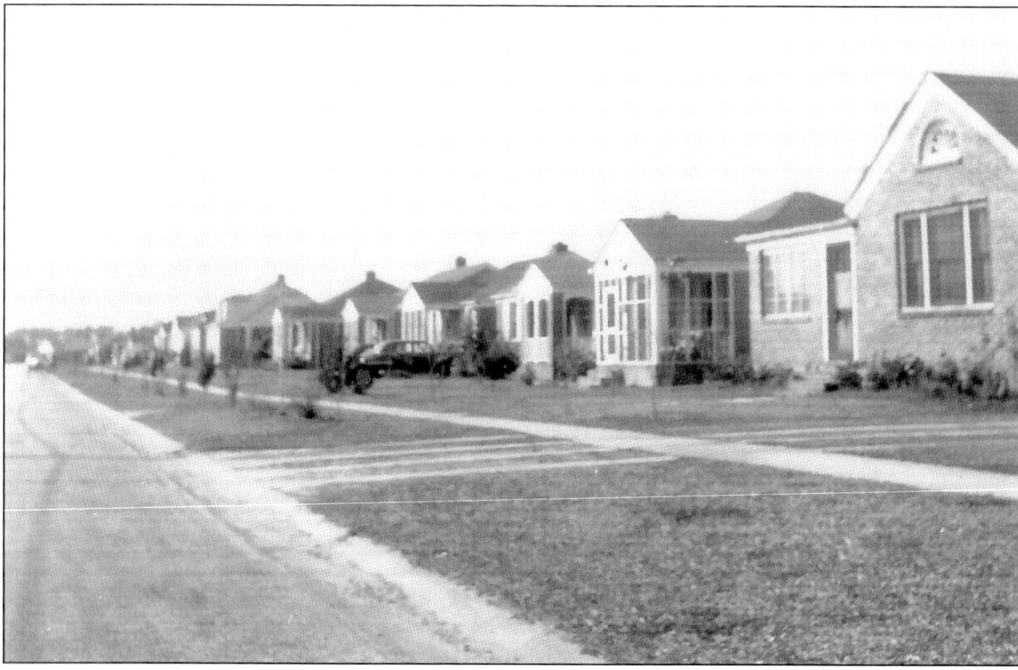

According to the *History Byrnes Downs Garden Club*, "One of the big projects of the Byrnes Downs Garden Club was the planting of the trees on many of the streets. The following pages show a few pictures where the trees were planted. Watch the great change in these pictures a few years from now." The top photograph is labeled "On Yeamans (later changed to Yeadon) looking South," and the bottom photograph is labeled "Looking Southwest from Corner of Nicholson and Craven Sts." In 1995, the neighborhood was featured in a *Post and Courier* article titled "Byrnes Downs is Golden." The article included "then" and "now" pictures of the streets, illustrating this "great change." (Both courtesy of Margaret Thorne Seidler.)

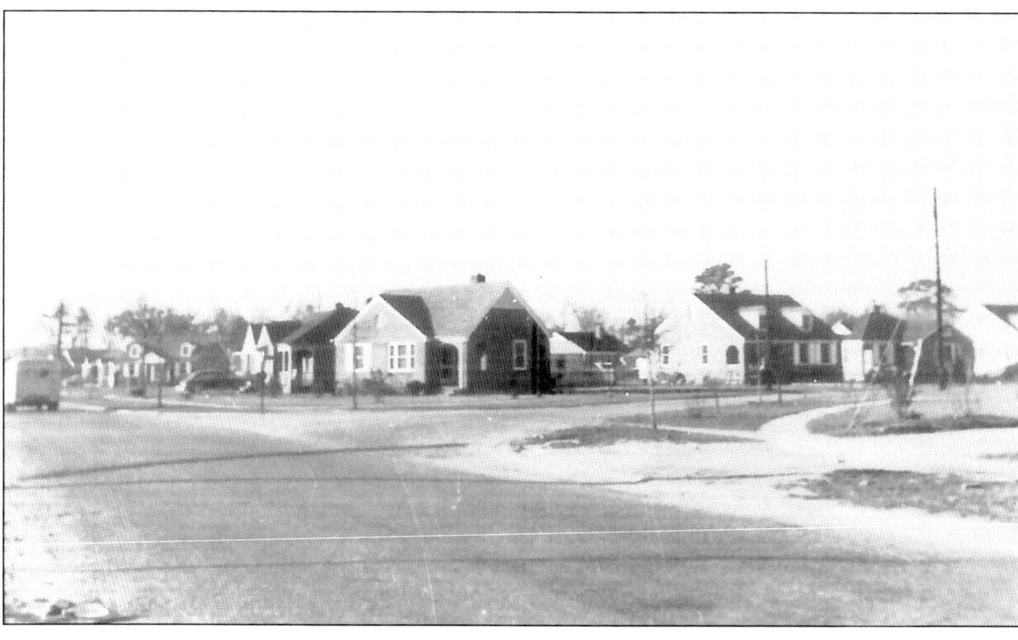

Two

THE GARDEN CLUB

Is it possible to preserve a piece of time that holds for the future a wish? A wish that one discovers and to the wonder of all realizes has come true? May T. Rossiter, the historian for the Byrnes Downs Garden Club from 1949 to 1950, wrote a foreword to the scrapbook she was preparing for the newly formed Garden Club. This foreword is reproduced in its entirety in this chapter, and it is the privilege of this author to grant her wish. With incredible attention to detail, a flair for graphic accent, and a need to "preserve for future reference all matters of interest which in any way pertains to the Garden Club of Byrnes Downs," she created this scrapbook to allow the reader to relive the day-to-day life of the beginning of Byrnes Downs. The Garden Club was serious about its mission to beautify Byrnes Downs. One of the first projects was the erection of street signs. "Money had to be raised. But nothing daunted the energetic ladies of the Garden Club, so the necessary funds were raised by means of a Card Party, held at the Exchange Building," she said. Next the ladies planted azaleas, nandinas, and ligustrum at the neighborhood entrances. They cleared the vacant lot at the corner of Savannah Highway and Nicholson Street and planted the lot with grass. Today Fire Station 10 occupies this site. Finally, "One of the finest accomplishments of the Club is the sale and planting of One Hundred Seven (107) oak trees in Byrnes Downs." The land had originally been part of Harrison Farms, and trees were scarce. Today the urban canopy of Byrnes Downs is treasured and closely guarded by the residents. There were also tea parties and chicken dinners on the Coburg Dairy Farm, Garden of the Month awards, Spring Flower Show entries, and regular meetings. Rossiter writes in "A Club is Born," "From that moment on, their activities have never ceased."

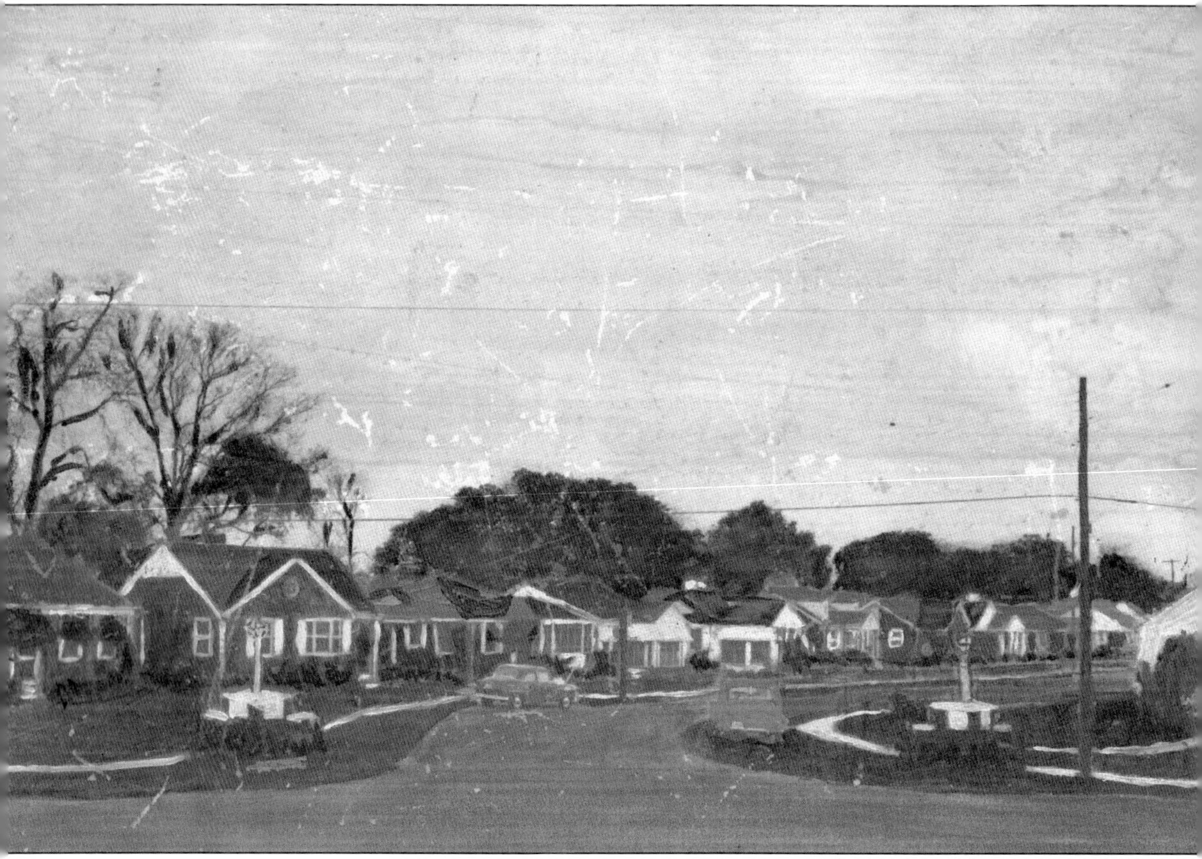

May T. Rossiter expressed the following sentiment in the section "A Club is Born" of *History Byrnes Downs Garden Club*: "One fine sunny day in the month of January, 1948 (it was January 15th, to be exact) a small group (fifteen in number) of representative ladies, all residents of Byrnes Downs, met at the home of Mrs. W. H. Mikell, Jr., at 7 Craven Street [*sic*], with the thought in mind that Byrnes Downs should have a Garden Club." This painting decorates the cover of the scrapbook prepared by May T. Rossiter for the Garden Club. On the back cover is a painting of a pink dogwood blossom. (Courtesy of Margaret Thorne Seidler.)

FORWARD

The purpose of this Book is to preserve for future reference all matters of interest which in any way pertains to the Garden Club of Byrnes Downs; in other words, a History of the Club's activities, so that all may know we are and always hope to be a real live organization.

That through our assembly, we will benefit ourselves and each other, and thus stimulate an interest in gardening, and in time hope that Byrnes Downs will become known as one of the Garden Spots in the Garden City of the World, for that is the reputation already attained by the City of Charleston, South Carolina.

None of us at present are native born Byrnes Downians. Folks have come from the four corners of the earth to make this their home. Some will leave Byrnes Downs. Others will take their places, but the Byrnes Downs Garden Club will go on and on and on.

It is through our Garden Club that we want to continue to make and to keep Byrnes Downs a beautiful and delightful place, so that it will always enjoy an enviable reputation as a good place in which to live.

May T. Rossiter

Historian 1949-50

The foreword speaks for itself. It is a beautiful statement about the drive, creativity, and determination of the ladies who desired to make Byrnes Downs a wonderful place to live. (Courtesy of Margaret Thorne Seidler.)

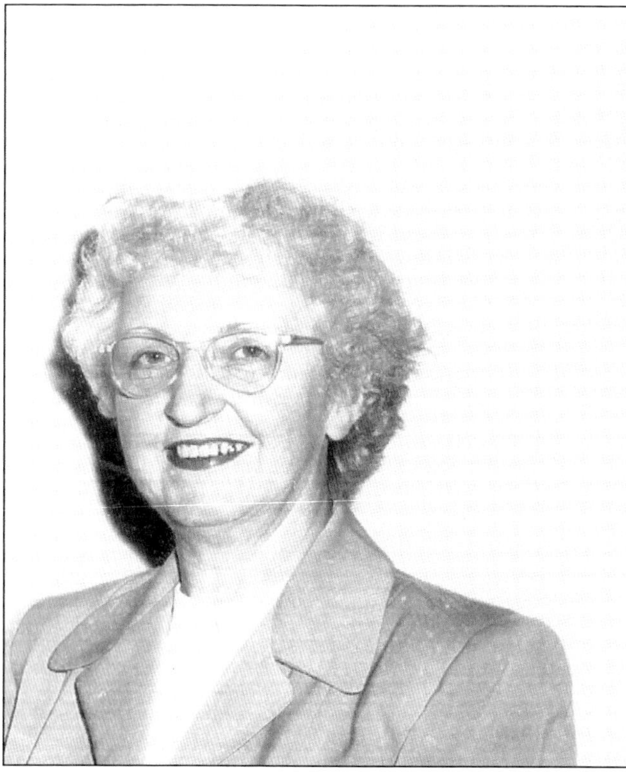

May Rossiter (pictured at left) titled her section on the beginning of the Byrnes Downs Garden Club "A Club is Born." She writes of the Garden of Eden, the gardens of Europe and Asia, the local gardens of Middleton, Magnolia, and Cypress, and then adds: "Now we want to talk about the Gardens closest to our hearts, the Gardens of Byrnes Downs, Charleston County, South Carolina, and the Organization founded as a result of those Gardens." Accenting her writing and photographs are numerous pen drawings of flowers, garden tools, a bee, butterfly, birdhouse, street sign, the entrance column, and a gaslight. The drawing of a dogwood blossom is shown below. The drawings are unsigned, so one can only assume Rossiter drew them. (Both courtesy of Margaret Thorne Seidler.)

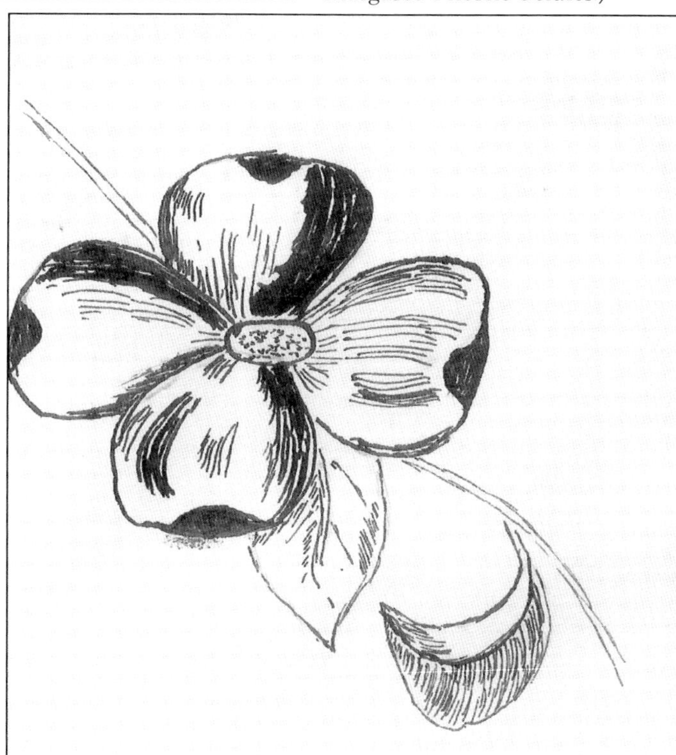

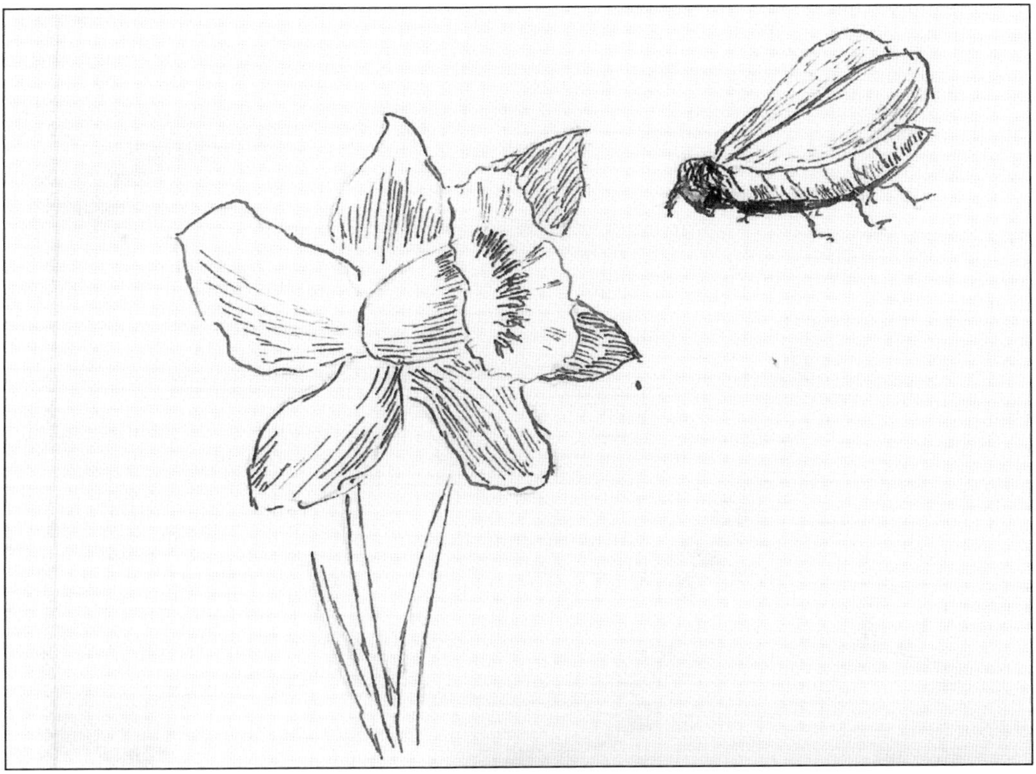

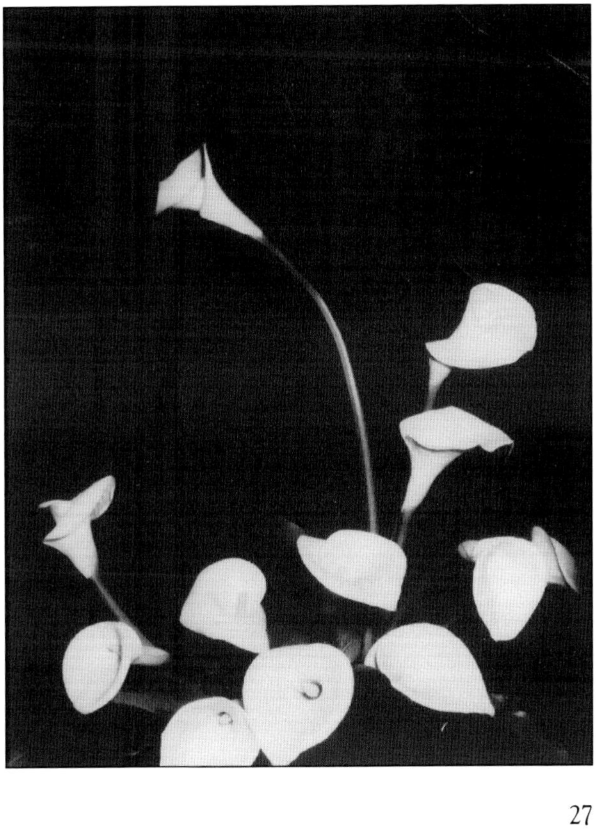

In addition to the delicately drawn graphic accents like the daffodil and bee shown here, there are pictures of award-winning flower arrangements decorating the scrapbook. The Garden Club entered a niche arrangement of calla lilies in the 1949 Charleston Spring Flower Show and won a blue ribbon for its period arrangement exhibit. The calla lilies were arranged in a clear crystal container with a dark-green background. (Both courtesy of Margaret Thorne Seidler.)

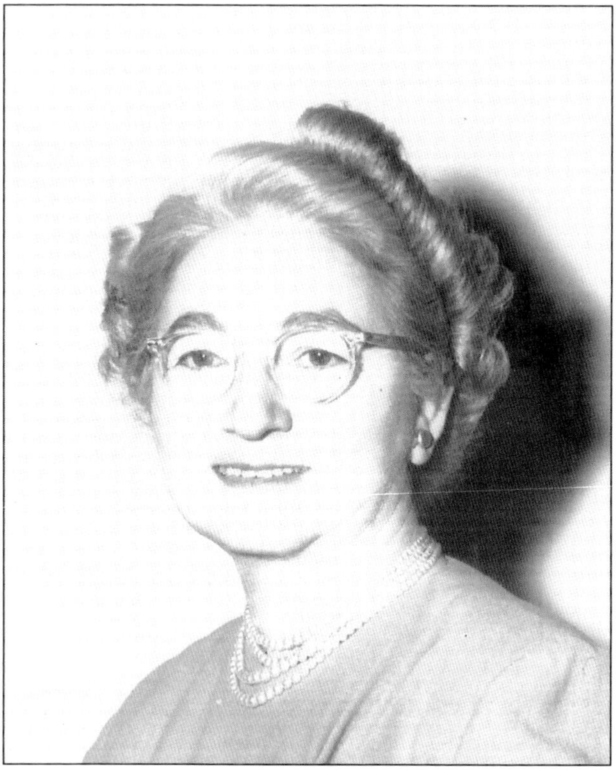

On January 15, 1948, Anne Thorne acted as the temporary chairman at the first meeting, where it was decided to form a club and elect officers. Mrs. W. H. Mikell Jr. was elected president, and the group laid out an ambitious plan of activities. On April 15, 1949, Thorne was elected president. The photograph of her at left is centered amid her other officers on page 18 of the scrapbook. Thorne worked very diligently, not only on the club's behalf for the neighborhood, but also on her gardens. There are numerous photographs featuring her house and gardens in the scrapbook. The lower photograph shows the flagstone walk between houses bordered with flowers and shrubs. (Both courtesy of Margaret Thorne Seidler.)

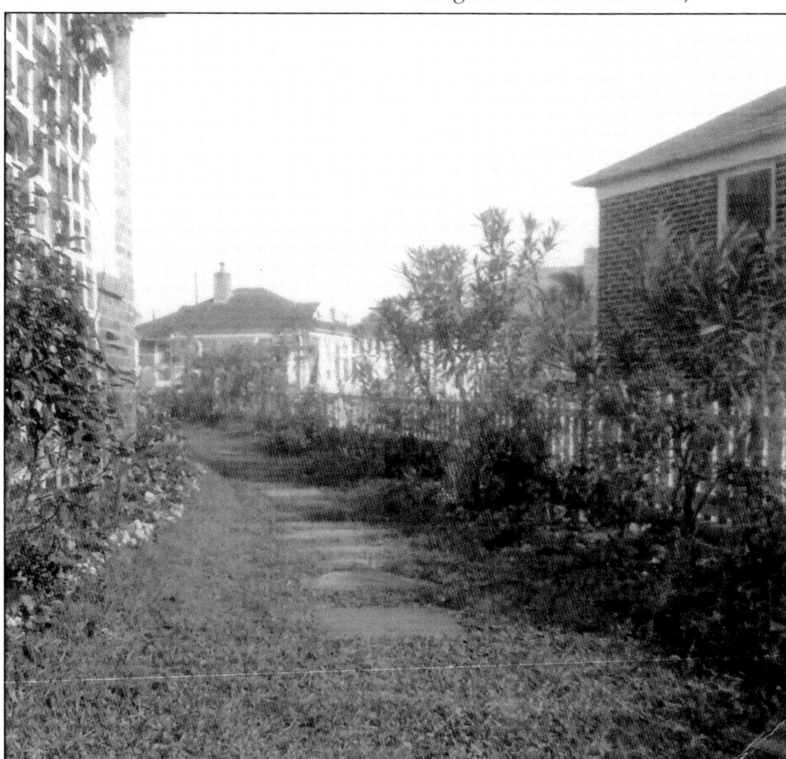

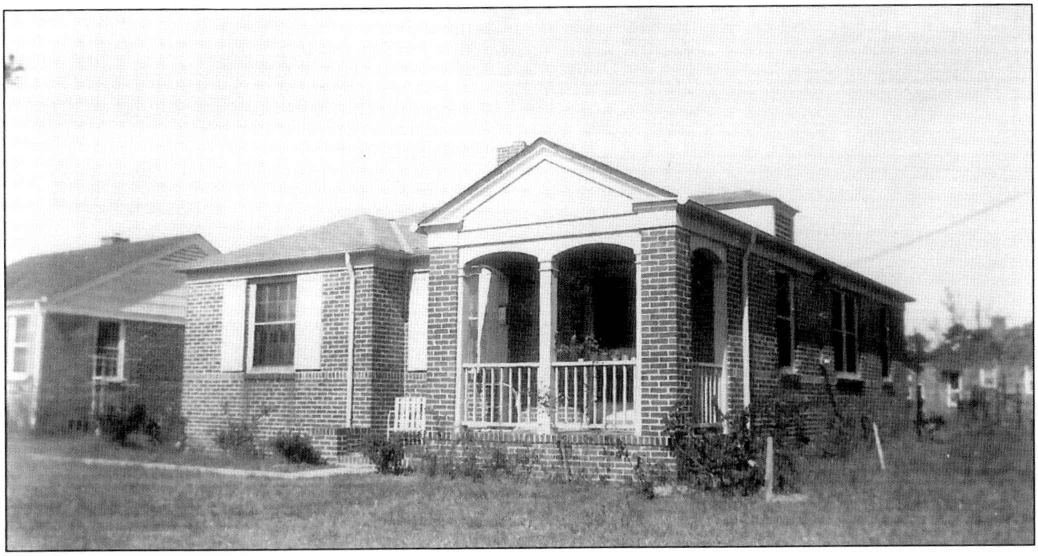

May T. Rossiter introduced the section on before-and-after pictures with this quote: "To preserve for future reference we were able to obtain several pictures of homes when the present owners first bought them and also some pictures, all showing landscaping and gardening, of the same homes as they are today." Anne Thorne's house at 4 Sothel Drive is seen above as it appeared in 1946. The lower photograph, taken in 1950, illustrates Thorne's addition to the home, awning accents, and numerous shrubs and trees planted in the front and side yard. Thorne was instrumental in the success of the Garden Club, and her dedication to the neighborhood and Garden Club is documented in the scrapbook titled *History Byrnes Downs Garden Club*. (Both courtesy of Margaret Thorne Seidler.)

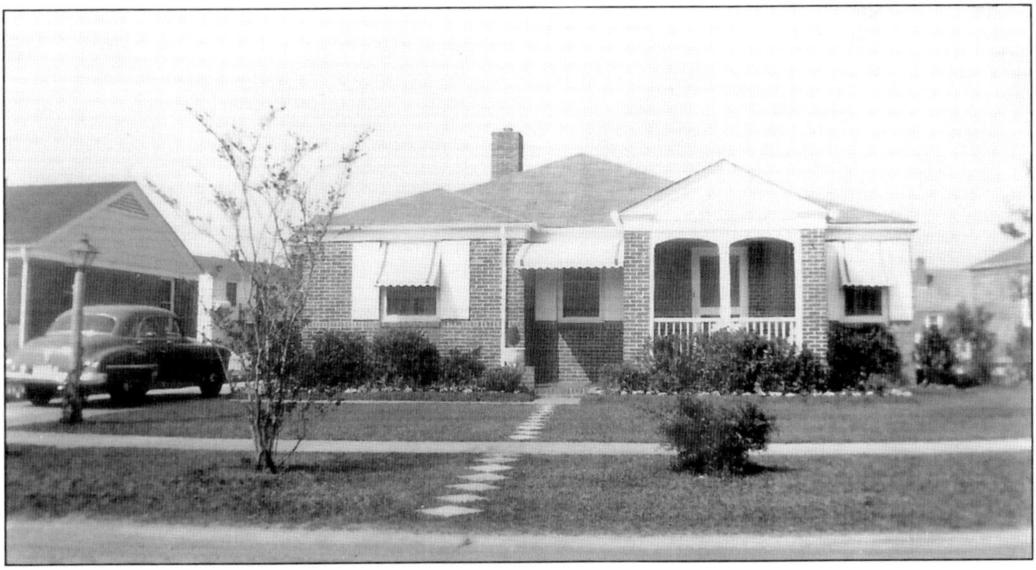

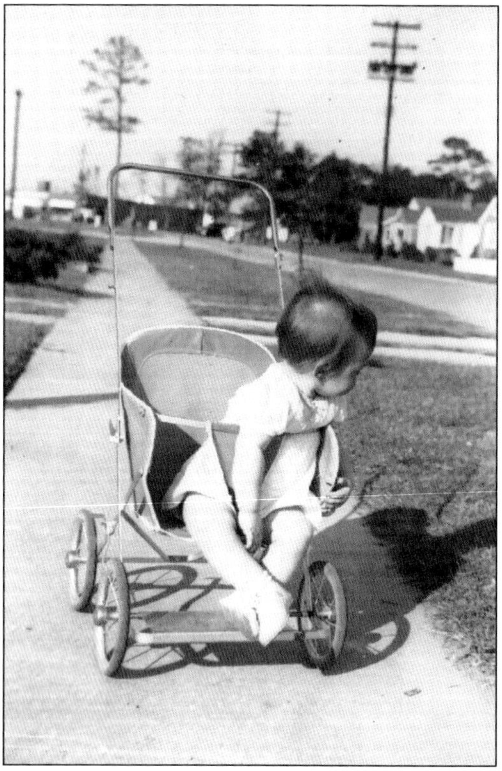

On a fall day in November 1949 (at left), Lynda Thorne, seated in her baby stroller, gazes up Nicholson Street toward Savannah Highway. If one looks carefully, one will notice three tree seedlings planted in the area between the sidewalk and the street. Anne Thorne chaired the committee that sold and planted 107 oak trees in the neighborhood. She sold 50 of these trees herself. In the background, one can also see the storefronts along Savannah Highway. On a spring day in April 1950, Anne proudly holds her granddaughter, Lynda, all dressed up in her Easter bonnet. (Both courtesy of Margaret Thorne Seidler.)

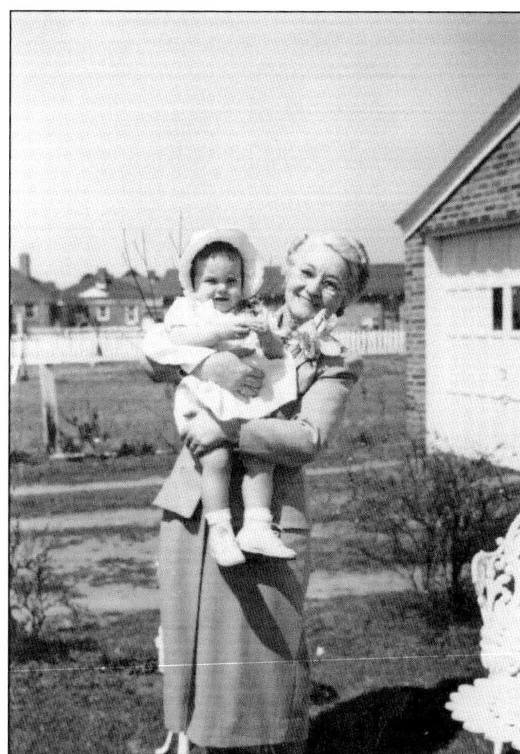

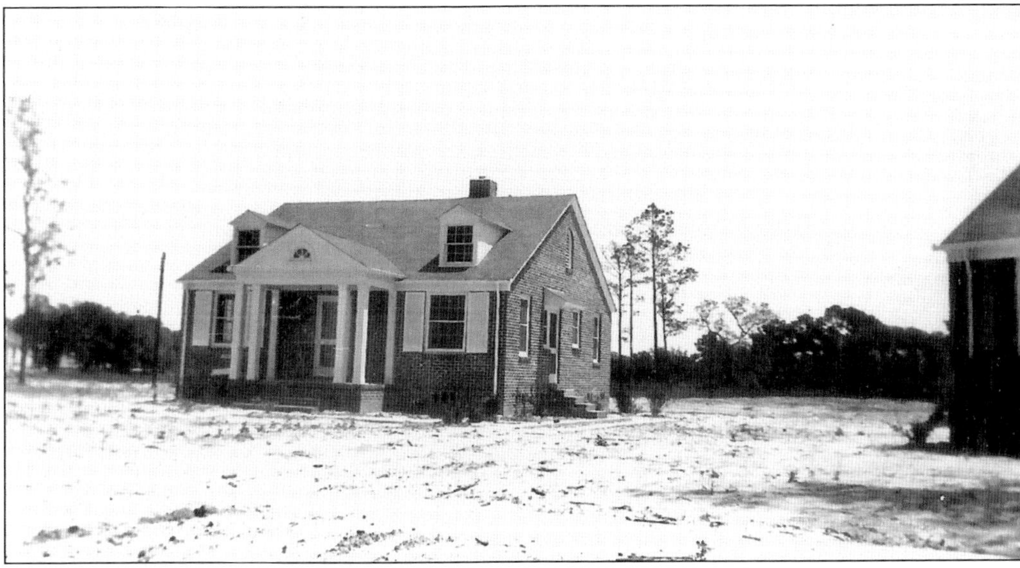

Mrs. B. Rivers Carroll was another very active member of the Garden Club, serving as the first vice president and as secretary under Anne Thorne. Her husband had his office, B. Rivers Carroll Real Estate, at the corner of Daniel Street and Savannah Highway. "If you want to buy or sell across the river see B. Rivers Carroll at 191 Savannah Highway," states an advertisement. A story is told that he was allowed to pick out the "best house in the neighborhood" for his work in selling homes in Byrnes Downs. These photographs illustrate how the Carroll home at 72 Colleton Drive looked in 1945 (above) and in 1950 (below). The transformation of this property is amazing. The wonderful footnote to this story and a testament to the efforts of this original group of ladies is that the house looks this beautiful today. (Both courtesy of Margaret Thorne Seidler.)

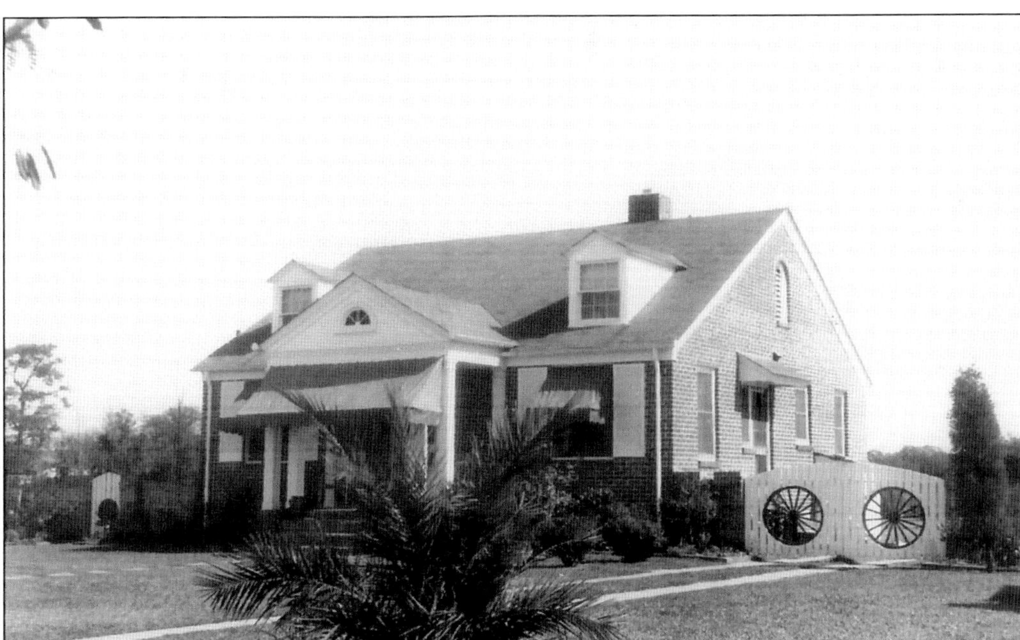

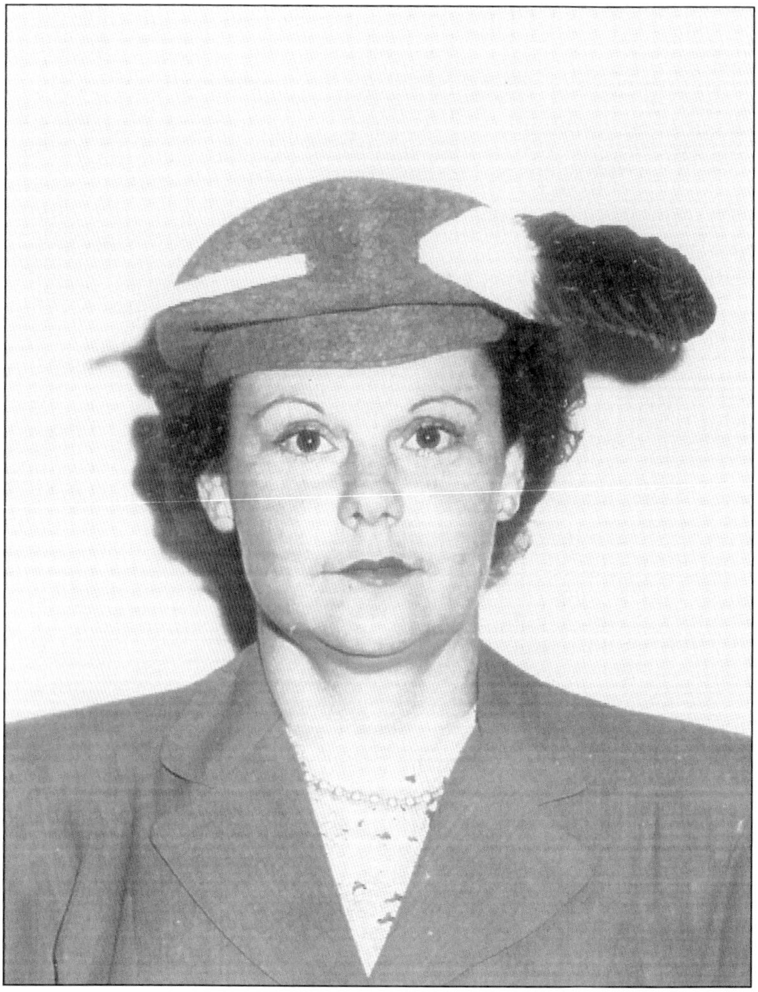

Mrs. Carroll, sporting a lovely hat, poses for her photograph (left) to document in the scrapbook her tenure as the first vice president of the Garden Club. Her home was located on the marsh that fingers its way into Byrnes Downs; during a "marsh hen tide"—a local term for very high tide—one could have launched a canoe from the dock in the backyard and paddled out to Coburg Creek, which led out to the Intracoastal Waterway. Interestingly, when the Byrnes Downs Neighborhood Association was formed in 1990, Helen Momier, who lived at the time at 72 Colleton Drive, was one of the charter members. (Both courtesy of Margaret Thorne Seidler.)

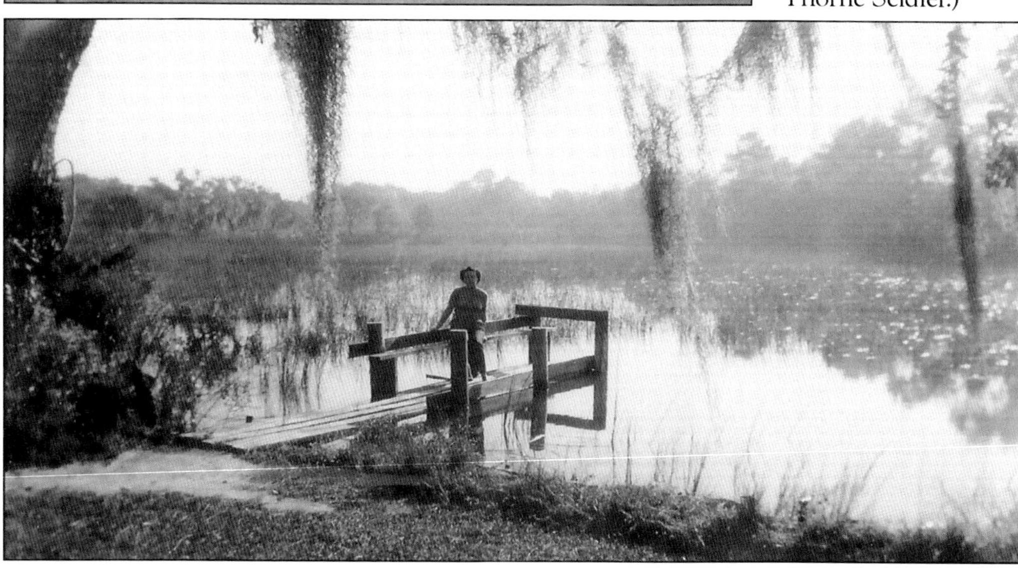

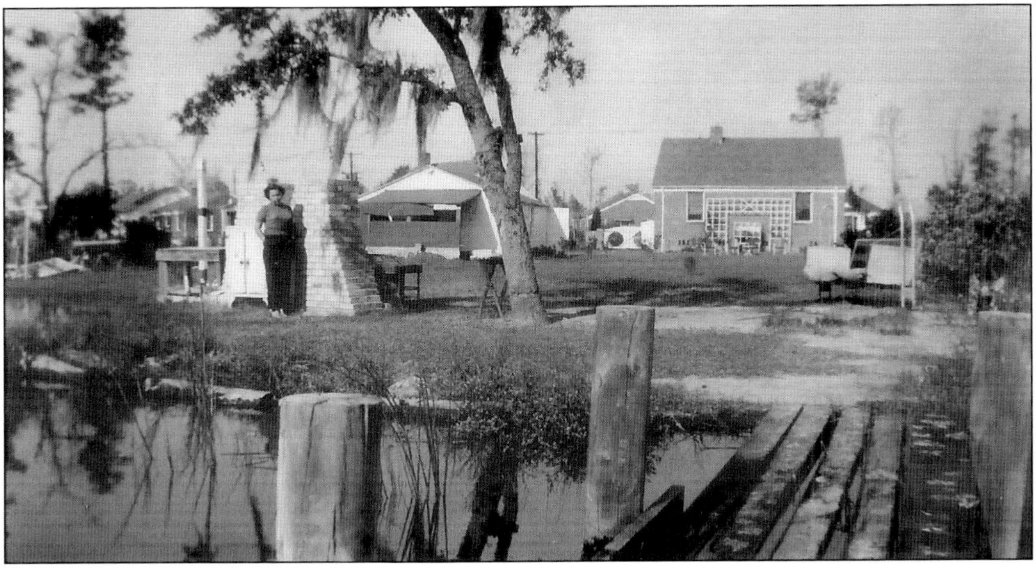

"Many residents of Byrnes Downs have done so much to make their homes more attractive, and thus make a better setting for the gardens surrounding them. Some have added rooms. Some have enclosed their gardens in fences. All these changes were made, with the thought in mind that the home, the center of all life, should bespeak of the grounds surrounding it, and thus add to the beauty of the gardens," reads *History Byrnes Downs Garden Club*. The B. Rivers Carroll home at 72 Colleton Drive best illustrates this quote. The barbecue pit and the landscaped backyard with the dock made this home the centerpiece of the neighborhood. (Courtesy of Margaret Thorne Seidler.)

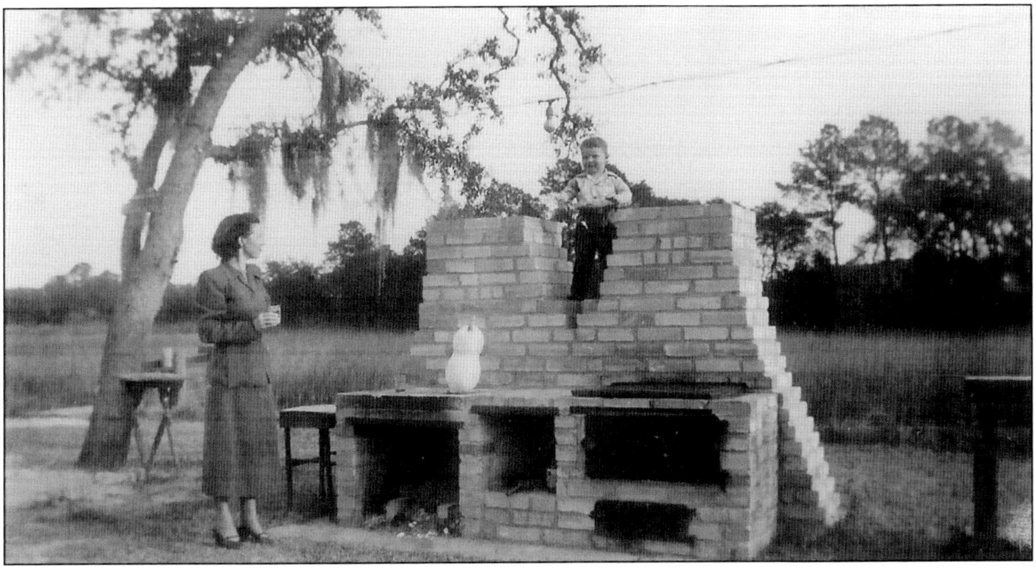

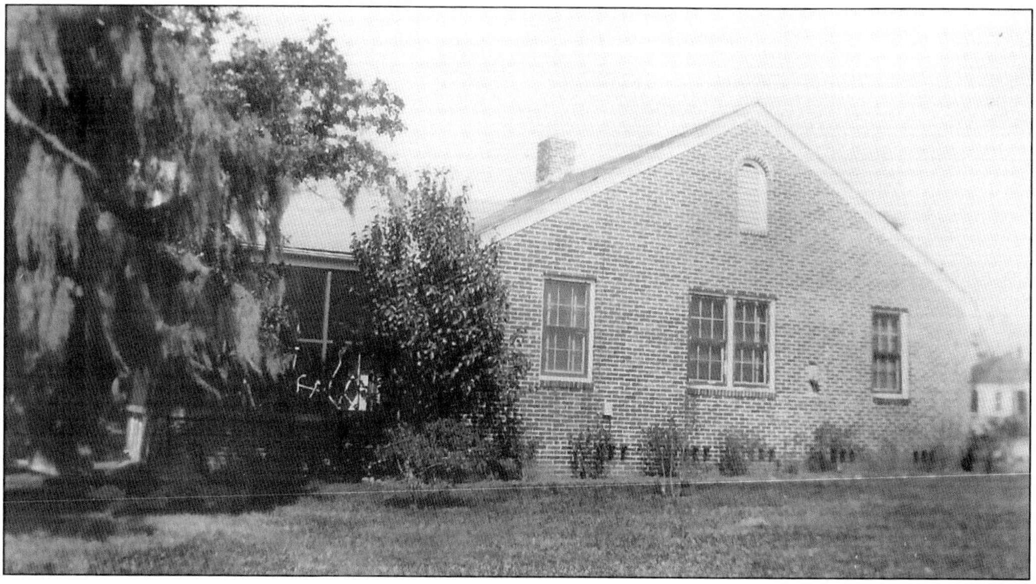

Dr. Leon Banov's home was located along the marsh on the cul-de-sac of Campbell Drive. On the marsh side of the house was a terrace and garden that the ladies captured on film for documentation in the *History Byrnes Downs Garden Club* as another attractive addition to a home. (Both courtesy of Margaret Thorne Seidler.)

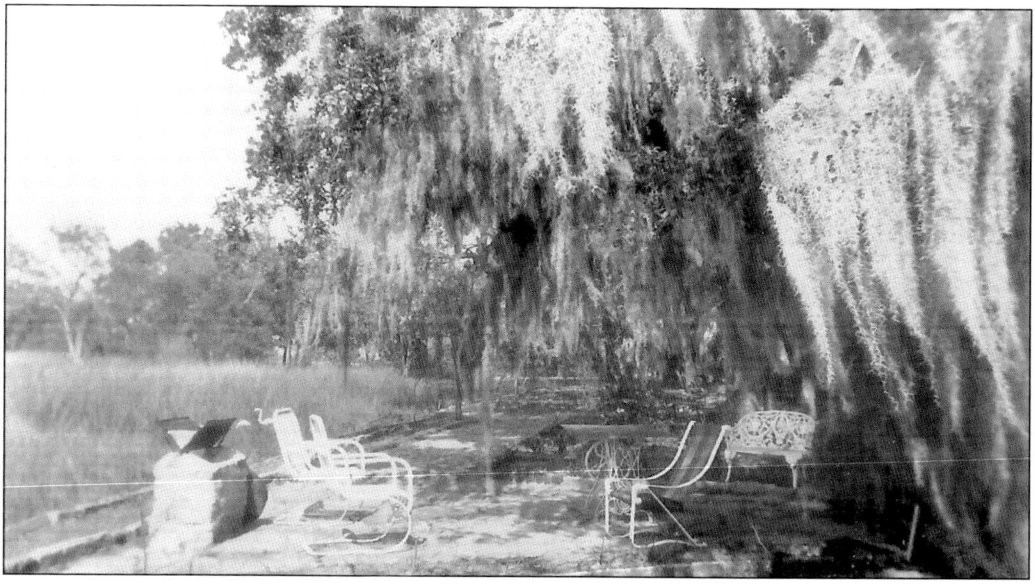

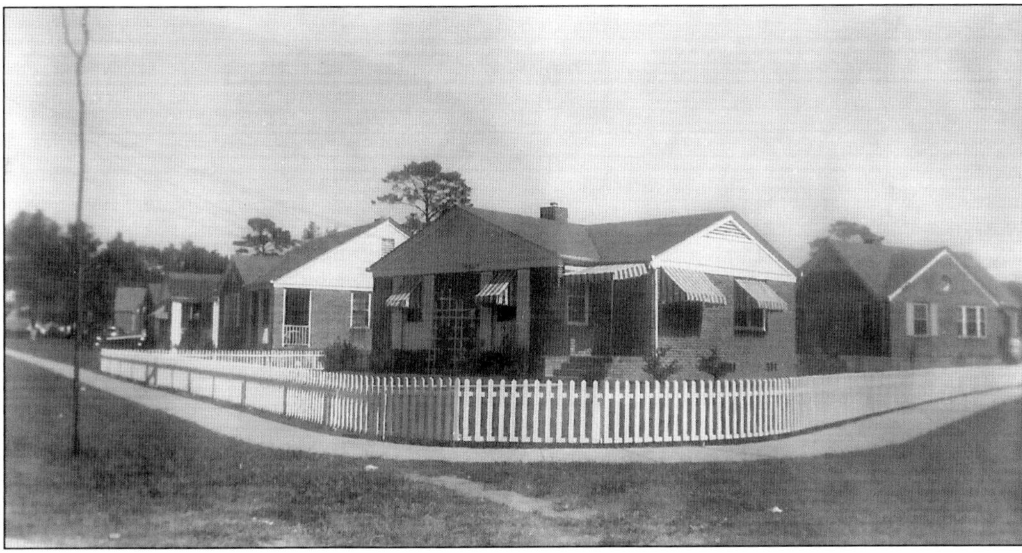

The home of George Breibart at the corner of Yeamans (now Yeadon) Avenue and Nicholson Street is bordered by a white picket fence. Today this house is still bordered by a fence accented with a hedge. Mrs. George Breibart was one of the founding members of the Garden Club. She was very active during the time she lived in Byrnes Downs, serving on several committees, including membership. The home of O. R. Friedell at 59 Campbell Drive is pictured in the lower photograph. Later this would be the home of Michael and Joanne Storen and their son Matthew. Joanne served as the chairman of the environmental committee, responsible for awarding the Yard of the Month and diligently tending to the common planted areas and entrance columns. The seeds planted by the original Garden Club took firm root. (Both courtesy of Margaret Thorne Seidler.)

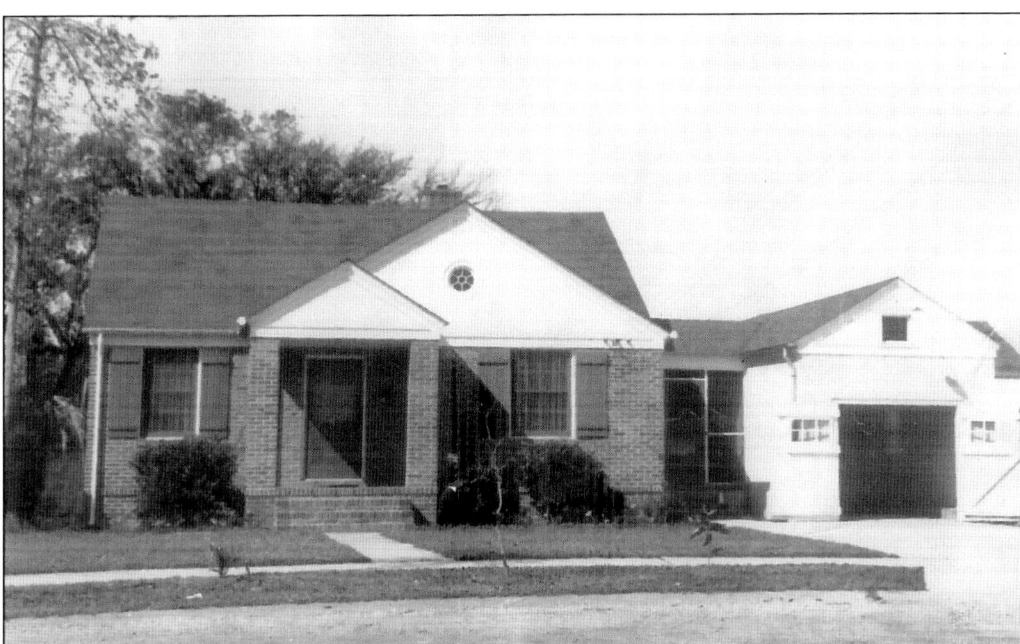

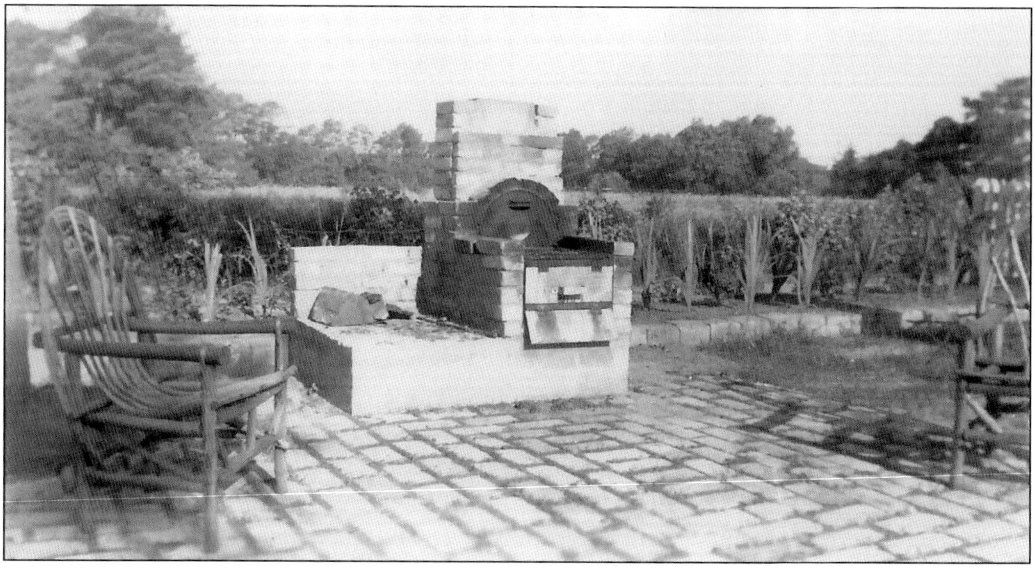

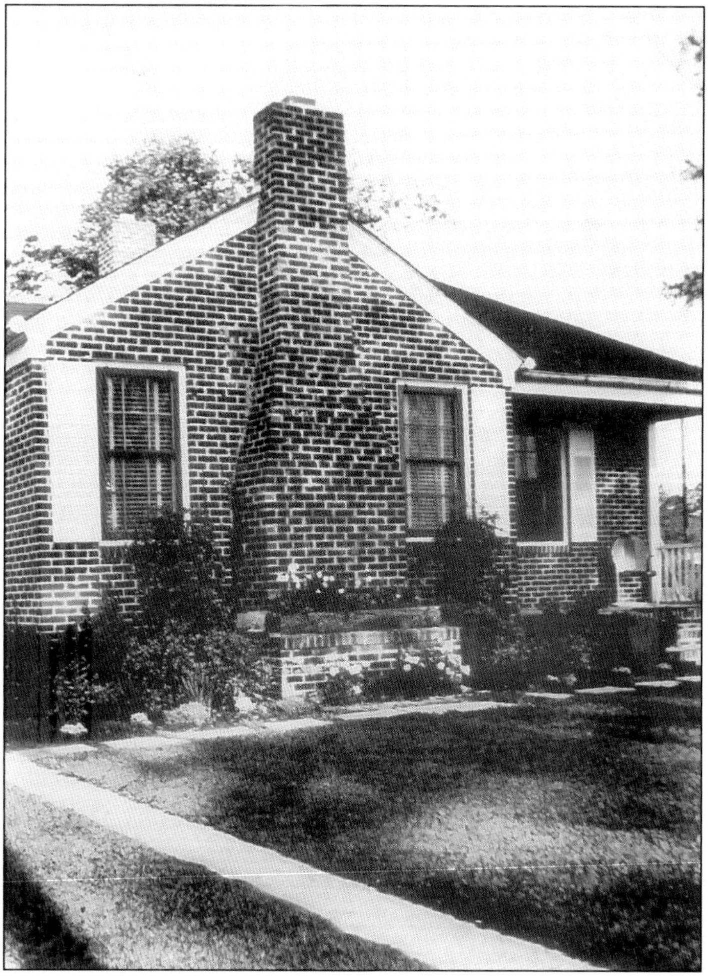

"The following pages show the changes made in some of the homes which made them different from others. There are many more homes in Byrnes Downs which have been changed than are shown here, but we caught these few with the camera as we rode through the Streets of Byrnes Downs," writes May T. Rossiter. Two more examples of these changes are reproduced here. Mr. and Mrs. Edward P. Holcombe Jr. of 47 Broughton Drive (now known as Timmerman Drive) built a barbecue pit and terrace in their back garden (above). Mr. and Mrs. Blair Prevost of 41 Broughton Drive added a chimney to the front of the home (left). "Such an added attraction," captions the photograph. (Both courtesy of Margaret Thorne Seidler.)

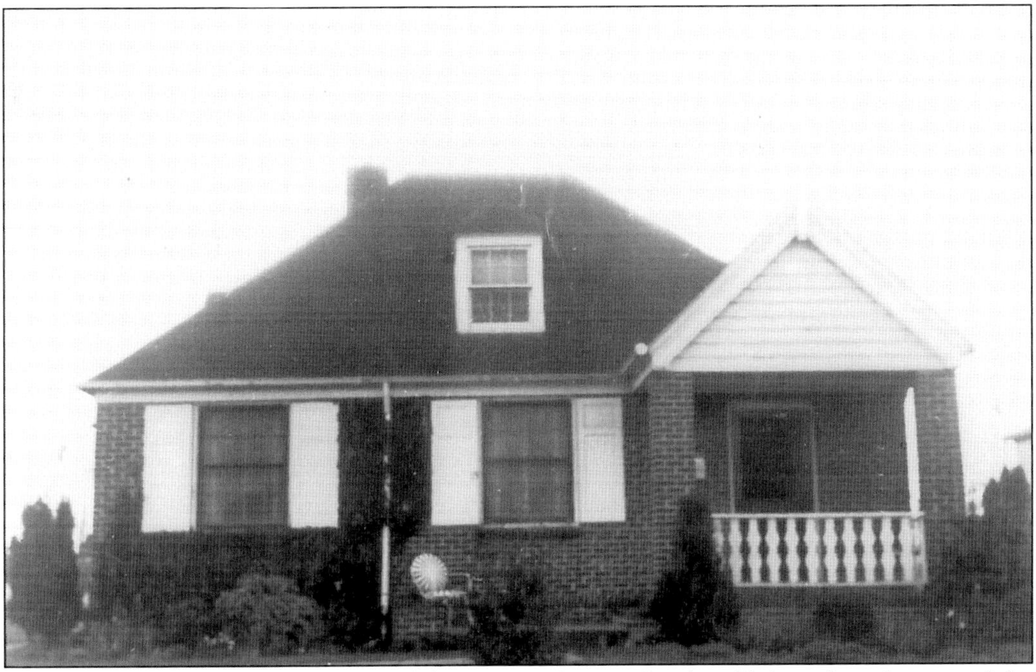

"Another interesting achievement of the Byrnes Downs Garden Club is the selection of the 'Garden of the Month'," read the scrapbook. In November 1949, the Garden of the Month was awarded to Mr. and Mrs. Wright of 15 Sothel Drive (above). In February 1950, the Garden of the Month was awarded to Mr. and Mrs. George Thompson of 28 Sothel Drive (below). Note the similarity between the home at 28 Sothel Drive and Mrs. Thorne's home at 4 Sothel Drive (page 29). There were only four or five basic house plans in the neighborhood, so it is easy to ride around and spot a look-alike. (Both courtesy of Margaret Thorne Seidler.)

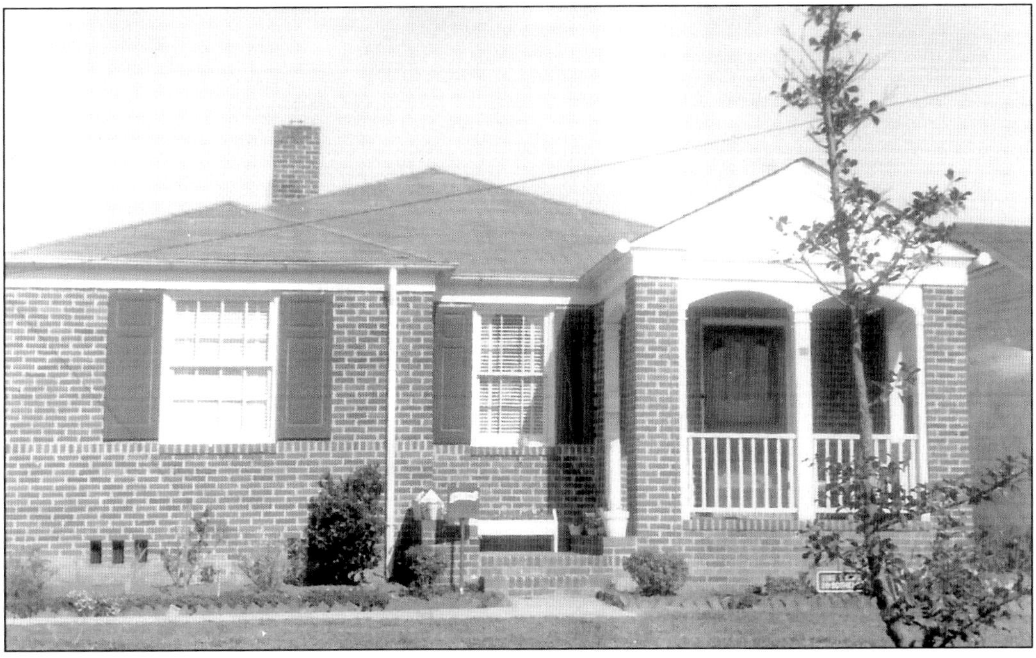

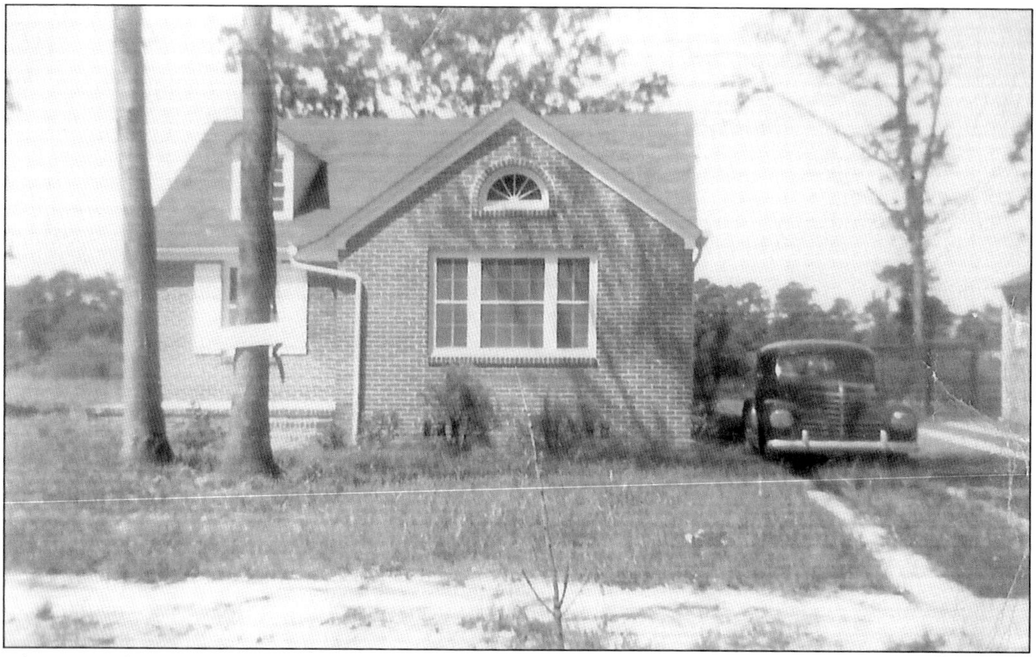

The most dramatic illustration of the "before" and "after" of a Byrnes Downs home are the 1945 (above) and 1949 (below) versions of the P. K. Thompson home at 43 Broughton Drive. Broughton was changed to Timmerman in 1963 in an effort to eliminate duplicate street names in Charleston County. Similarly, Yeamans was changed to Yeadon Avenue. The duplication of street names had become a problem to emergency agencies like fire and police as well as to the postal service. (Both courtesy of Margaret Thorne Seidler.)

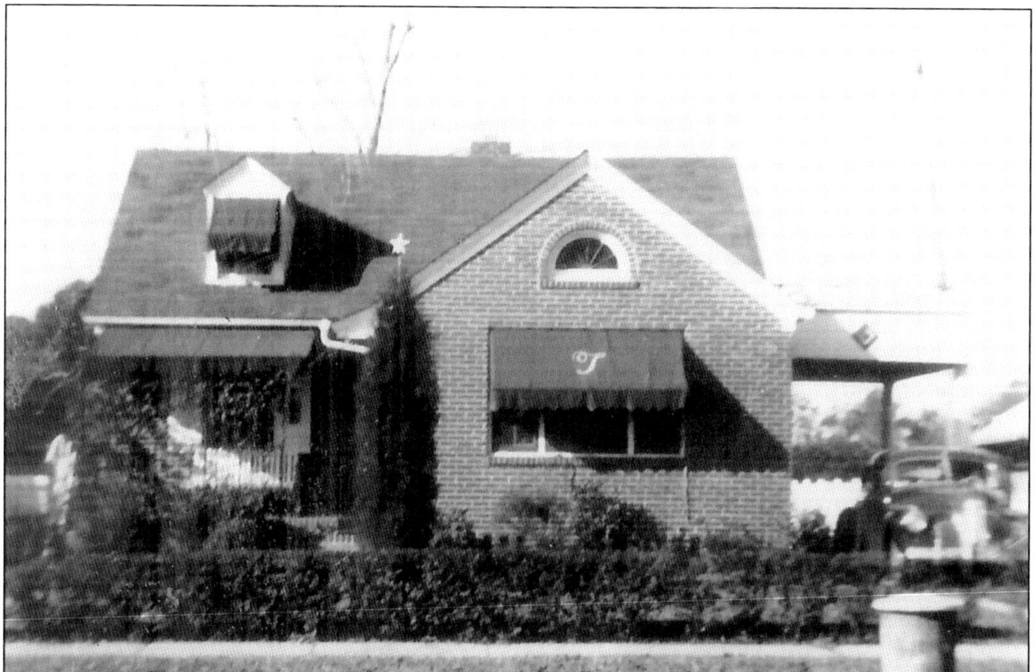

Three

THE NEIGHBORHOOD

The tree-lined sidewalks and streets of Byrnes Downs beckon the residents to push baby strollers, walk dogs, talk over fences, congregate on the sidewalks for a conversation, throw a street party, learn to ride a tricycle or bicycle, hunt for Easter eggs, or roast oysters. It is a place where everyone seems to know each other and can enjoy the simple pleasures of raising families and being good neighbors. Most who move here never want to live anywhere else and, if required to move, always speak with great affection about their life in Byrnes Downs. Because of this affection, Byrnes Downs has been able to maintain a strong sense of place in the community. In December 1953, a newspaper article announced that the Byrnes Downs Garden Club would now be known as the West Ashley Garden Club. This opened membership for all West Ashley residents to the Garden Club. *The History of St. Andrew's Council of Civic Clubs* from 1955 to 1969 lists Byrnes Downs as a member club. Several neighborhood issues prompted the residents of Byrnes Downs to reorganize a chapter of the St. Andrew's Council of Civic Clubs in the 1980s. The main issue to be addressed was the closing of the connector road between Byrnes Downs and South Windermere beside St. Andrew's Elementary School. The road was primarily for the school buses and had morphed into a connection between the two areas. Numerous residents were passionate about this issue; in the end, a new road was formed and named for the principal of St. Andrew's Elementary School, Charles B. Culbertson. This civic club, having addressed the immediate issues of the day, became disorganized. In the summer of 1990, the Byrnes Downs Neighborhood Association was formed under the leadership of Margaret Thorne Seidler and continues today as an active association. One interesting story emerges from the organizational meeting. Mendel Caldwell was the treasurer of the civic club. When the group disbanded, there was money in the treasury. Caldwell transferred the money to his savings account and monitored the accrued interest and balance in a separate column of his ledger. When the group voted to form an association, Caldwell raised his hand and told of the money. He was immediately elected treasurer and held the position until 1998.

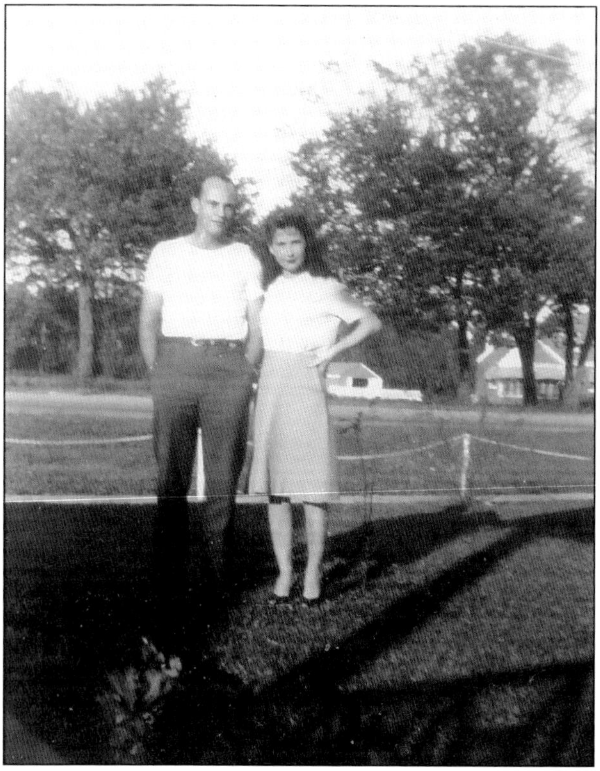

Mildred Weathers Barron and her husband, William H., pose in the front yard of Mildred's parents' home on Savannah Highway in 1949. Mildred's father, J. B., passed away in 1951, and it became important for them to move in with her mother, Carrie, at 119 Savannah Highway in Byrnes Downs. They lived with her mother for a couple of years before purchasing their home in Riverland Terrace. (Courtesy of William H. Barron Jr.)

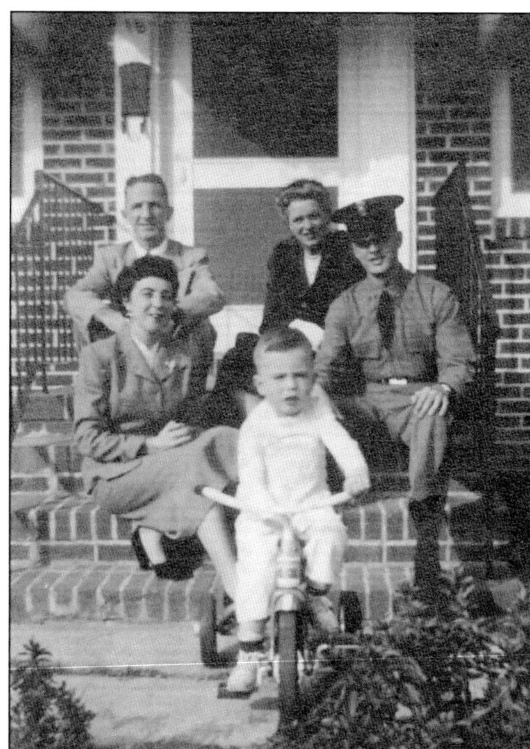

The Lannan family moved to Craven Avenue in the early 1950s. Pictured on the top step of the front stoop are parents Joseph and Mildred, and on the middle steps are Barbara and her brother Michael, who attended the Citadel. Their brother Timothy is on the tricycle. When Timothy grew up, one of his adventures was spending summers in Alaska as a tour guide. Barbara lives in the home today. (Courtesy of Barbara Lannan.)

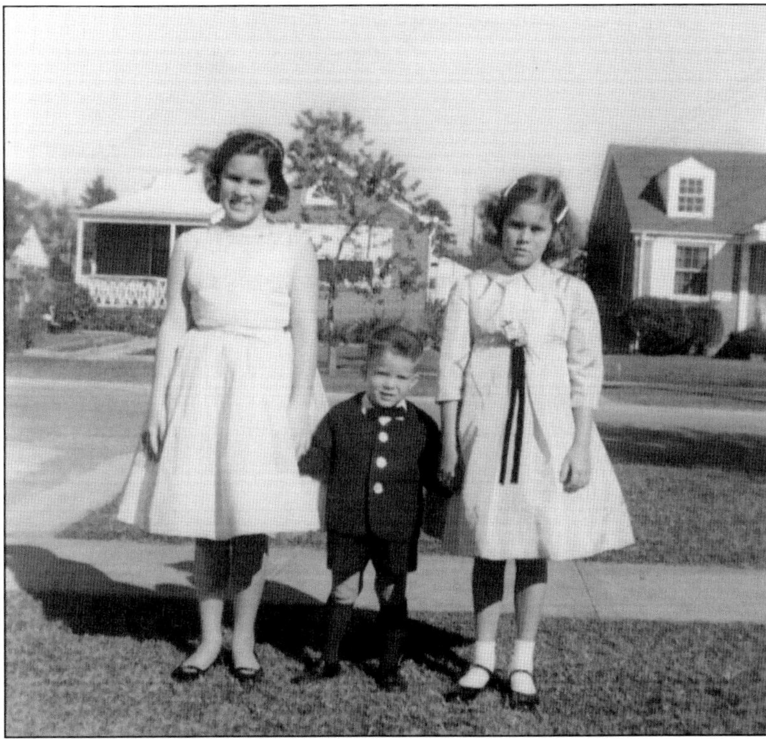

Easter time in Charleston is the perfect time to dress up the family and take a picture. Nancy (left), Larry, and Jeanne Hartnett hold hands and pose for their Easter photograph. One can see a tree in the background, then grown to about the height of the rooftop. In a few more years, a canopy of oak trees would shade the sidewalks and streets. (Courtesy of the Hartnett family.)

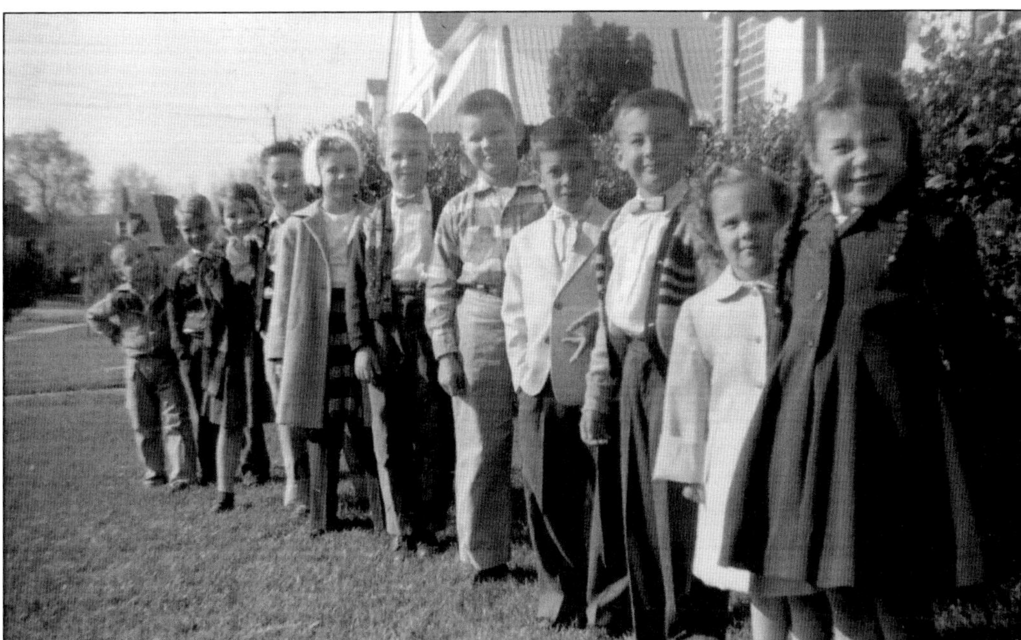

What better way is there to celebrate a birthday than with a party? The family and neighborhood friends gather with Mendel Caldwell Jr. to smile for the camera. From left to right are Henry Pregnel, Ron Caldwell, Peggy Caulfield, Skip Weldon, Patsy Touchberry, Mendel (wearing a bow tie), Robert Wilson, Charlie Calas, Craig McClure, Susie Norvell, and Sarah Ann Calas. Thanks to Mendel Jr. for remembering all the names. (Courtesy of the Caldwell family.)

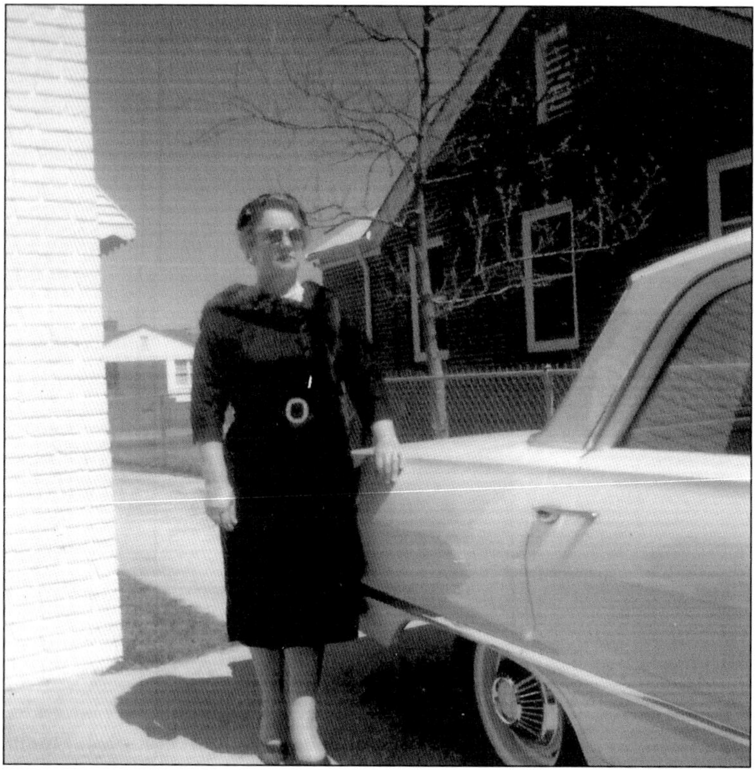

In April 1963, Lurena Hiers stands proudly beside the automobile in the driveway of her home. Lurena was Donald Charpie's great-aunt and resided at 43 Yeadon Avenue. Book L46, page 3 in the Register of Mense Conveyance office shows Lurena's husband, Herbert J. Hiers, purchasing Lot 6, Block L in December 1945. The "Personals" section of the *West Ashley Journal* describes their daughter Rena's birthday party with 49 children in attendance. (Courtesy of Donald Charpie.)

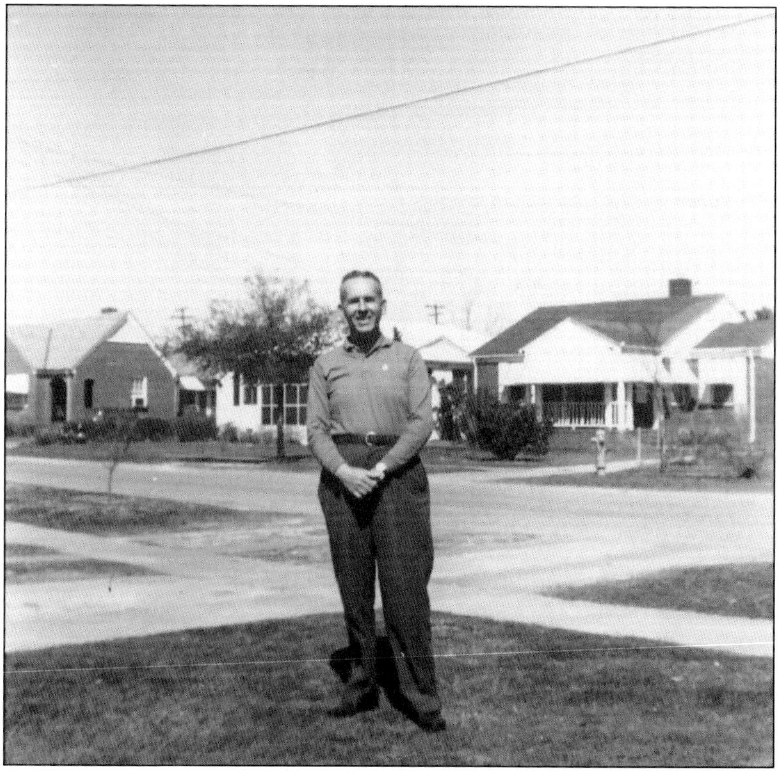

Lawrence Hartnett was the perfect father, according to Jeanne, his daughter, who has lived in Byrnes Downs since a very young age. He served in the U.S. Navy during the war; after World War II ended, he worked at the Charleston Navy Yard. The house on Yeadon Avenue was the first and only house he and his wife, Doris, bought, and they lived there for the rest of their lives. (Courtesy of the Hartnett family.)

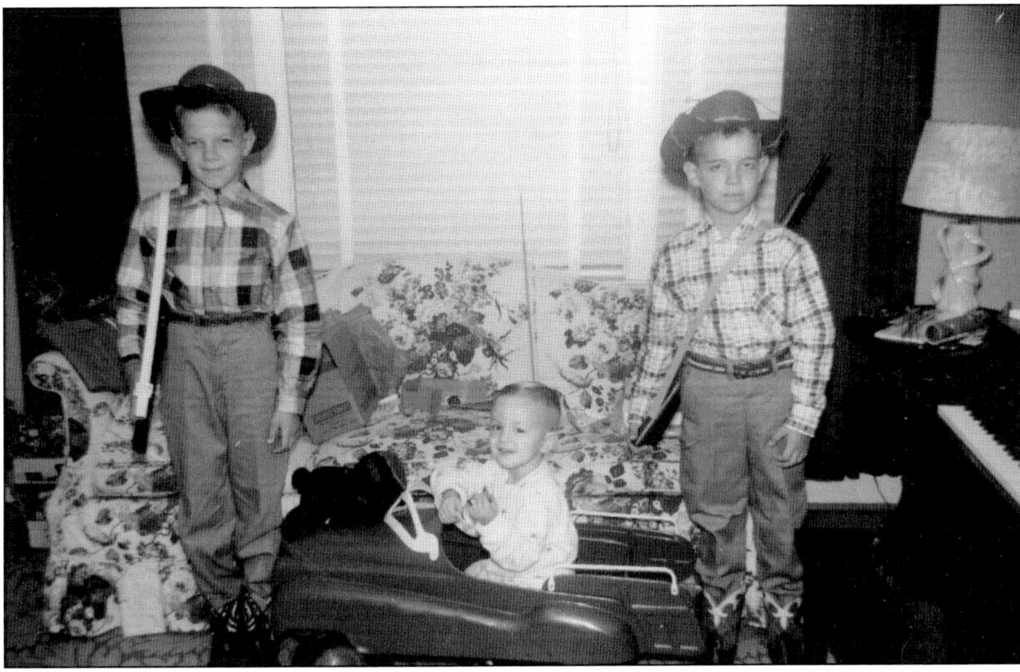

The Caldwell "Cowboys"—Mendel Jr. (left), Gary (in the car/wagon), and Ronnie—prepare for the "Wild West Frontier" in the living room on Colleton Drive. In reality, growing up in Byrnes Downs was like living in a *Leave it to Beaver*–type neighborhood according to Mendel Jr. (Courtesy of the Caldwell family.)

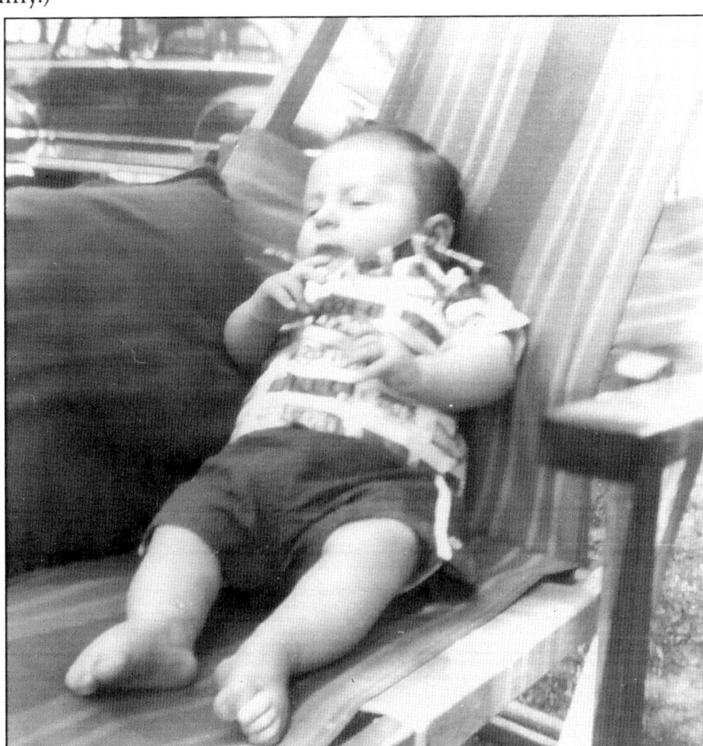

Nell Harvey lived across the street from Camilla Blanton on Colleton Drive, and they were great friends. In this 1955 photograph, Nell's son Bobby poses in a lawn chair. In 1992, Byrnes Downs raised the money to build three new entrance columns for the neighborhood. Bobby offered to cast the nameplates for these new columns from nameplates that had been recovered and saved by Rutledge Corvette from a destroyed entrance column. (Courtesy of Camilla Blanton.)

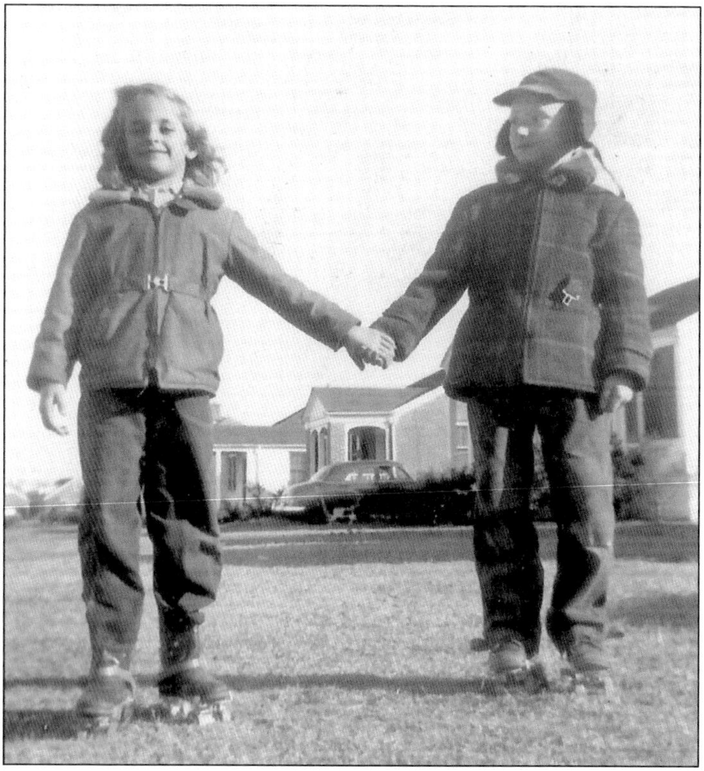

Felix Nepveux III (right) lived at 28 Craven Avenue, and Patty McCrary (left) lived at 13 Craven Avenue. Her mother, Mrs. C. F. McCrary, was a member of the Garden Club, as was Mrs. McCrary's sister Evelyn McConnell, who lived at 9 Craven Avenue. McConnell's son, Glenn, would be elected to the South Carolina Senate to represent District 41 (which includes Byrnes Downs) in 1981. Senator McConnell continues to represent the area and now serves as the president pro tempore of the S.C. Senate. In the lower photograph, Felix (right) stands with another neighborhood boy as the camera gives a view along Craven Avenue. (Both courtesy of Ethel Nepveux.)

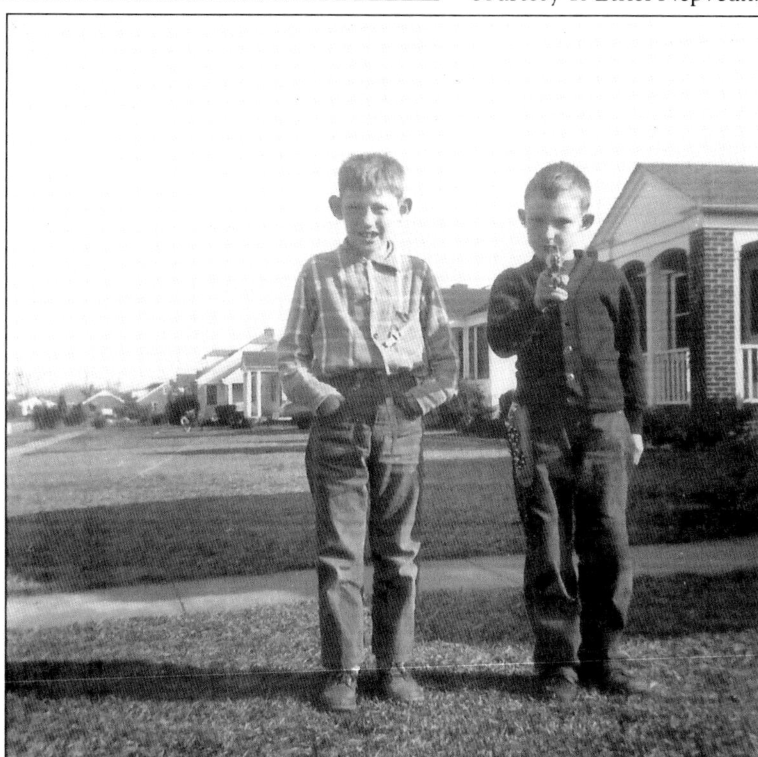

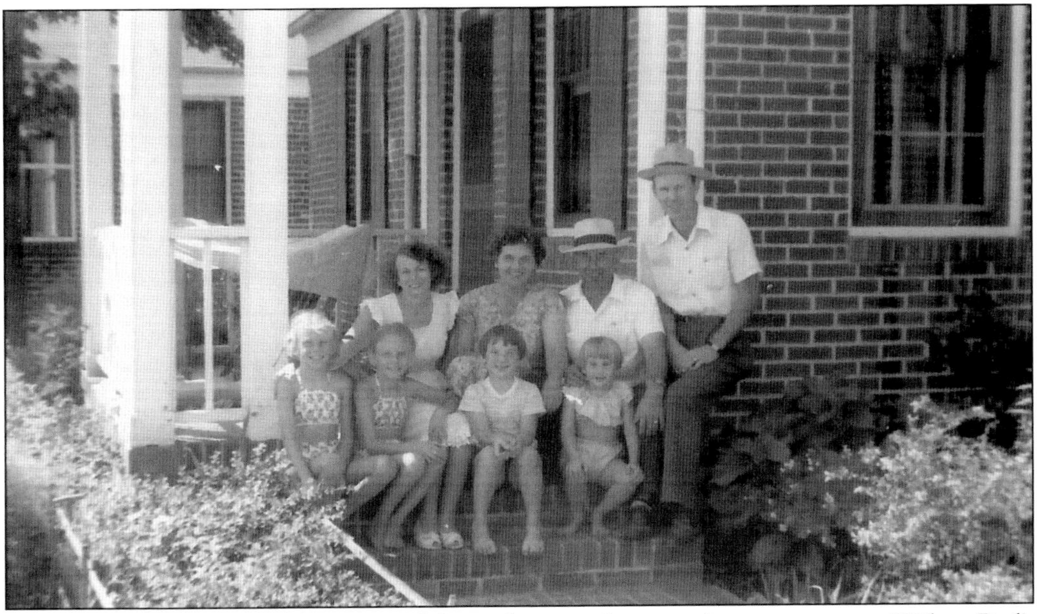

The Blantons loved to gather a crowd for a photograph or maybe even a party. "When Red's brother Marchant and his family came for a visit from Woodruff, South Carolina, it was a reason to celebrate," recalls Camilla Blanton. The family gathered on the Blantons' front porch for a photograph. From left to right are the following: (first row) Judi and Susan Blanton, and Marchant's daughters Brenda and Margaret Blanton; (second row) Camilla, Sara (Marchant's wife), Marchant, and Red. (Courtesy of Camilla Blanton.)

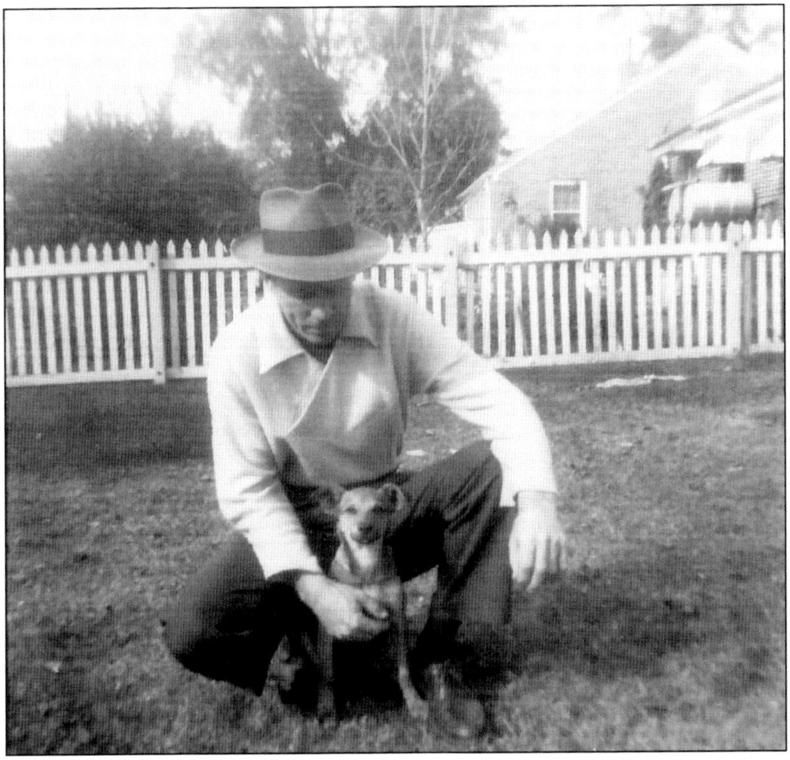

The Blantons owned a dog, Yogi, named by Susan and Judi after the cartoon character Yogi the Bear. Red corrals Yogi for a photograph in the backyard. (Courtesy of Camilla Blanton.)

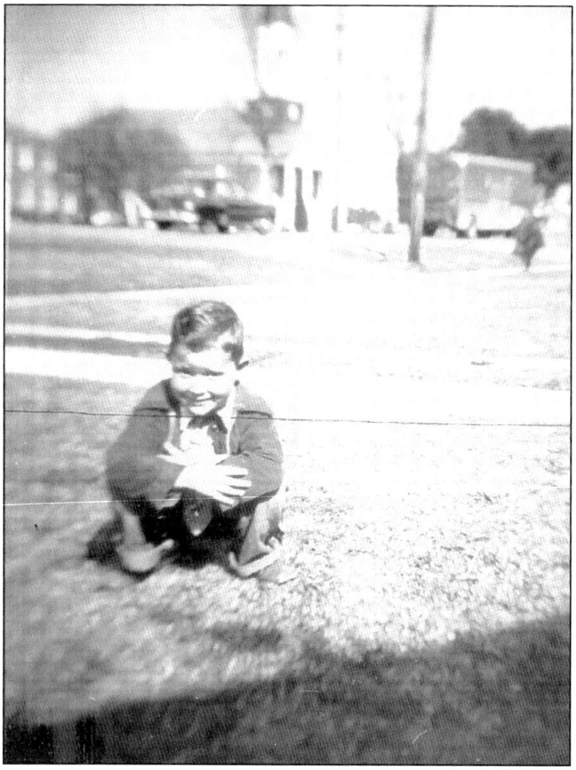

Bobby Barron was Mildred and William Barron's only son, born in October 1946. In 1952, when the family moved in with his grandmother Carrie at 119 Savannah Highway, he attended St. Andrew's Elementary School. Bobby smiles for the camera in the front yard of his grandmother's home with the John Wesley Church in the background (at left). Below, he is in the backyard with his dog, Chiquita, and a friend (in back). The backs of the homes along Yeadon Avenue are easily visible in this photograph. (Both courtesy of William H. Barron Jr.)

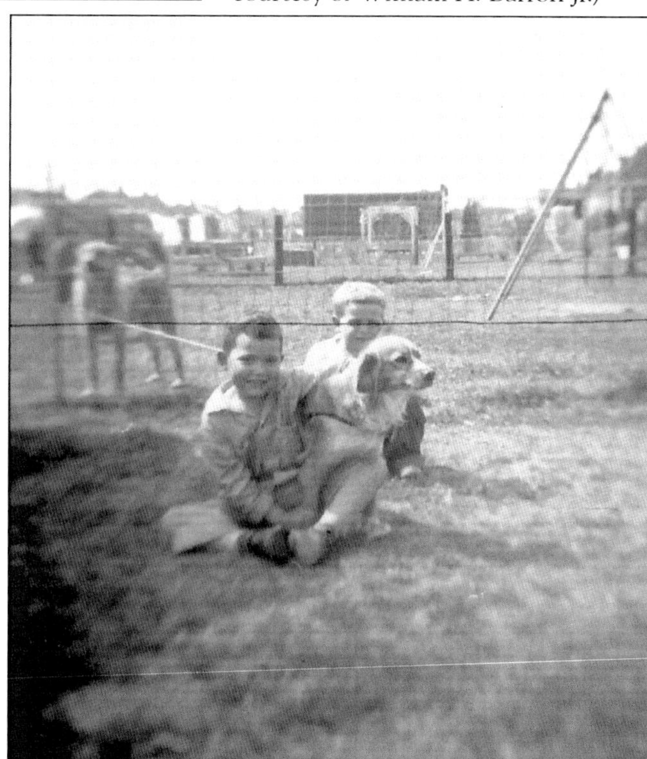

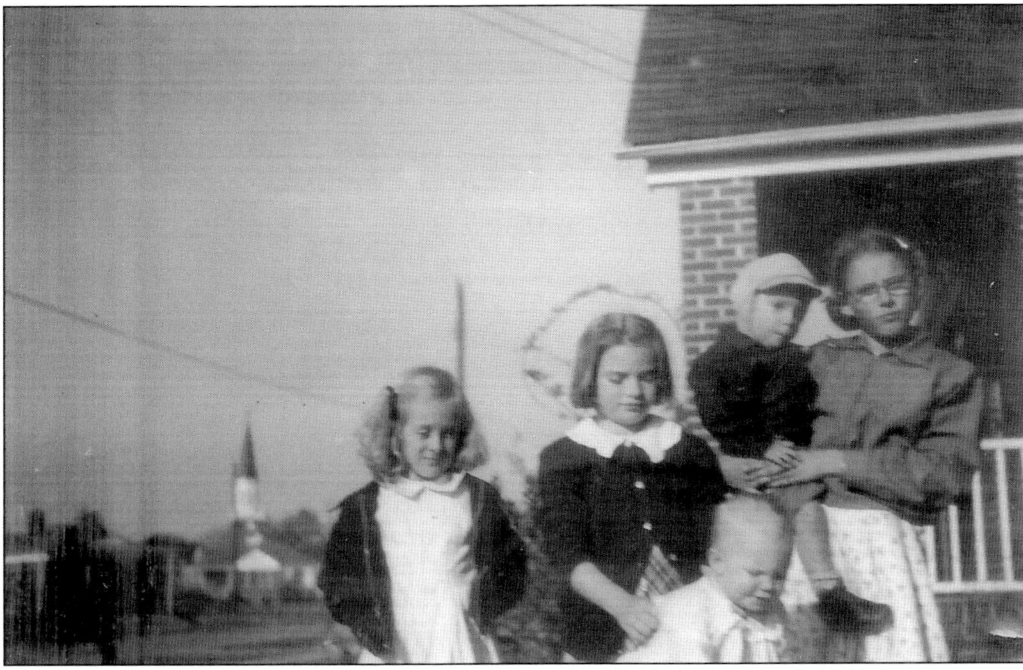

Neighborhood kids pose with Beth Corvette on her first birthday in March 1952. Beth's parents, Rutledge and Margaret Corvette, and grandparents, John Emiel and Ruth Fariey Corvette, lived on Campbell Drive and were very active in the John Wesley Methodist Church. The oak trees planted by the Garden Club are not quite mature enough to block the view of this church in the background. (Courtesy of Rutledge and Margaret Corvette.)

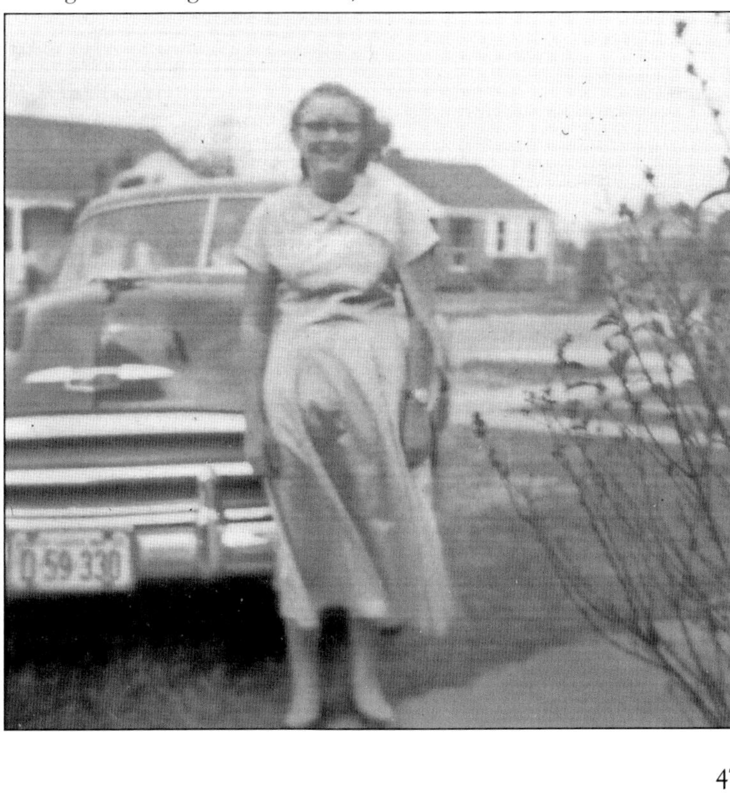

Francis G. Melfi purchased Lot 14, Block J on Campbell Drive in March 1945 for $3,500. Rookie, Francis's wife, poses on a windy day in her front yard. She would soon give birth to her son, George. As a side note, Rookie's parents, Henry O. and Marie Hasselmeyer, were the owners of Henry's, the famous restaurant located in the Market. (Courtesy of Frances and Joe Roy.)

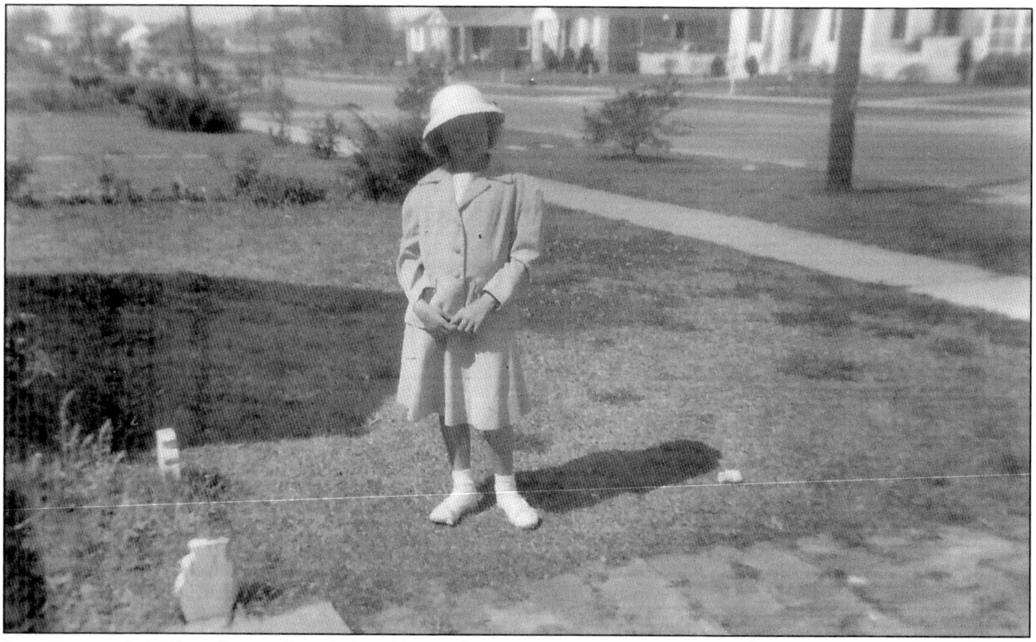

Jan Craven Melfi is dressed with her Easter bonnet on a sunny spring day and is ready for the egg hunt to begin. The gardens of the neighborhood are still young, as are the families. (Courtesy of Frances and Joe Roy.)

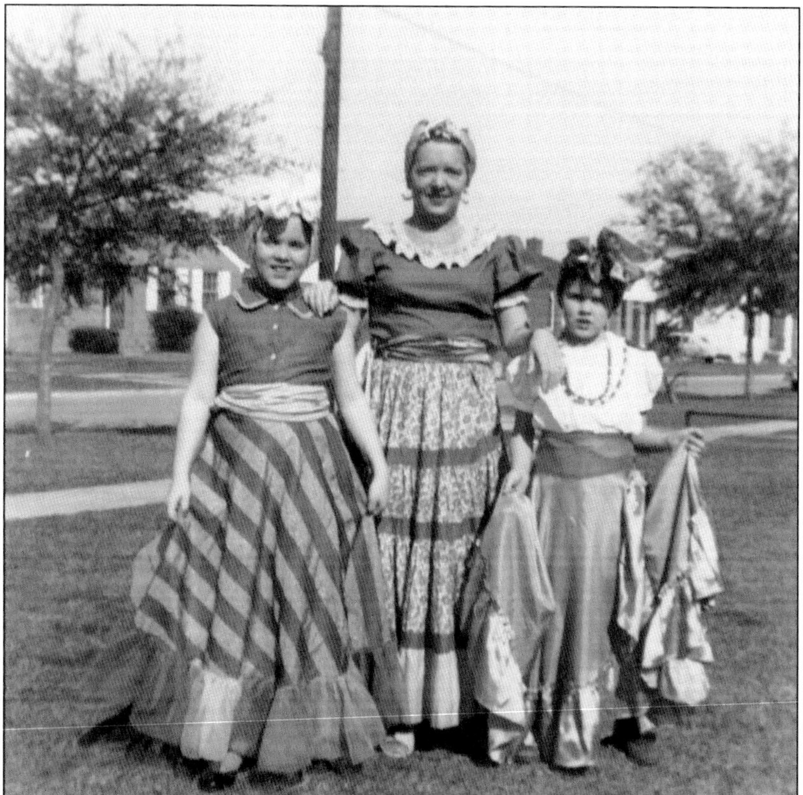

Doris Hartnett was an excellent seamstress, making all of her children's clothes except their socks. When Halloween costumes were needed, out came the fabric, needle, and thread. Nancy (left), Doris (center), and Jeanne model Doris's creations. Notice the trees in the background—they are really beginning to take shape. (Courtesy of the Hartnett family.)

Shane Austin, son of Jim and Saundra Austin, received a tricycle on his first birthday in July 1975. By the winter of 1975, he was a tricycle professional, pedaling down the driveway of their Yeadon Avenue home. (Courtesy of Jim and Saundra Austin.)

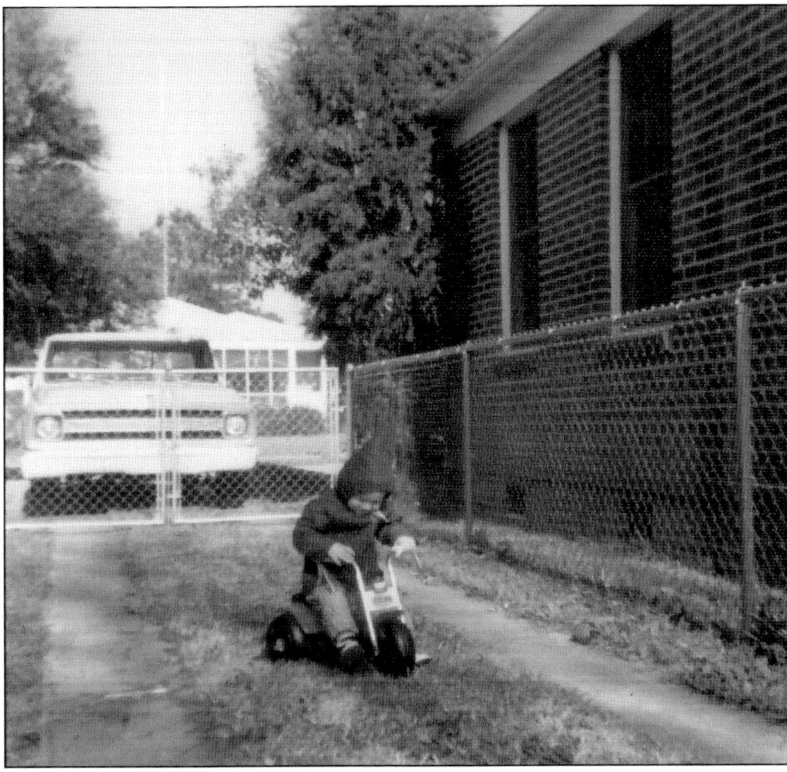

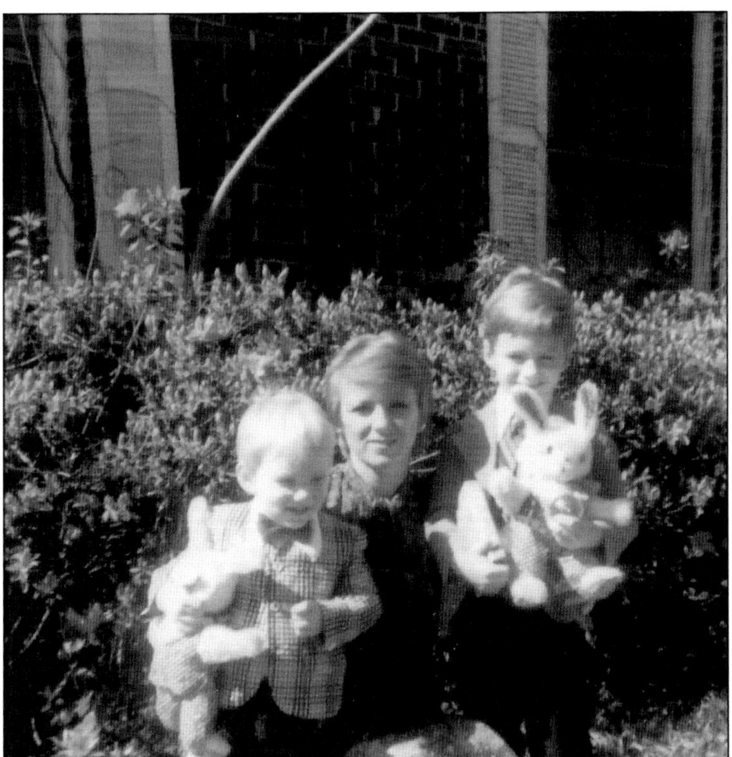

Aaron (left) and Shane Austin pose with Easter bunnies in their arms and with Saundra's arms around them. All dressed up for Easter Sunday church services is the perfect occasion for a photograph. Today Aaron and Shane are both married with children and live in the Charleston area. (Courtesy of Jim and Saundra Austin.)

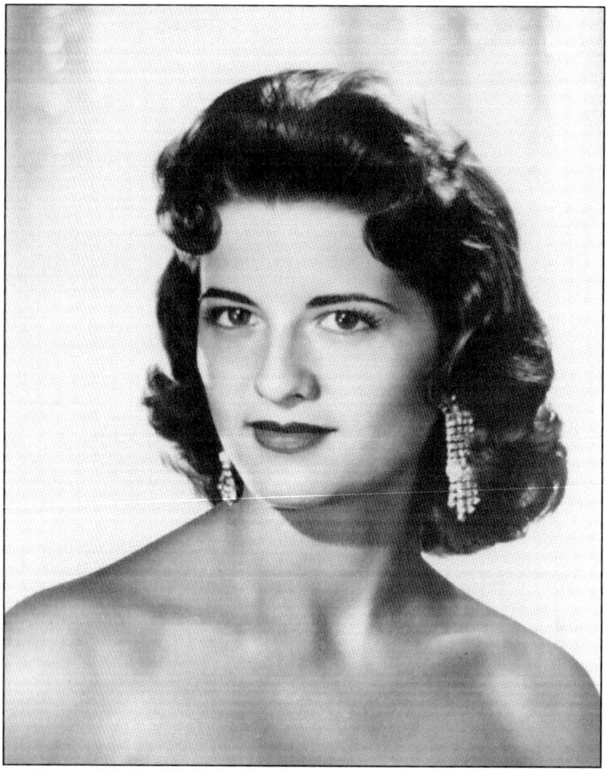

Gene Lenoir Wilson, the daughter of Bob and Sally Wilson of 48 Colleton Drive, was crowned Miss Charleston for the 1958–1959 season and Miss South Carolina in 1959. According to the *News and Courier* article featuring Gene, her parents were expecting a boy—"even their doctor predicted a male child." Her photograph ran with the headline "A Shock for Father—This is a Gridiron Hero . . . ?" (Courtesy of Sally Wilson.)

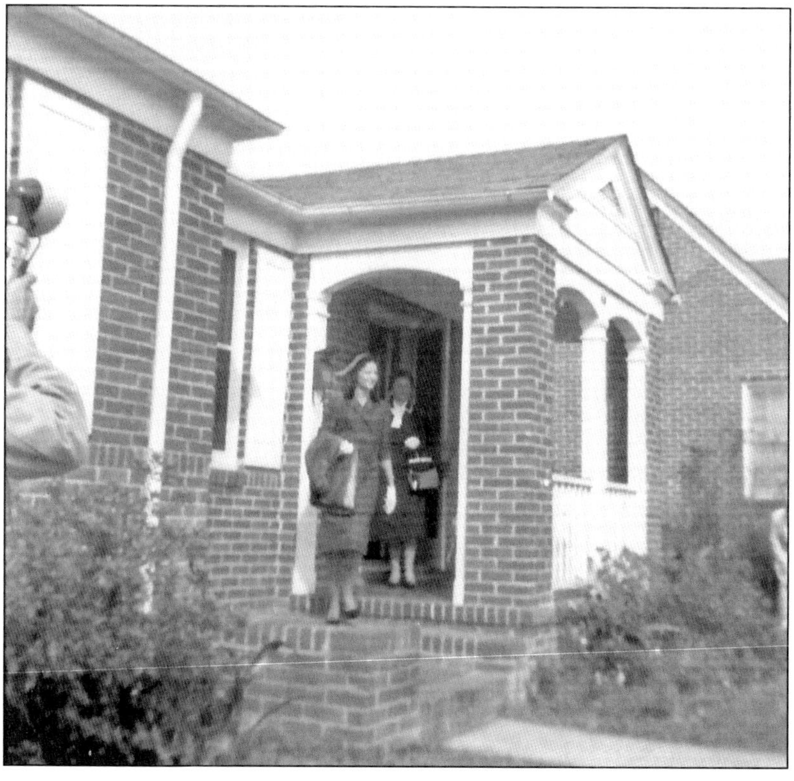

With a lot of pomp, fanfare, paparazzi, and a 35-car motorcade, Gene and her mother, Sally, leave their Colleton home in Byrnes Downs for the airport. As Miss South Carolina, she would represent the state in the Miss America contest, held in Atlantic City. Gene was the Charleston Civitan nominee to the Miss Charleston pageant. This nomination was her first step on the road to the Miss America pageant. (Courtesy of Camilla Blanton.)

Gene poses with her dad, Robert B. Wilson, for the many professional and amateur neighborhood photographers in her father's front yard. Several hundred people were present to wish her well on her journey and bid for Miss America. Her father and brother Robert drove to Atlantic City to attend the ceremonies. (Courtesy of Camilla Blanton.)

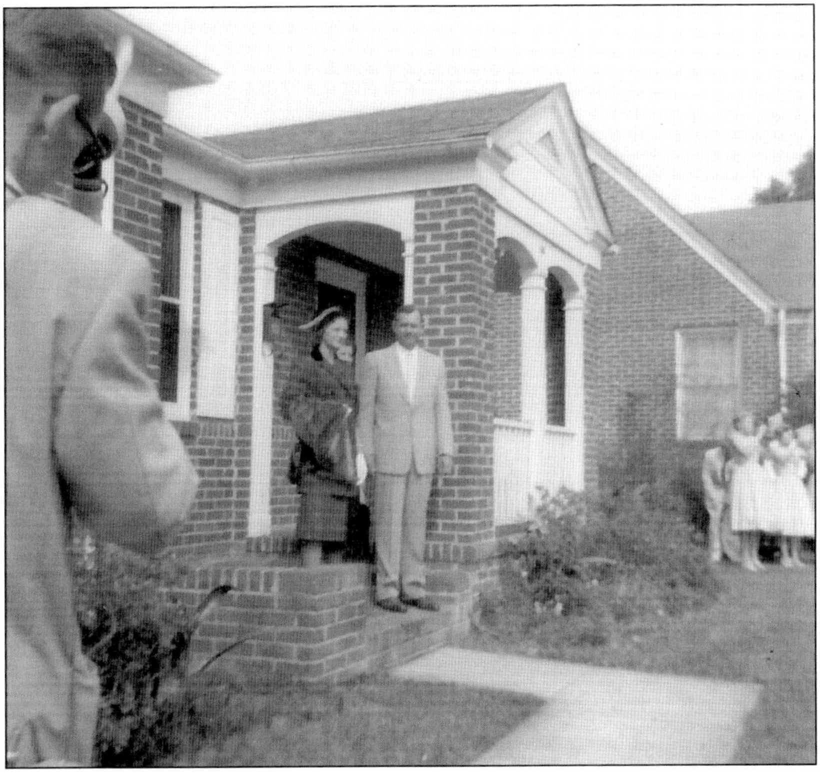

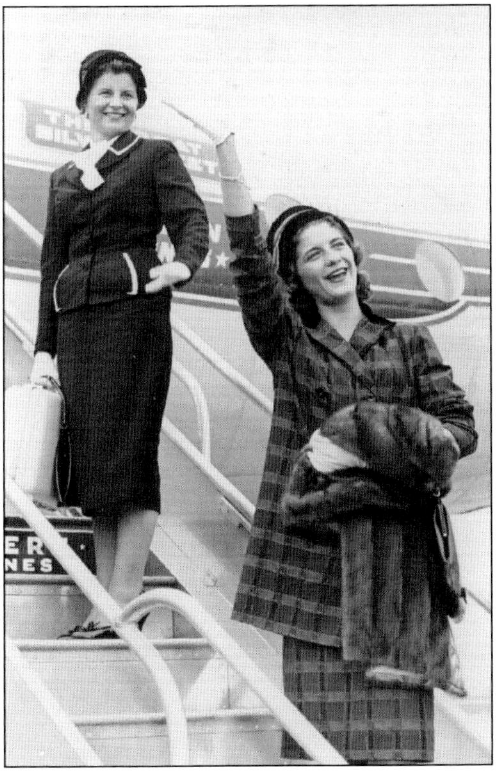

Gene waves to the well-wishers as she and her mother, Sally, board the airplane to Atlantic City. Gene was not successful in her bid for Miss America. She did, however, win first place as the most talented classical or semi-classical singer with her rendition of "If I Loved You" from *Carousel*. She received a $1,000 scholarship for this accomplishment. After her tenure as Miss South Carolina, Gene finished her degree at Converse College. Prior to pursuing her music and voice interest at Converse, she loved to sing in local churches, particularly her church, Ashley River Baptist Church. (Courtesy of Sally Wilson.)

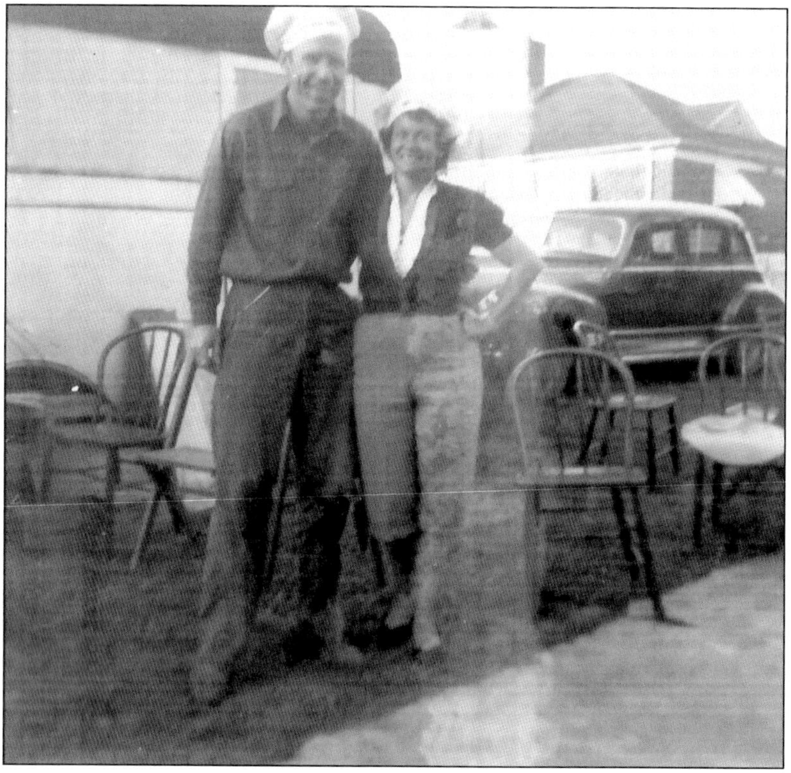

Red and Camilla Blanton (left) take a minute from party preparation to pose for the camera in their chef's hats. The tables and chairs are set up in their backyard, and the neighbors gather to roast some oysters. Mack Blanton, dressed in an apron; Red, still in his chef hat; Marion Harvey, sampling a freshly shucked oyster; Nell Harvey; and George Calas, with his signature hat, are some of the neighbors gathered for the oysters. (Both courtesy of Camilla Blanton.)

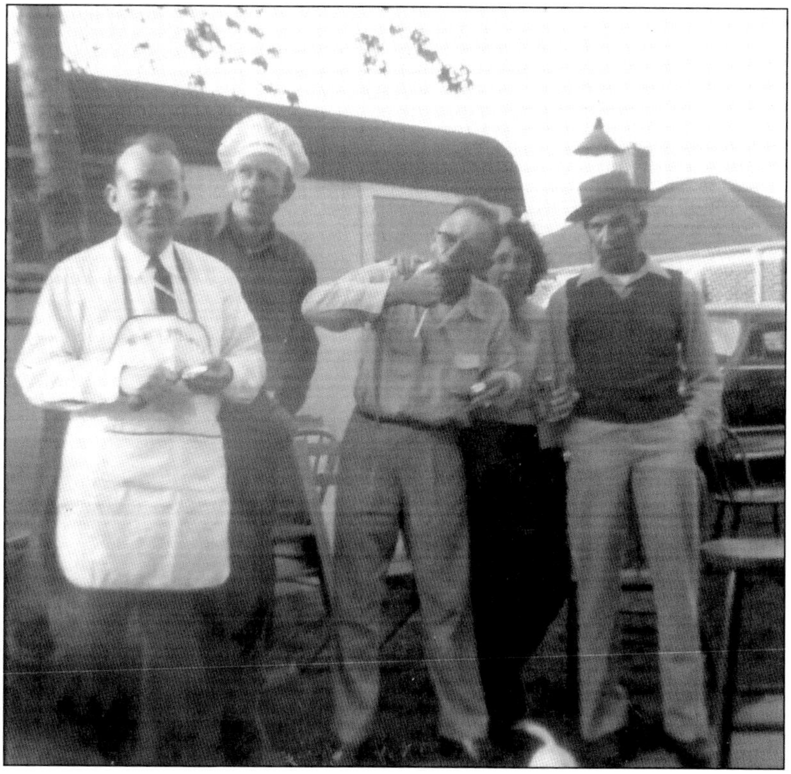

Julian and Barbara Kiel purchased 4 Nicholson Street in Byrnes Downs for their daughter Barbara Ann. Standing on the porch of the home is Barbara Ann and her son Michael. This house is directly across from Fire Station 10. Every morning at approximately 8:00 a.m., the firemen drive the fire trucks out of the station and conduct a test of all the alarms. What a wake-up call! (Courtesy of Julian and Barbara Kiel.)

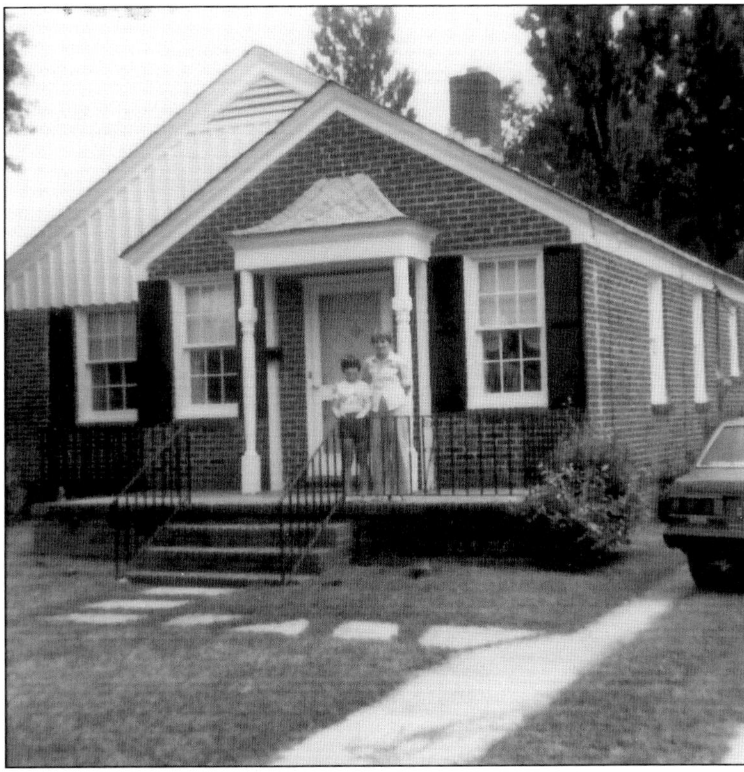

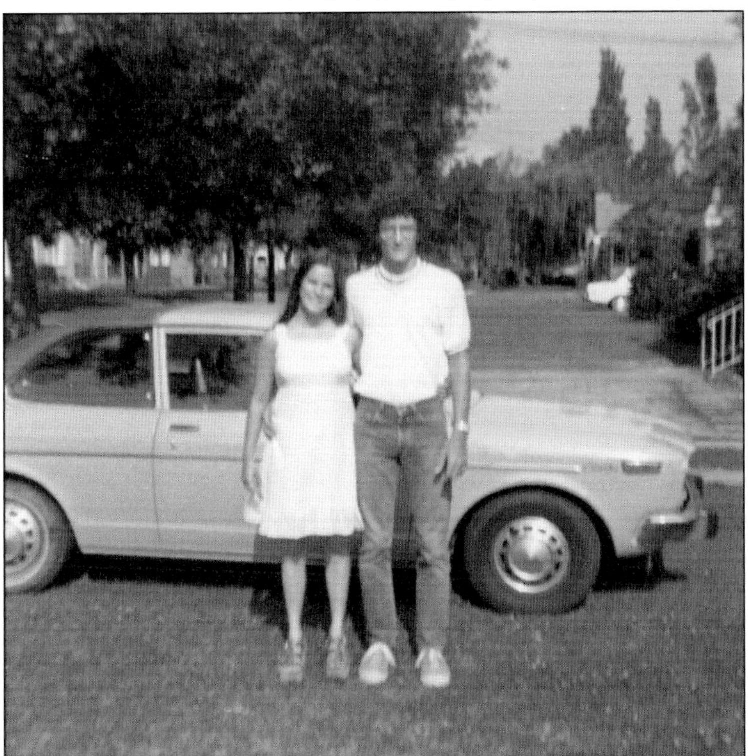

In 1976, Joyce Hartnett and Marvin Kirkland were high school sweethearts. Upon graduation, Joyce attended the College of Charleston and Marvin went to the Citadel. Life took them on separate paths until later, when they rekindled their high school romance and are now married. Although they reside in Georgia, they still own the family home on Yeadon Avenue. (Courtesy of the Hartnett family.)

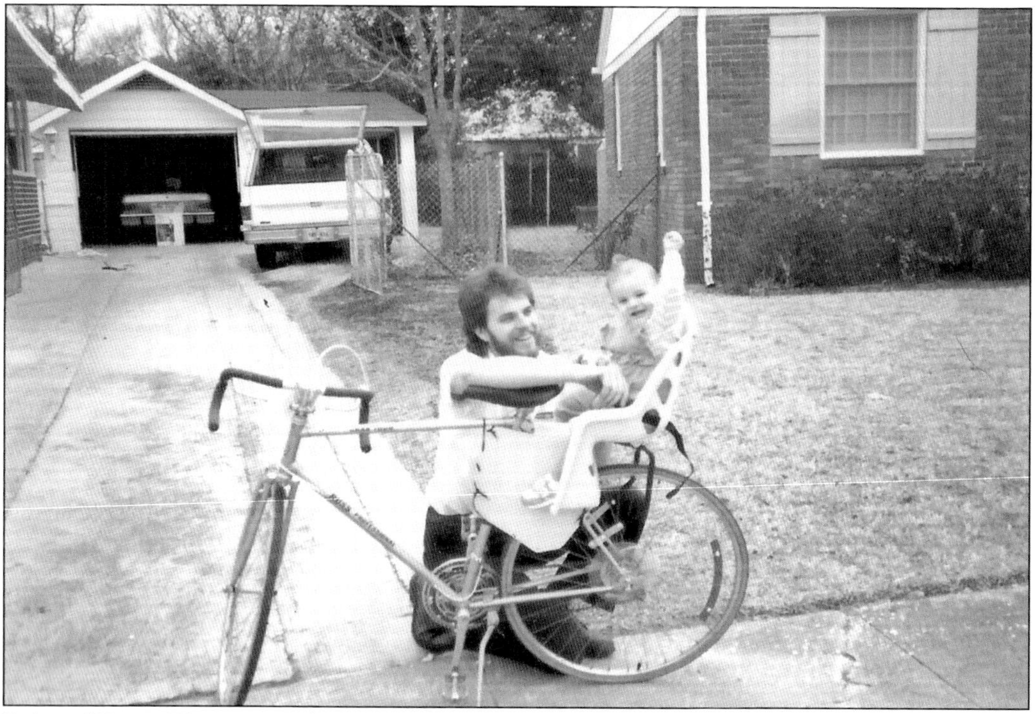

Bob and Karen Thames purchased their home on Lyttleton Avenue in October 1981. Amy, their only daughter, was born in May 1984. Almost a year later, it was time to cruise the neighborhood on the family bicycle. In the upper photograph Bob is the cyclist, and in the lower one, Karen decides to pedal. Either way, Amy is having fun riding. Bob Thames is a famous local artist known for his illustrations of the *Hermy the Hermit Crab* books. A series of three books recounts Hermy's adventures in the Lowcountry. (Both courtesy of Bob and Karen Thames.)

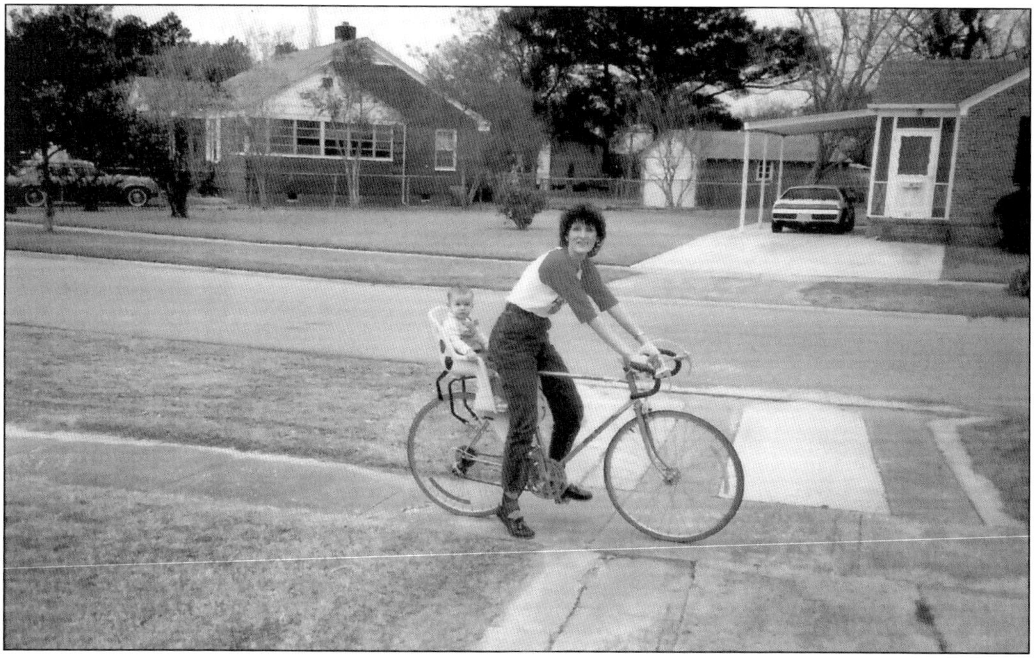

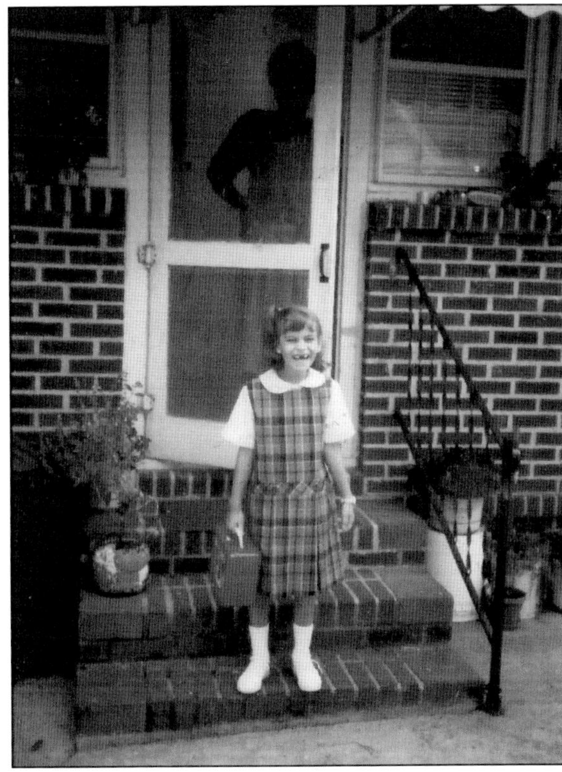

Amy Thames (at right) is all smiles as she leaves to walk to her first day at Blessed Sacrament School in the fall of 1990. Two years later, Amy is dressed and ready for her First Communion service at Blessed Sacrament Church (below). She poses in her front yard with her friend Jennifer Grant (left). Amy has been involved from an early age with neighborhood activities. Today she serves on Byrnes Downs Neighborhood Association's social committee while furthering her studies in the School of Pharmacy at the Medical University of South Carolina. (Both courtesy of Bob and Karen Thames.)

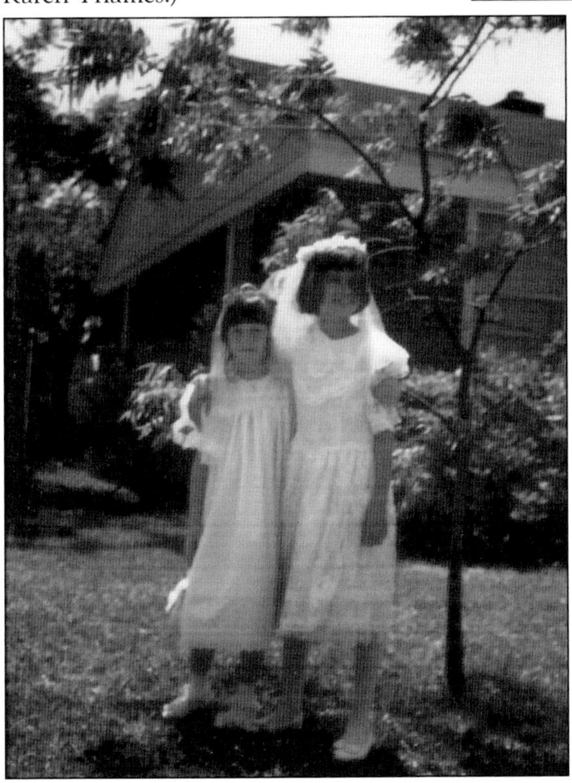

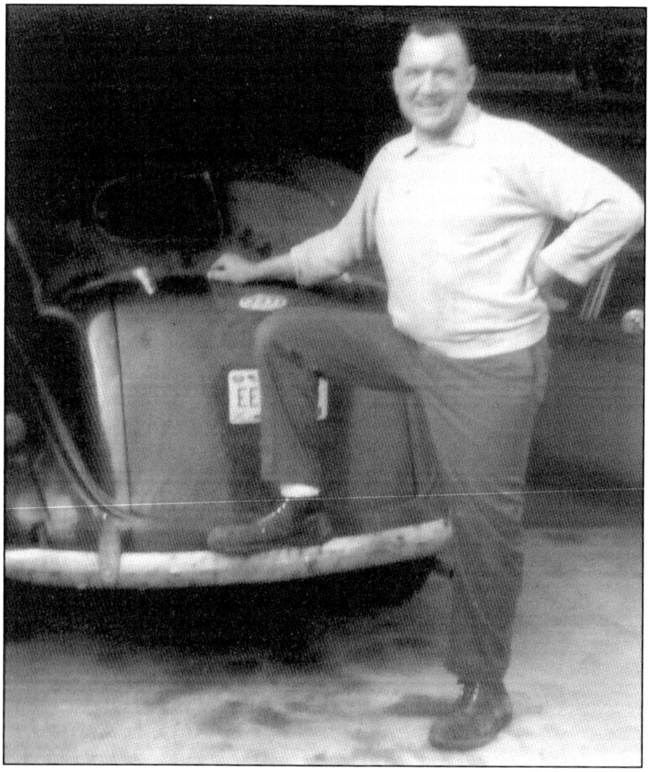

Tom Kwiatkowski fell in love with Frances "Frankie" Hargette, and on July 27, 1968, they were married. Frankie owned her home at 6 Craven Avenue. Tom also loved Rambler cars. Over time, he converted a section of the backyard into a mechanic's dream with a shop and car bays for repairing and renovating cars. In the photograph at left, Tom stands with his foot on the bumper of his 1938 Plymouth. In the lower photograph, his red 1961 Rambler is out for display in front of his home with the flag waving in the wind. Look closely at the right back corner of the photograph to catch the edge of the car bays that extended the width of the backyard. Today Tom lives on Rambler Way in Huger, South Carolina, and still owns this 1961 Rambler. (Both courtesy of Tom Kwiatkowski.)

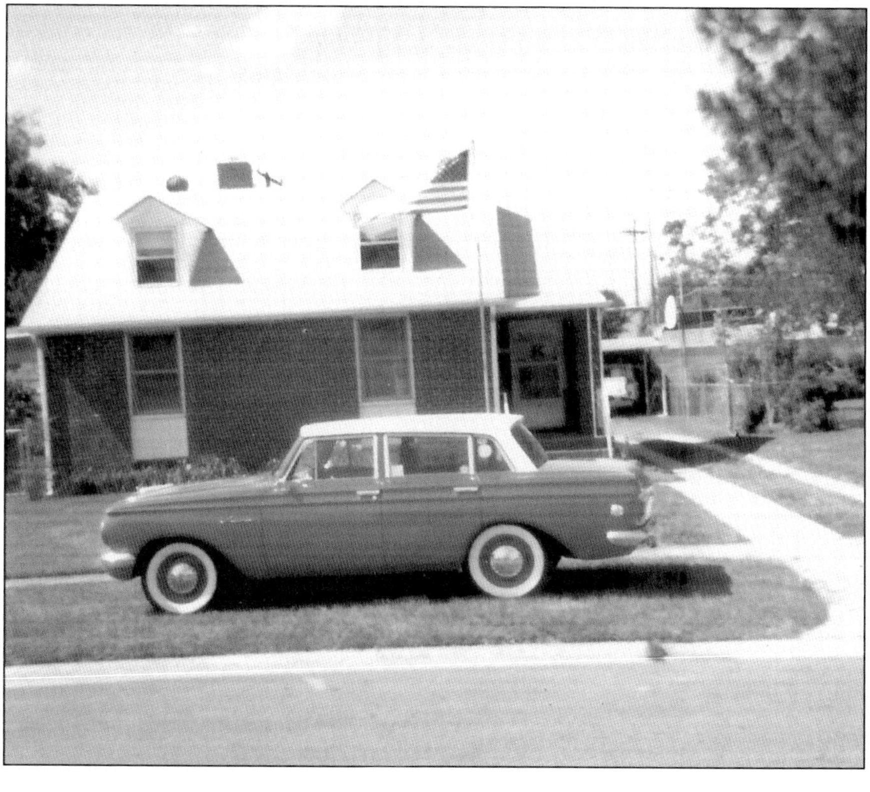

Buddy Hargette is Frankie's son and lived with Tom and Frankie at the Craven Avenue home. On this day, he is excited about his first motorcycle. Buddy also drove a school bus for some extra spending money. The bus was parked at home so he could be ready to roll early in the morning. Buddy also ran errands and deliveries for the Pure Oil Station, which used to be at the corner of Nicholson Street and Savannah Highway where Fire Station 10 is now located. He shared fond memories of Roy Hart's, the walk-up diner that was across the street. On occasion, his mom would send him across the road for dinner. (Both courtesy of Tom Kwiatkowski.)

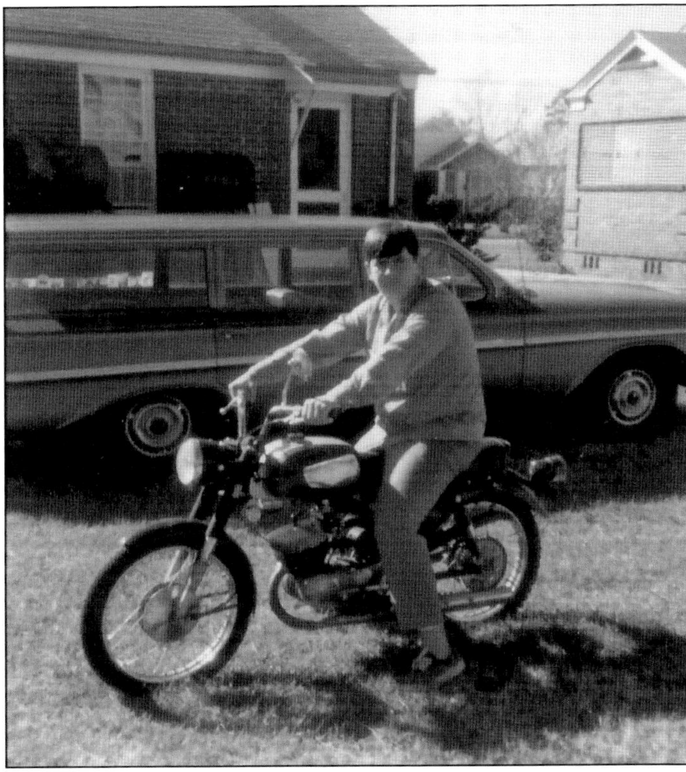

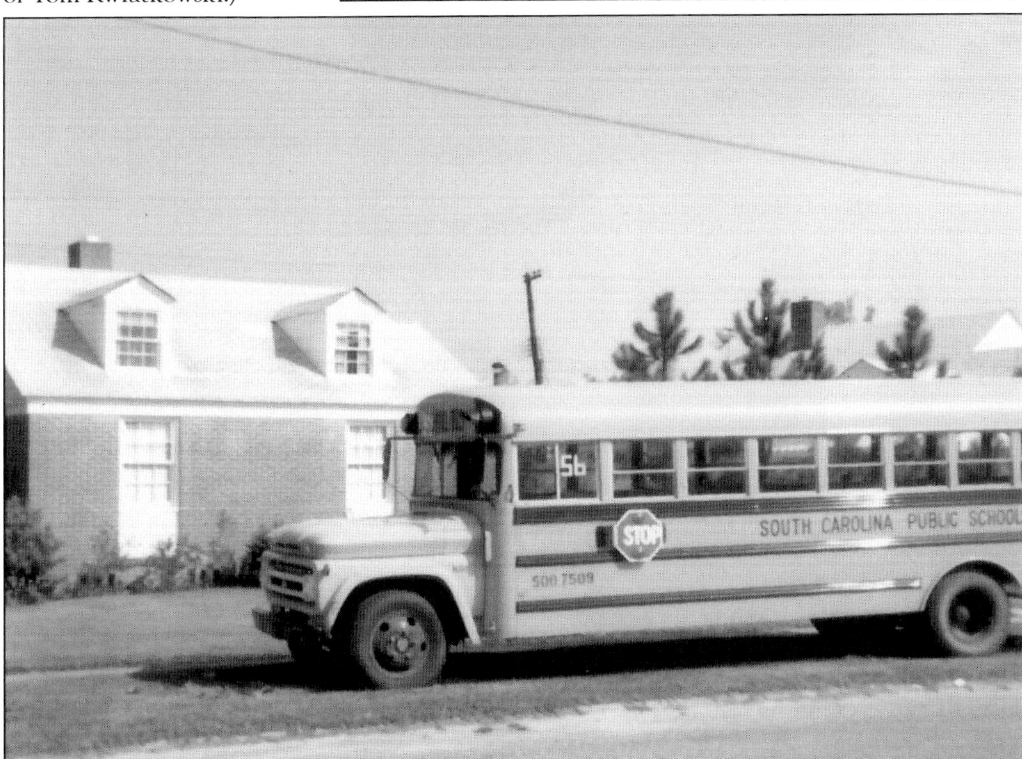

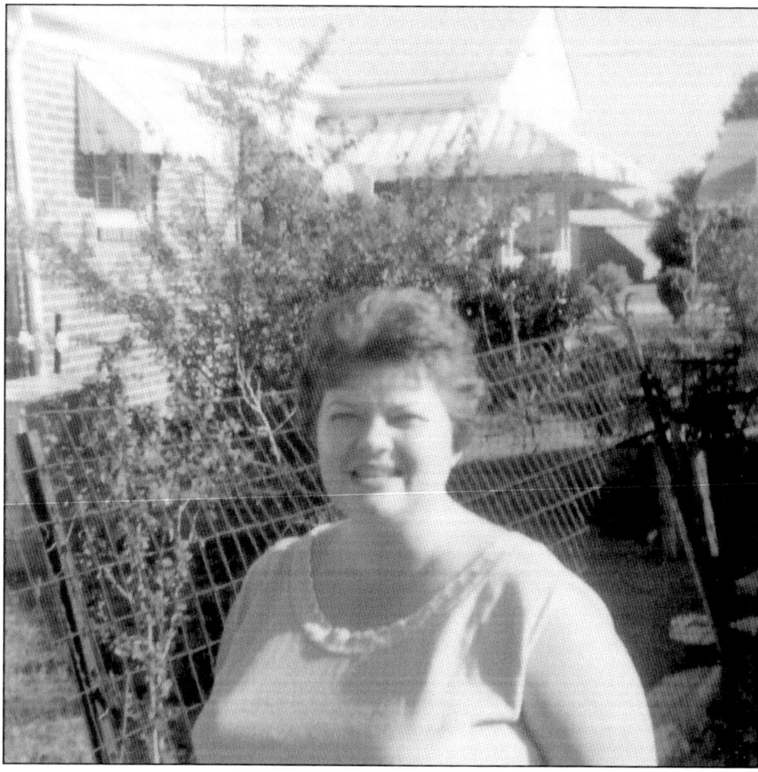

Frankie and Tom were constantly working at improving their home at 6 Craven Avenue. Frankie is all smiles standing in her backyard in 1970. By 1978, there was a large flower bed planted on the land along the border of 6 and 8 Craven Avenue. Gardening is still a passion for the current residents. Randy Todd owns 8 Craven Avenue, where his sister Saundra Austin and her husband, Jim, now live and continue to love the home and the yard. (Both courtesy of Tom Kwiatkowski.)

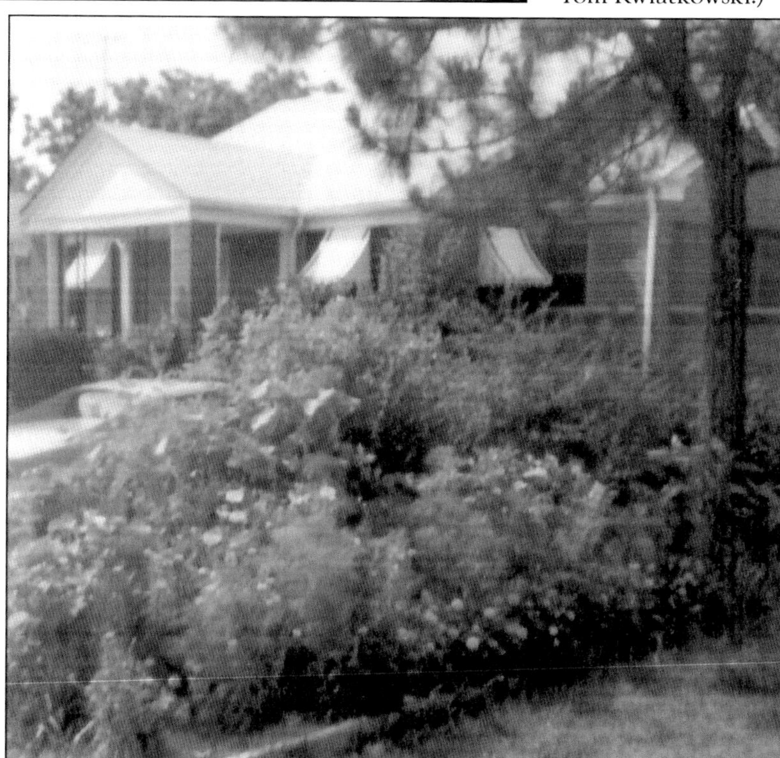

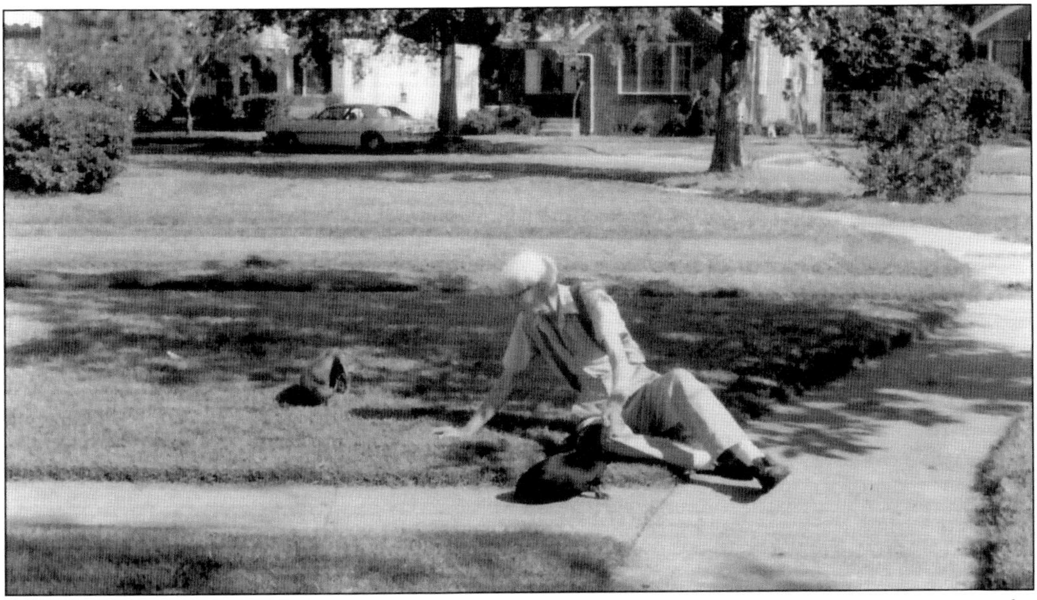

Emiel Corvette, Rutledge Corvette's father, purchased his home at 28 Campbell Drive in 1944 for his wife and family. When he purchased the home, it was not quite finished, so he and his wife were able to choose the paint colors used in the home. Later they moved to a home at 55 Campbell Drive and lived out the remainder of their lives. In the upper photograph, Emiel plays with his dogs in his front yard. The lower photograph shows Rutledge and Margaret Corvette's home at 27 Campbell Drive. On the back of the photograph, Rutledge notes, "Our home for 50 years (looking nice)." Rutledge and Margaret purchased 27 Campbell Drive for $6,995 with a 20-year GI Loan No. 48 from First Federal Savings and Loan in September 1946. The monthly payment, including taxes and fire insurance, was $38.18. (Both courtesy of Rutledge and Margaret Corvette.)

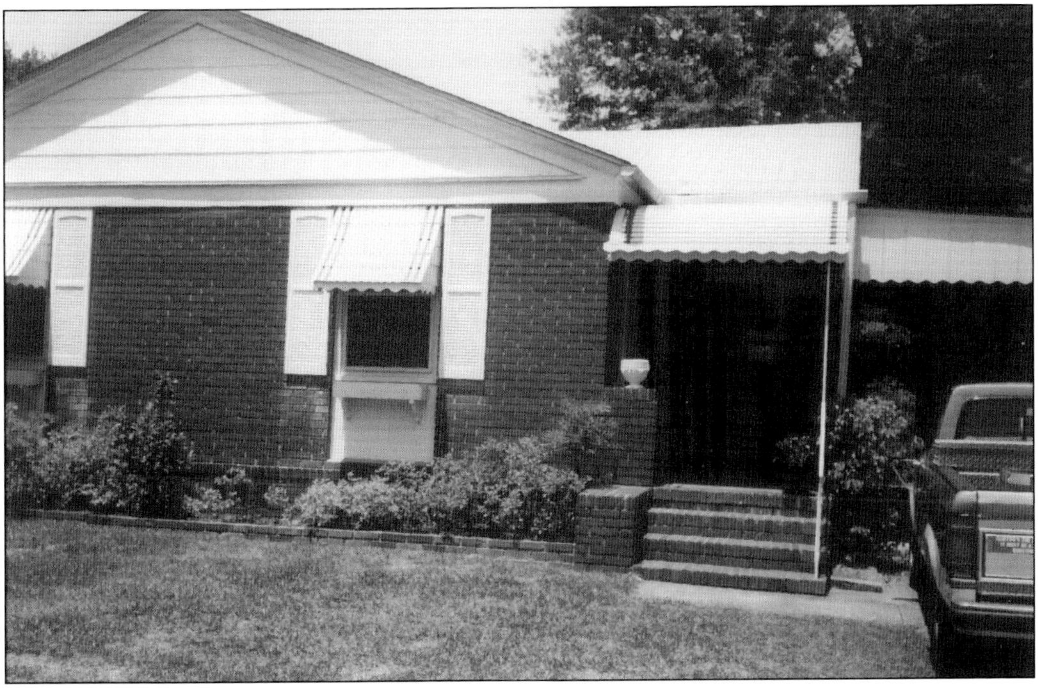

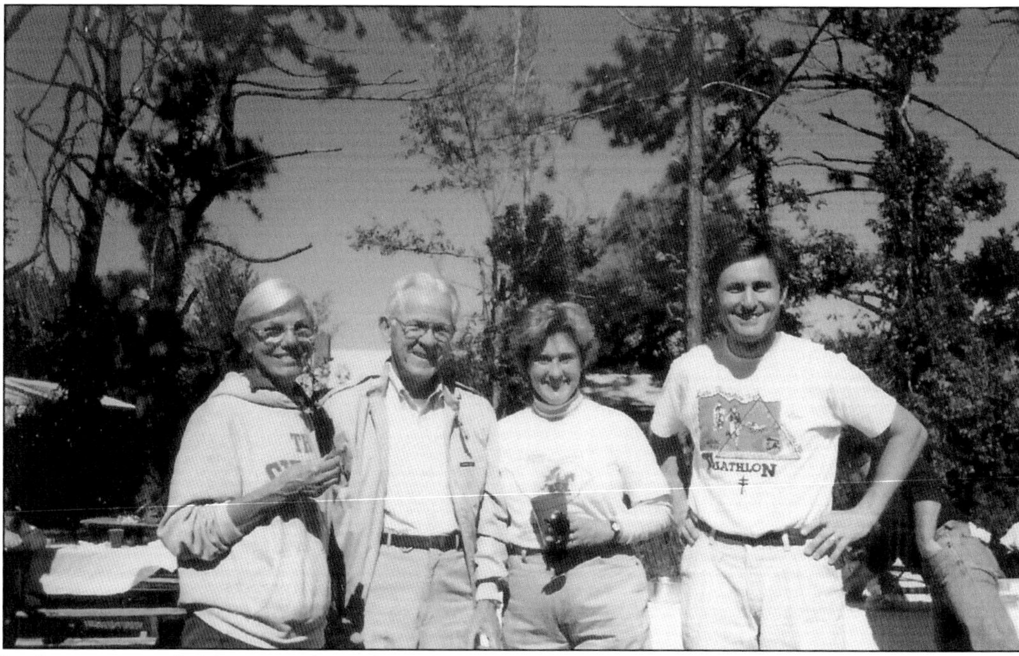

In the summer of 1990, several people gathered at Margaret Seidler's home to discuss the formation of a neighborhood association. On June 25, a meeting was held at the St. Andrew's Center. Yvonne Evans, Byrnes Downs city council representative, and city staff guided residents on the organizational process. The first officers are pictured from left to right at the Neighbor Day Picnic: Martha Cromer, secretary; Mendel Caldwell, treasurer; Margaret Seidler, president; and Tom Lyon, vice president. (Courtesy of Shannon Hurley.)

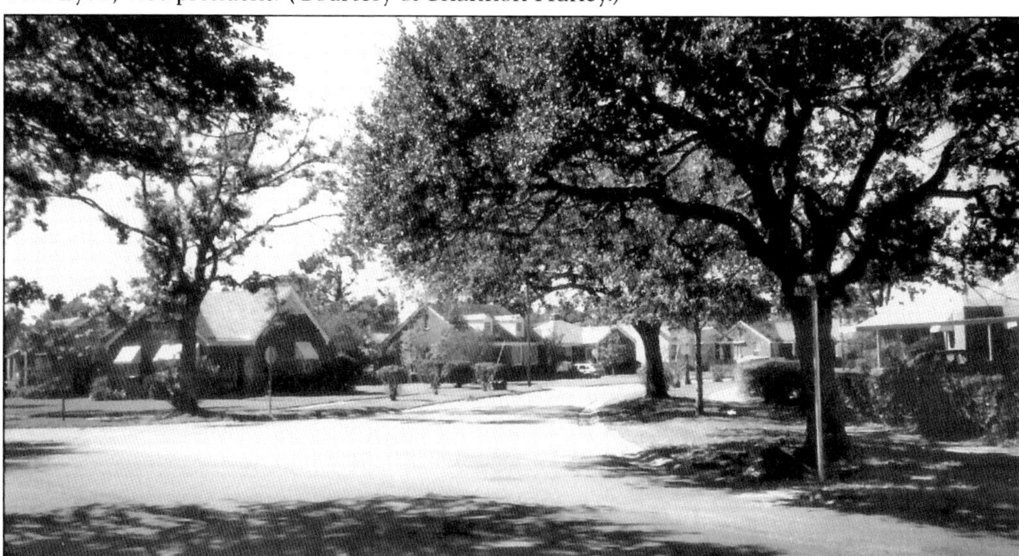

Fifty years later, "Looking Southwest from Corner of Nicholson and Craven Sts." is quite a different view, illustrating the expected changes to the Byrnes Downs neighborhood by the ladies of the Garden Club. What foresight they had to lay the groundwork for this amazing transformation. The fun part is that many of the original owners got to enjoy the fruits or rather "shade" of their labor.

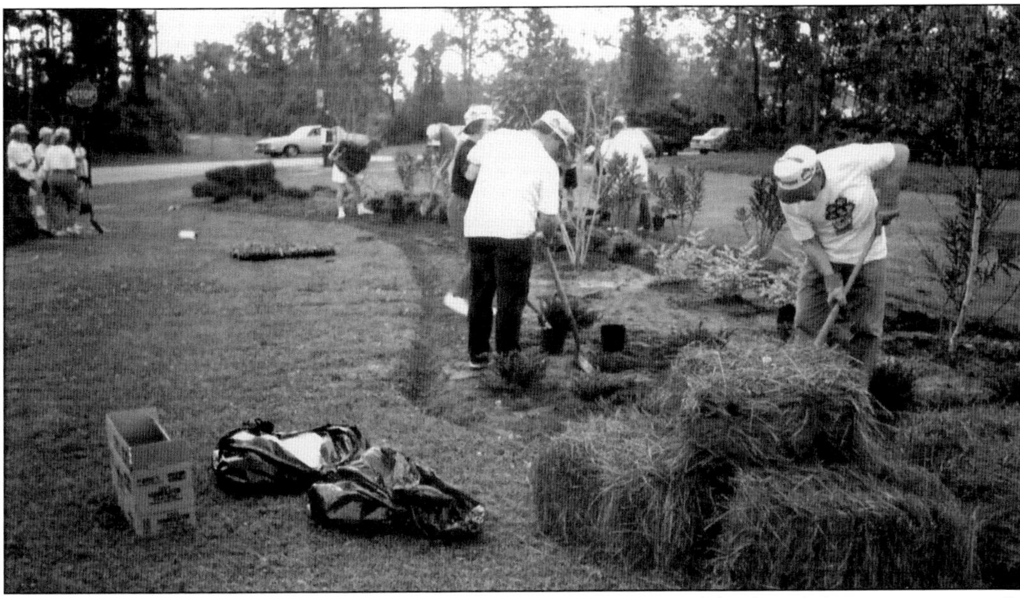

One of the many ambitious projects for the Byrnes Downs Neighborhood Association was the planting of a nondescript piece of land at No Name Street along the West Ashley Greenway. The street is named this, for it is actually a private piece of property and was turned into a street, in order for the neighbors to be able to drive to the St. Andrew's Center. Randall Shealey, who lived on Nicholson Street, designed the planting, and the neighborhood association organized a "Neighbor Day" event for April 13, 1991, to install the trees, shrubs, and flowers. The association won first place and $250 in the beautification category of Charleston's Clean City Sweep. The neighborhood celebrated with a picnic. In the lower photograph, Gordon Hay and Amy Blyth are busy cooking hot dogs and hamburgers for the hungry workers and neighbors.

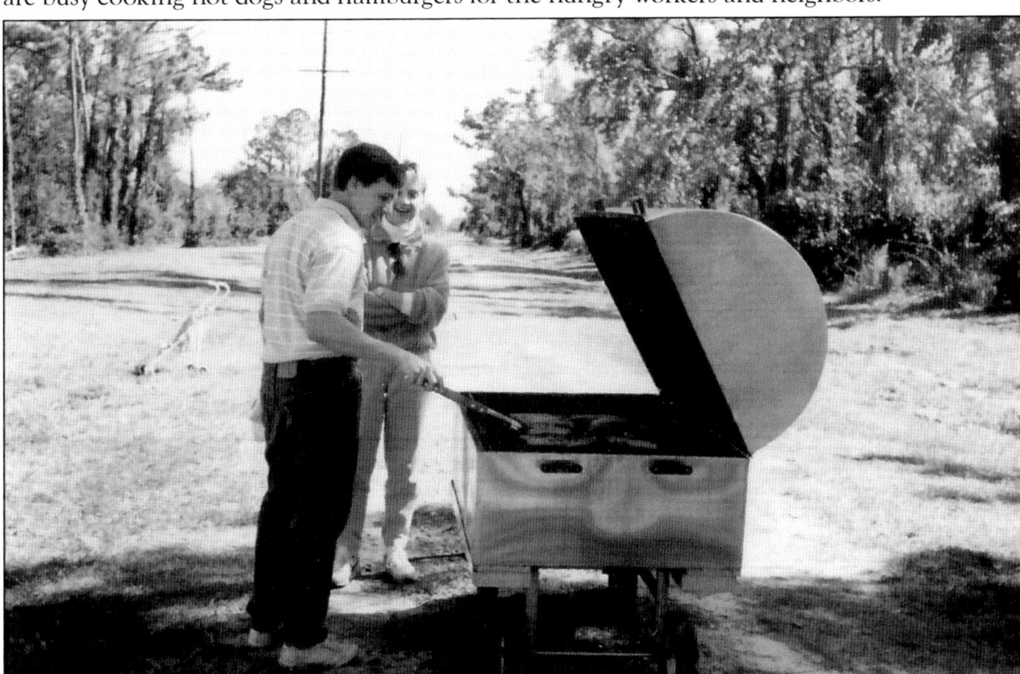

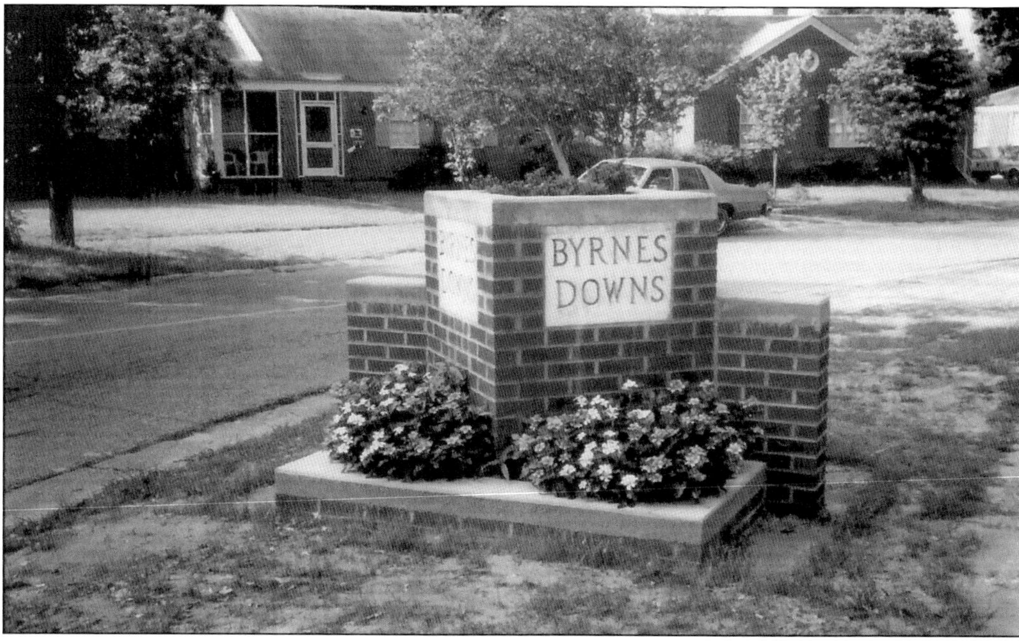

Another ambitious project was to replace the entrance column at the corner of Campbell Drive and Savannah Highway. The original column graces the cover of this book, but it succumbed to a car in an accident. Rutledge Corvette had the foresight to recover the concrete nameplates and keep them safe at his home. When the neighborhood association decided to raise the money for not only the replacement of this column and but also the construction of two new ones at Culbertson Street and at No Name Street, he came forward with the nameplates and $200 toward the fund-raising. In 1992, the column at Campbell Drive and Savannah Highway once again beautifully announces the neighborhood (above). The new column at Culbertson Street brings definition to this corner of the neighborhood (below).

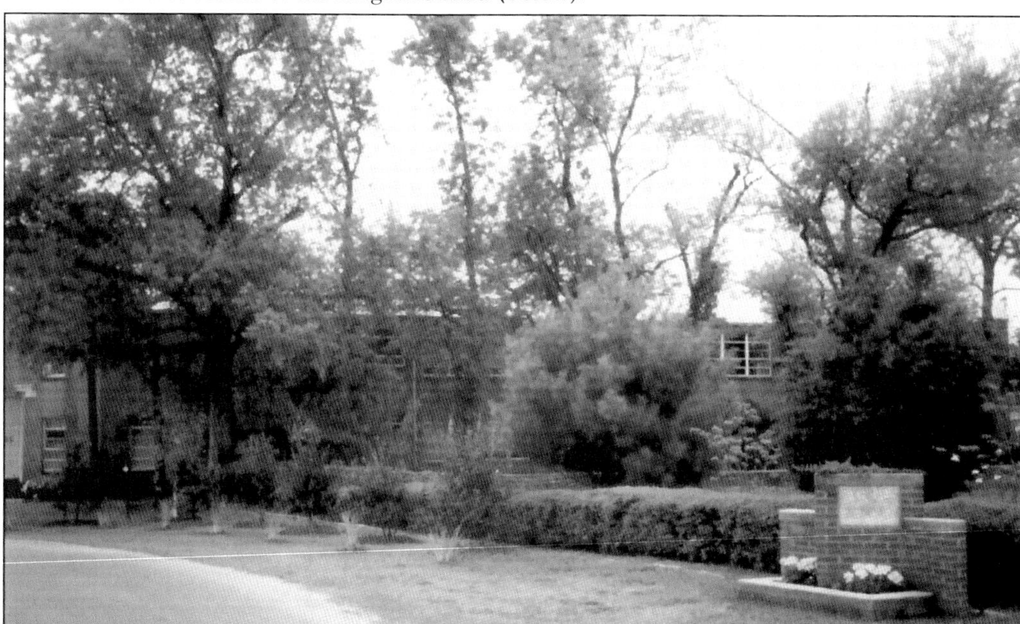

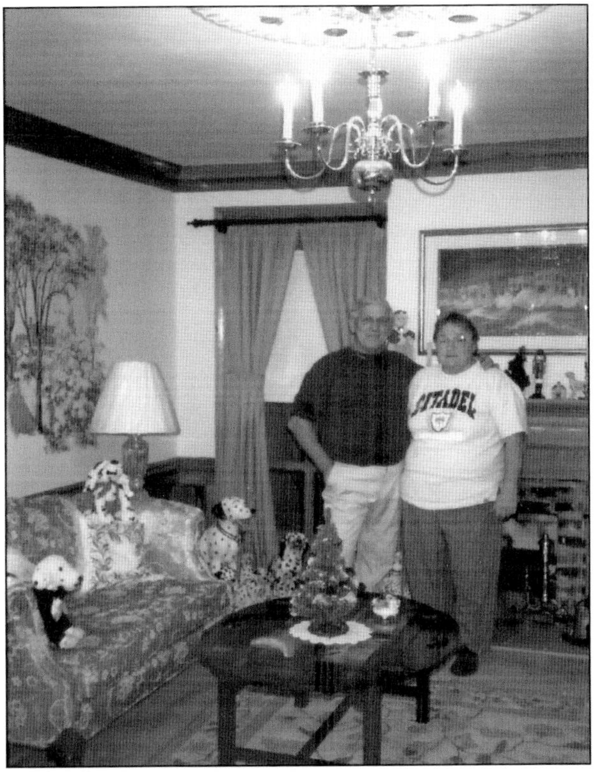

The neighborhood association also organized the Christmas Tour of Homes. It was a wonderful way for neighbors to meet neighbors and to find out how some of the homes had been renovated, upgraded, and added on to over the years. By 1992, Joe and Frances Roy had extensively renovated, upgraded, and added on to their home at 26 Campbell Drive. At right, they stand in their living room ready to showcase their labors of love for the neighbors to see. In 1998, Mendel Caldwell was ready to "pass the calculator" as treasurer, and Donna Jacobs accepted the position. They are ready to greet neighbors (below) as they check in for the Christmas Tour of Homes that year at 6 Craven Avenue.

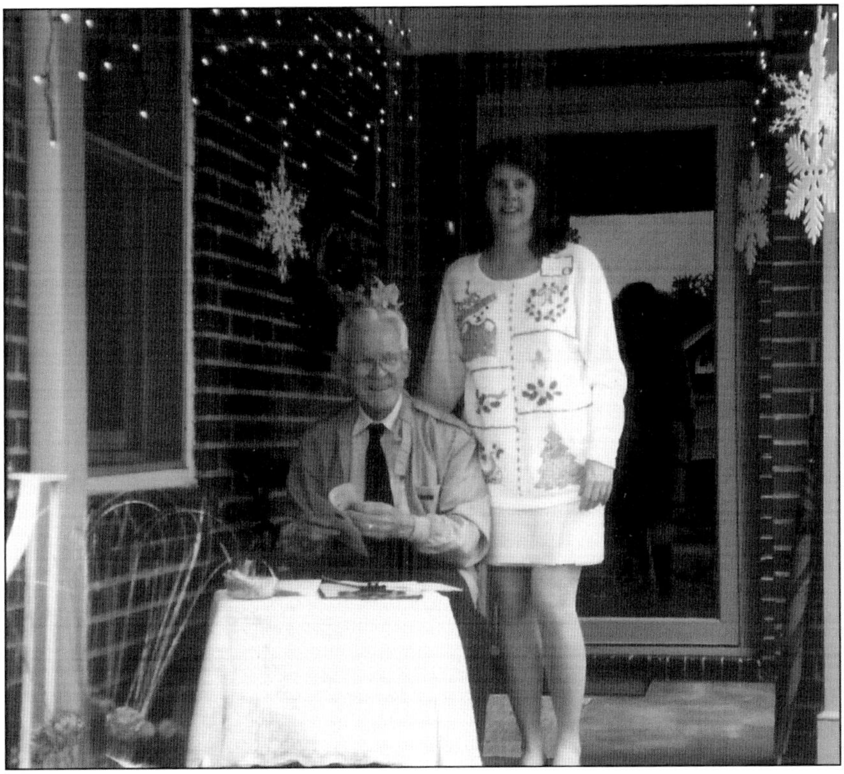

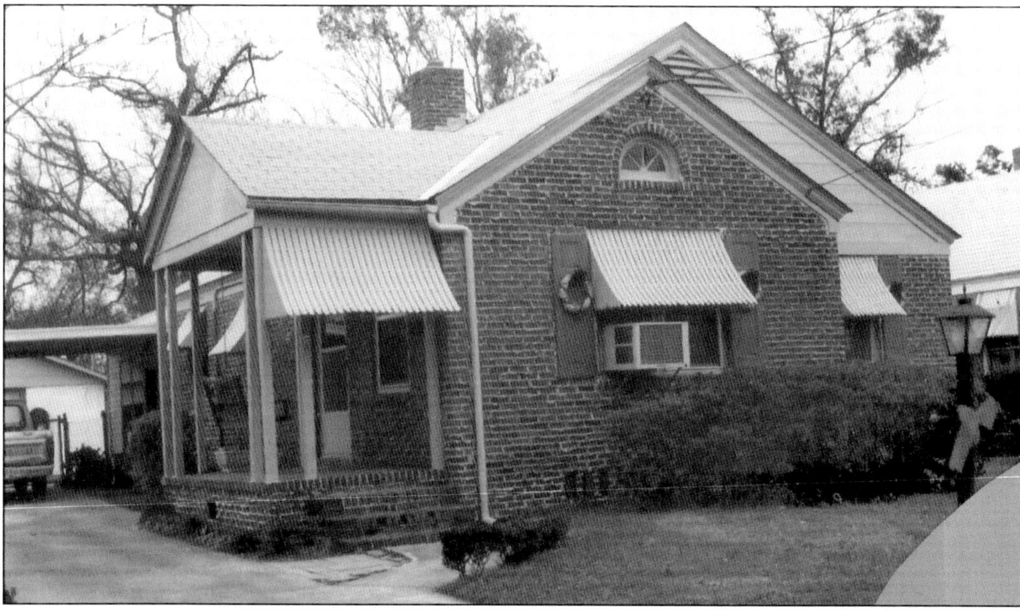

Ted and Ernie Salvo lived at 8 Tynte Street and had a beautifully decorated home and a well-appointed yard. They were delighted to be invited to participate in the first Christmas Tour of Homes. Ted served as president of the neighborhood association from 1993 to 1994. Ernie was the chair of the committee that organized the 50th birthday party. It was her dream to have an annual reunion of people who had lived in the neighborhood. In the lower photograph, Ernie (left) serves Christmas treats to Barbara (center) and Mildred Lannan of Craven Avenue. The home at 8 Tynte Street was also featured in the *History Byrnes Downs Garden Club* scrapbook in the "before and after" section. At the time, Mr. and Mrs. R. G. Thomas owned the home.

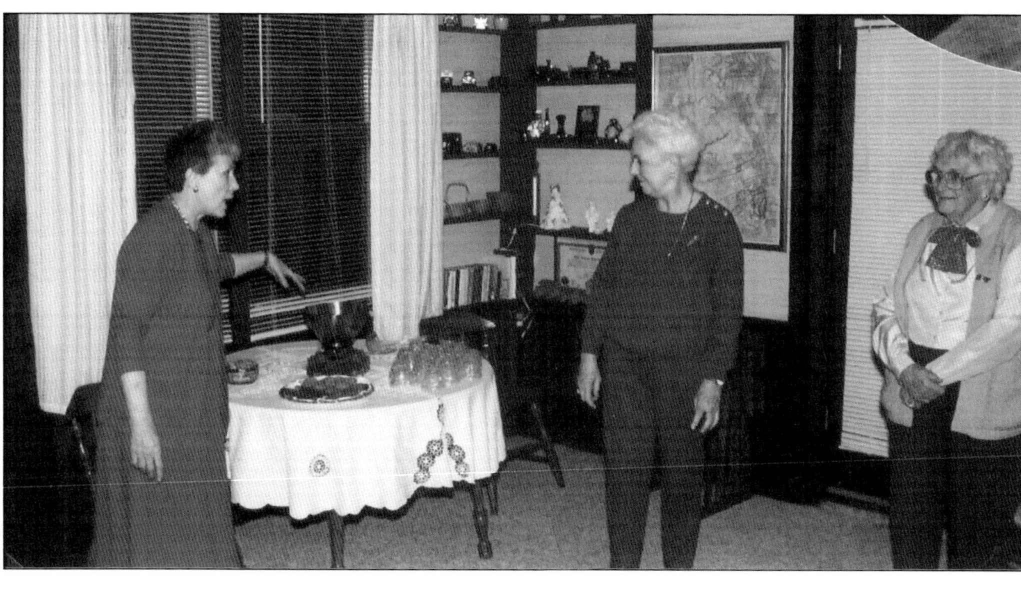

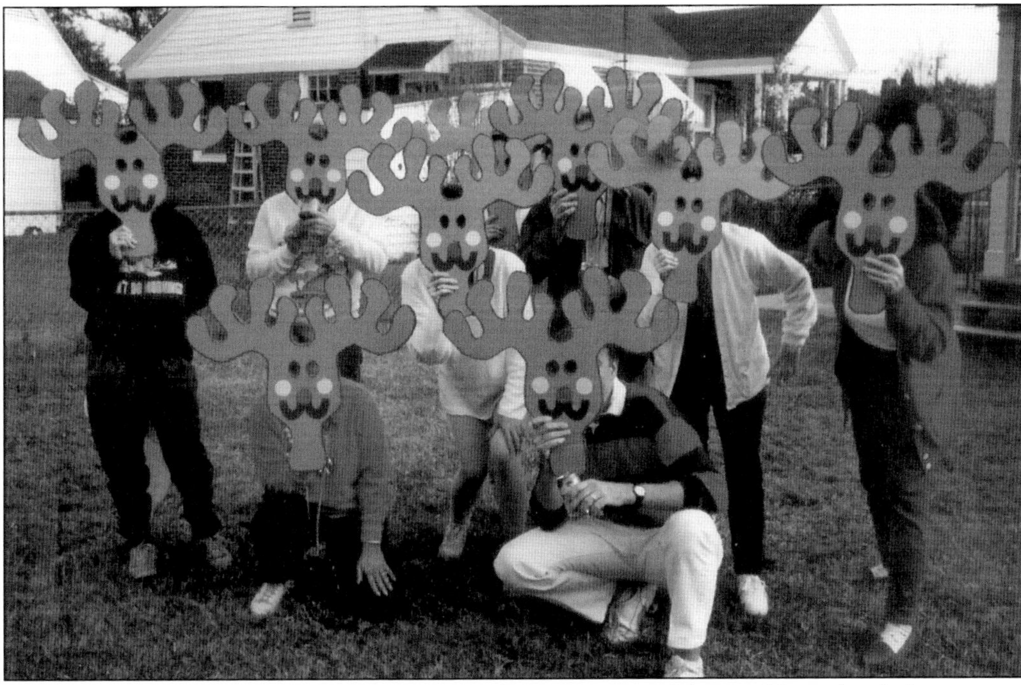

In addition to organizing the Christmas Tour of Homes, some of the neighbors decided to organize a group for the Reindeer Run, a charity event held annually at the beginning of December. Creativity was not lacking with this group. Santa's sleigh and reindeer masks were constructed for the participants. The group earned first place in the costume competition of the event.

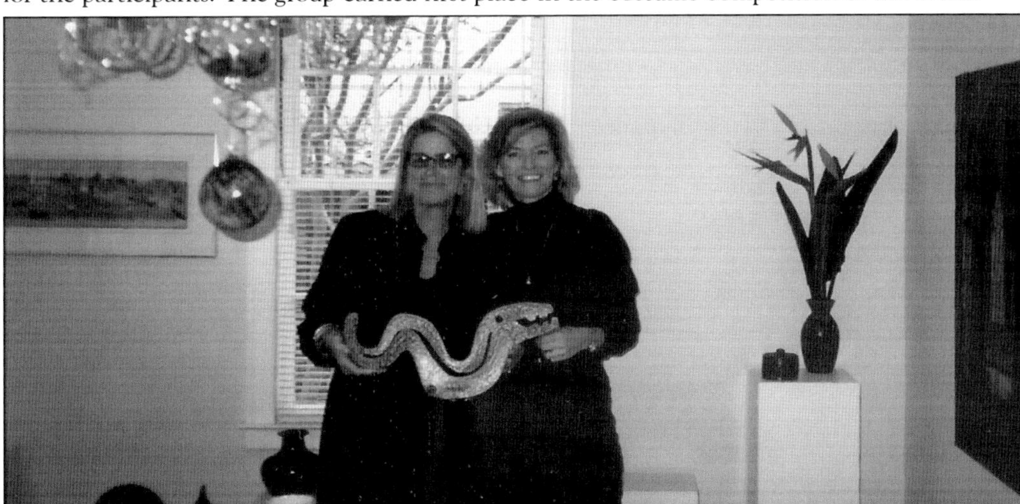

Another twist on the Christmas Tour of Homes came in 2000 when an art tour was added to the event. Several local artists resided in the neighborhood, so it was decided to feature artists' homes and their artwork. All Art, Nicole Elswick's gallery on Savannah Highway, also participated as well as the Java Moon, the funky, artsy coffee shop owned by her husband, Bryon Jessee. In this photograph, Allison Ladd (left) and Kathy Hawkins hold some of Allison's pottery at her 10 Lyttleton Avenue home. Kathy and Ed Hawkins' home at 45 Lyttleton Avenue was also on the tour and showcased her pottery.

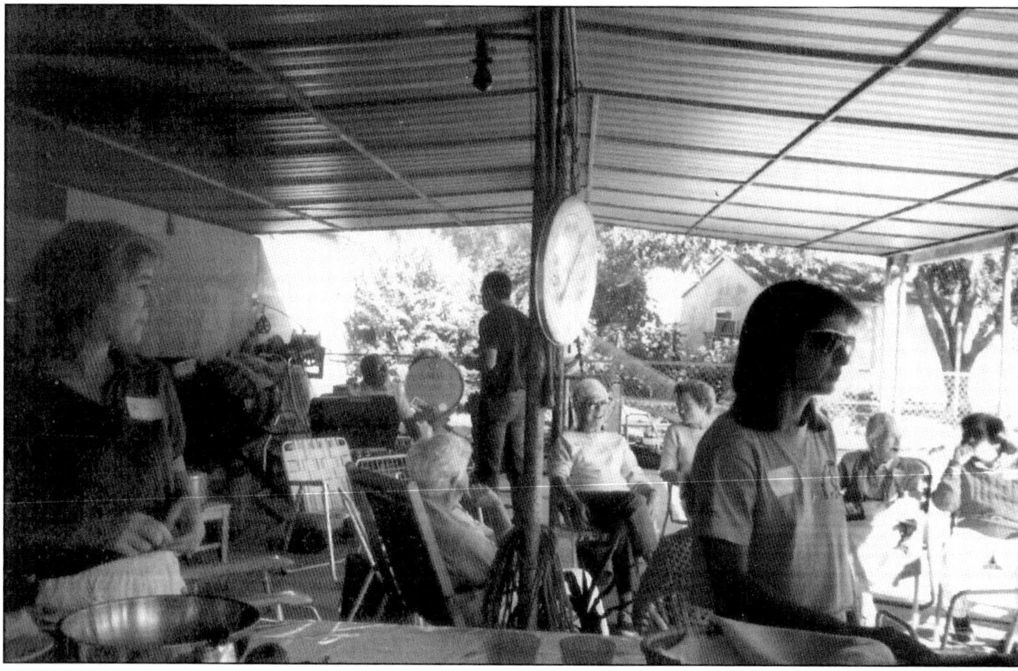

After Jeff and Donna Jacobs moved into their Craven Avenue home in 1985, they organized a street party to meet their neighbors. Invitations were sent to everyone on the street, and there was a 100 percent response. Some of the neighbors had lived on the street for a long time but had lost touch with their neighbors, so it became a reunion of sorts and developed into a tradition. Neighbors gathered under the shed, which had once been the home for Tom Kwiatkowski's vintage cars, for a potluck lunch. In the lower photograph are David and Kathy Gindhart, who lived at 4 Craven Avenue. Their home has been in Kathy's family for several generations.

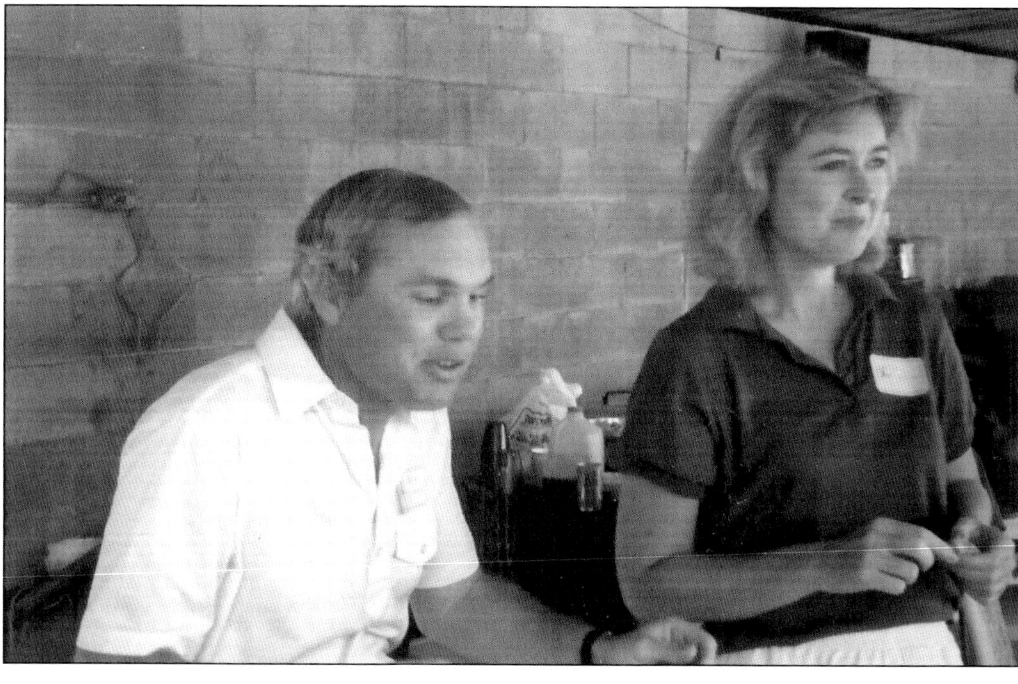

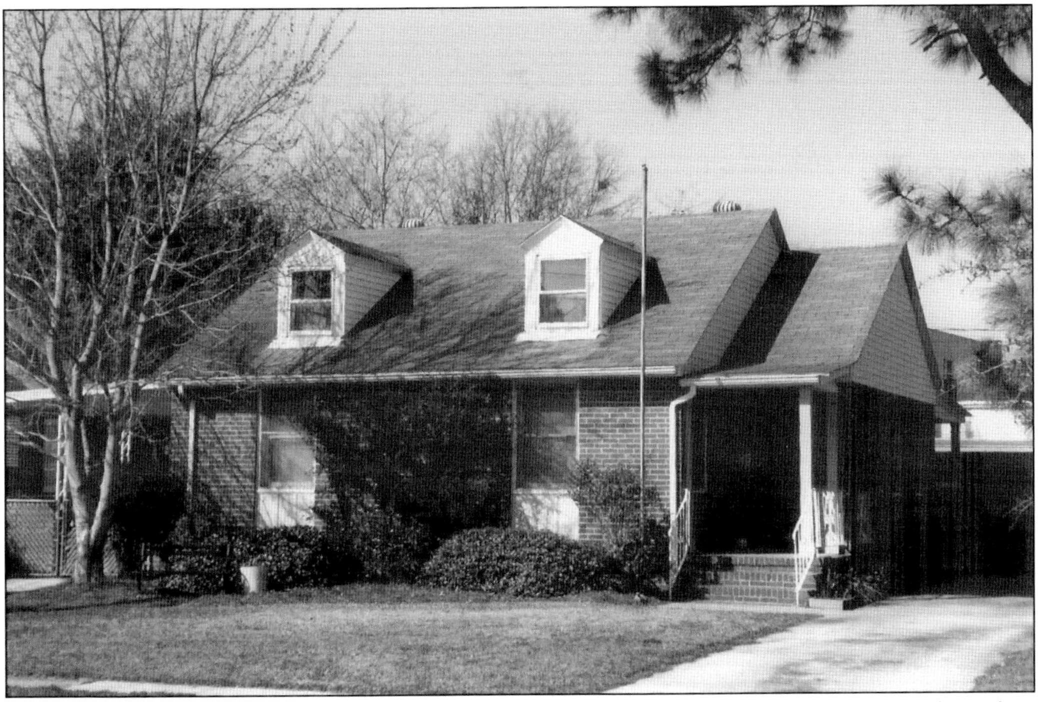

The Jacobses' home on Craven Avenue looks quite different in 1998 than it did when they purchased the home in 1985. They have continued the tradition of renovation and upgrading that flourishes in this community. The tree in the front yard was a housewarming gift from Donna's parents. The home is also the site of many parties. This one is an Easter egg hunt for relatives and neighborhood children. To the delight of the children, the Easter Bunny made a surprise stop at the party to entertain the children and pass out balloons.

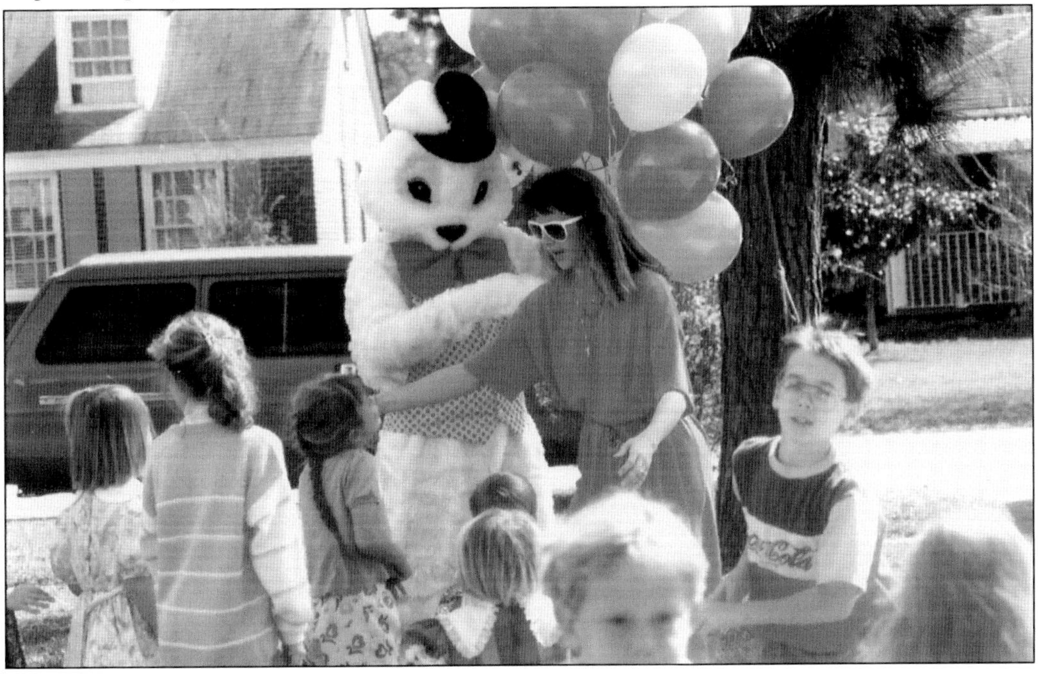

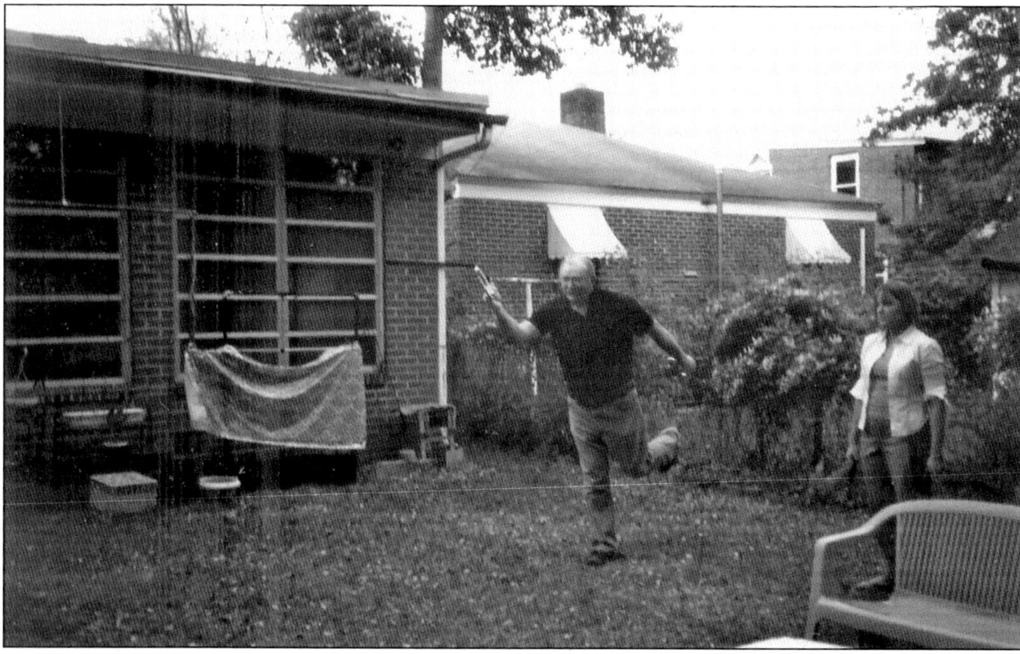

It is fun to discover photographs that bring things full circle. On page 12 is a 1946 photograph of Red Blanton's sister Dot pitching horseshoes in the backyard of Red's home. Fast-forward to April 2003, and some things never change. Judi's husband, Tony, is photographed pitching horseshoes in the backyard of the Blanton home. (Courtesy of Camilla Blanton.)

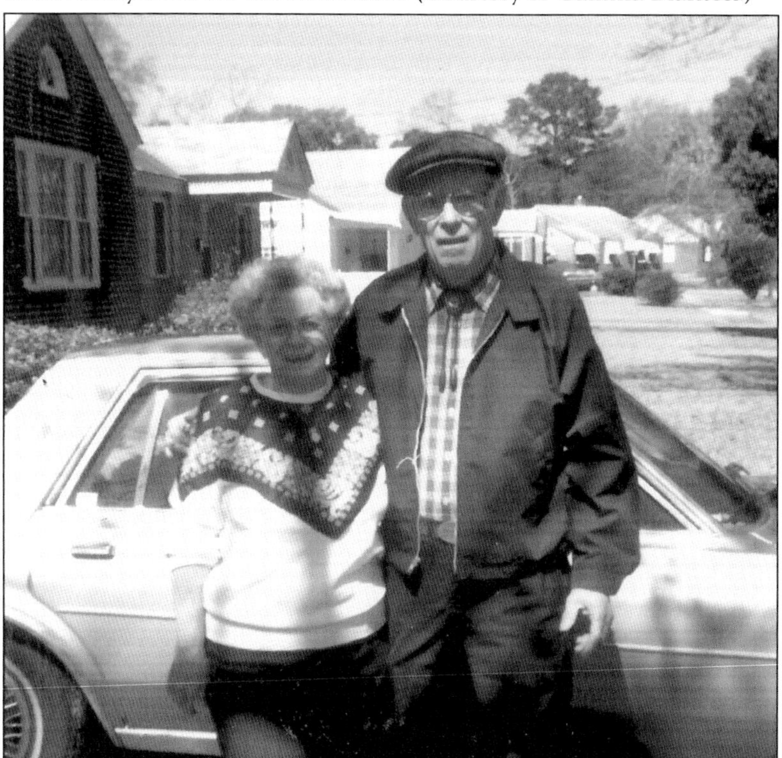

Camilla and Red Blanton met on October 31, 1936, at the Fountain Inn, a local hangout at the corner of Savannah Highway and Coburg Road. In December 1937, they were married. They had many adventures during their married life. One such adventure was to travel to all 50 states of the United States. (Courtesy of Camilla Blanton.)

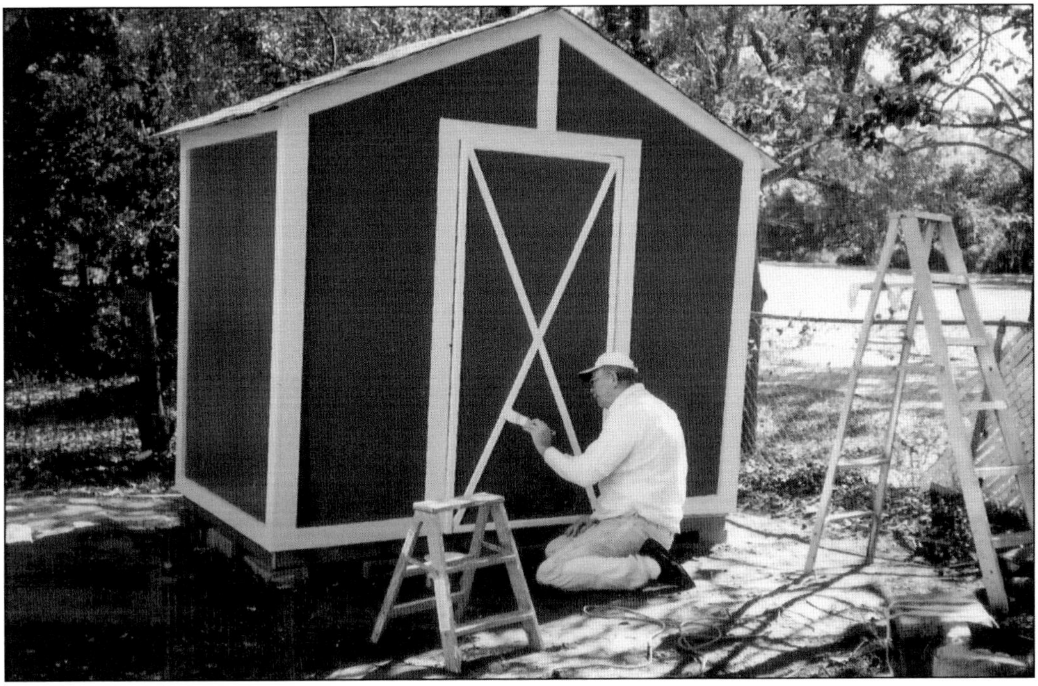

Tony Meyers, Camilla Blanton's son-in-law, works on "The Penny Shed." Red passed away in 2002. Camilla and her daughters, Judi and Susan, collected all the jars of pennies Red had saved in his lifetime. There were enough pennies to build this shed. It was only fitting that the structure be coined "The Penny Shed." (Courtesy of Camilla Blanton.)

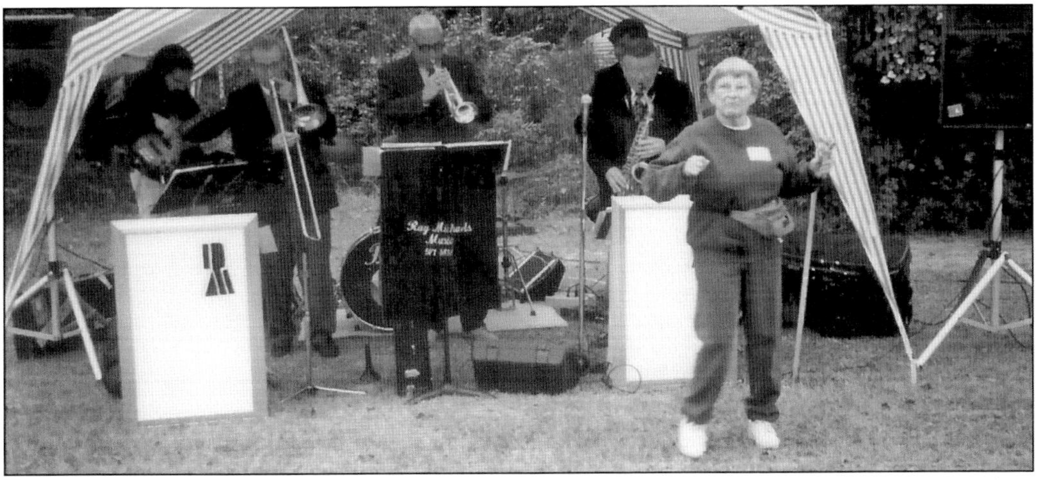

This photograph is captioned, "Sara Calas loves to swing." Sara Calas was a long-term resident of Byrnes Downs, and when the 50th birthday party rolled around, she was ready to celebrate. She is pictured swinging to the tunes of the Ray Michaels' Band as they played for the birthday party on the West Ashley Greenway.

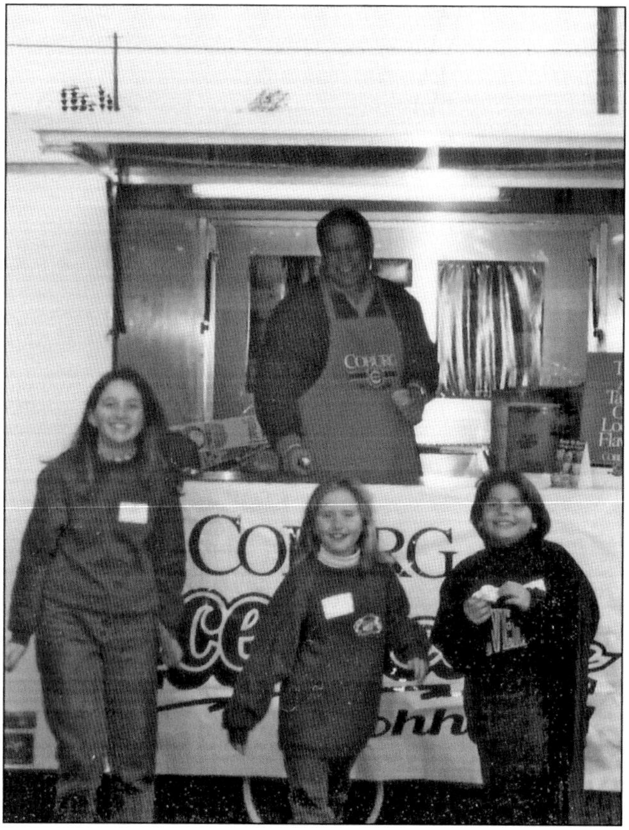

Byrnes Downs became Coburg Dairy's neighbor in the late 1940s. When Byrnes Downs celebrated its 50th birthday in November 1995 with a picnic on the West Ashley Greenway, Coburg employees came with the ice cream truck and served ice cream with the birthday cake. Mendel Caldwell, one of the oldest residents, and Winky Zeberlein's daughter Anna, one of the youngest residents, were asked to cut the birthday cake that had been generously provided by Liberty Café and Ashley Bakery. Neighbors came with their lawn chairs and picnic blankets despite the chilly weather. There were sandwiches provided by Subway, Larry's Subs, and Great Harvest Bread Company in addition to the birthday cake and ice cream. George McDaniel of the National Trust and Mayor Joseph P. Riley Jr. praised the neighborhood for its history and commitment to community.

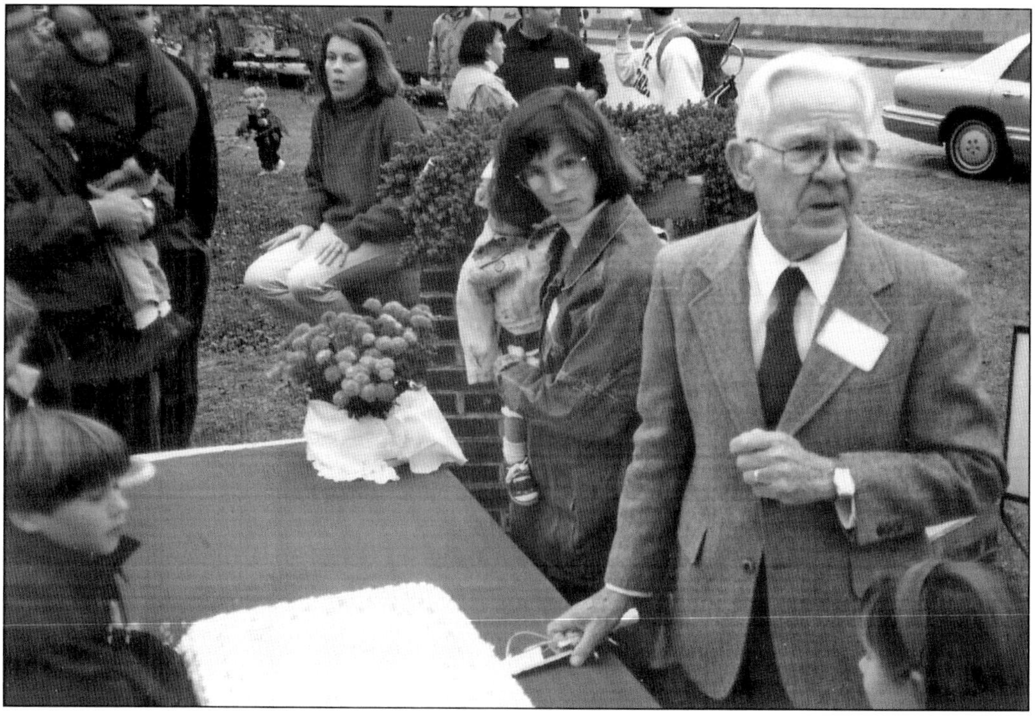

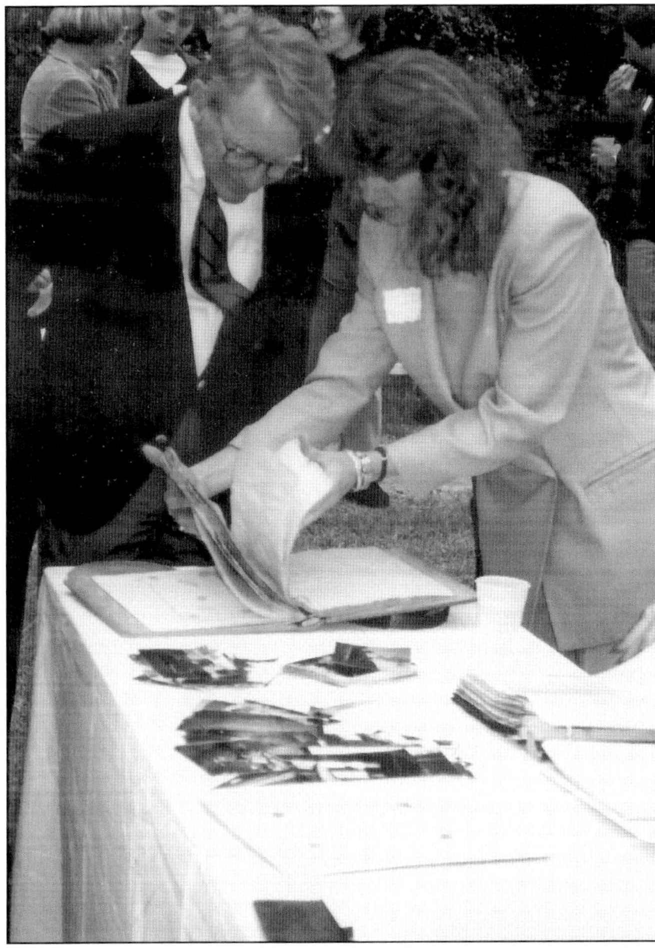

Margaret Seidler loaned *History Byrnes Downs Garden Club* to the neighborhood for the celebration. Donna Jacobs took the opportunity to share with Mayor Joseph P. Riley Jr. some of the amazing pictures of early Byrnes Downs in the scrapbook. One of the highlights of the celebration was the unexpected attendance by Charles Bennett (below, left) and Jerry Quinn, two members of the Little Helpers Club that had been featured in the 1949 newspaper article describing the Garden Club's first year of activities. They had seen the 1949 photograph in the November 2, 1995, article "Byrnes Downs is Golden," which had appeared in the *West Ashley This Week* section of the *Post and Courier.*

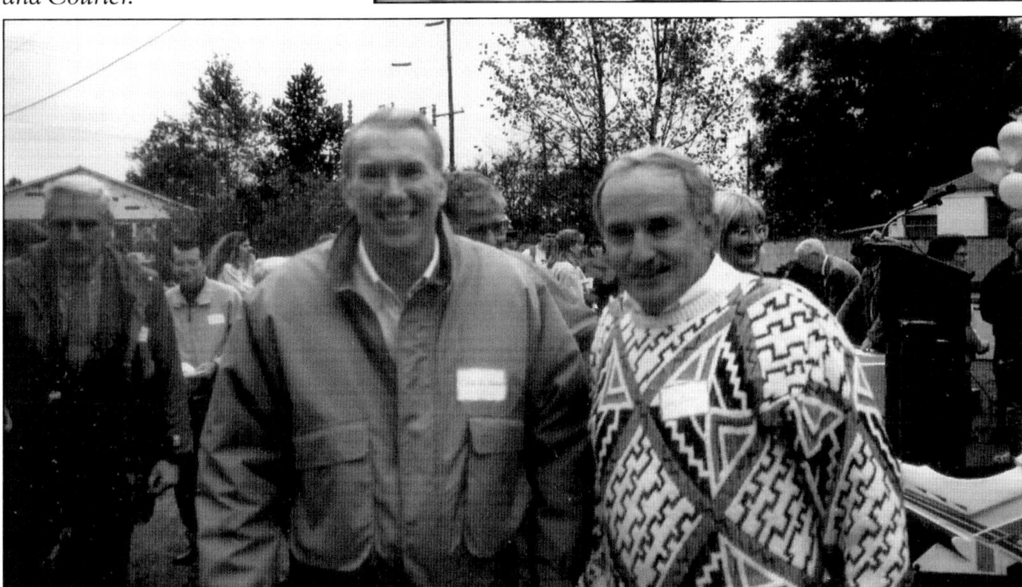

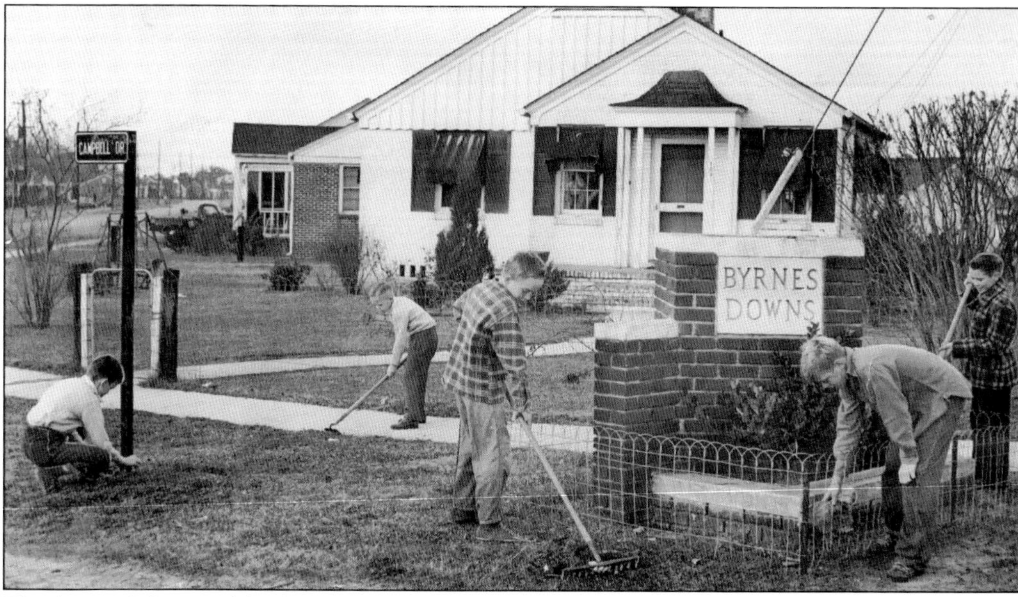

The boys of the neighborhood were organized into the Little Helpers Club, which assisted in beautification projects and keeping the neighborhood clean. Bill Regan spreads the dirt around the base of the Campbell Drive street sign. Herbert Koger uses a hoe to level the turf at the sidewalk. From left to right, Jerry Quinn, Sam Diggle, and Charles Bennett clear debris from the brick entrance column. (Reproduced with permission from the *Post and Courier*, by staff photographer Holcombe.)

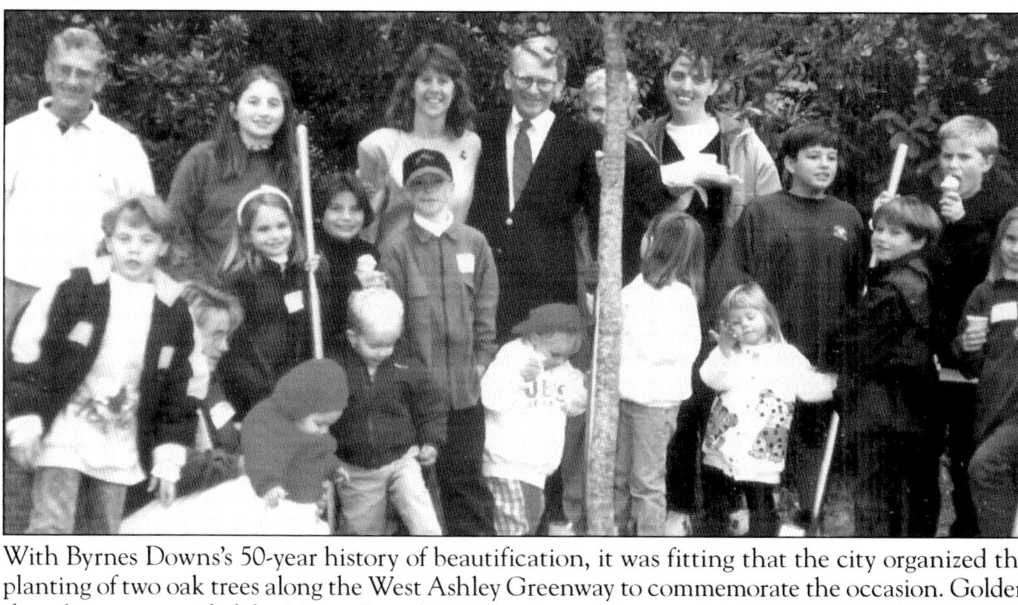

With Byrnes Downs's 50-year history of beautification, it was fitting that the city organized the planting of two oak trees along the West Ashley Greenway to commemorate the occasion. Golden shovels were provided for Mayor Joseph P. Riley Jr. and the residents to assist in the planting. Mayor Riley encouraged the children attending the party to return one day in the future and tell the story to their children of living in Byrnes Downs, celebrating its birthday, and planting these trees. Thirteen years have passed since this celebration, and the neighborhood association has continued to plant trees along the greenway and throughout the neighborhood. May Rossiter was right when she predicted, "From that moment on, their activities have never ceased."

Four

Our Neighbors

Byrnes Downs is nestled among several neighborhoods: Albemarle Point, The Crescent, Moreland, Old Windermere, South Windermere, Westwood, Wappoo Heights, and the community of Coburg. The World War I Memorial Bridge was constructed in 1926, replacing the privately owned wooden structure known as the "Ashley River" or "New" bridge that had been constructed in 1889 by the Charleston Bridge Company. The memorial bridge was magnificent. Now St. Andrew's Parish was easily accessible for people yearning to move out from the congested peninsula. Albemarle Point was owned by Thomas C. Stevenson Jr., who subdivided the area and built his home there in the 1940s. The Crescent traces land ownership back to 235 acres owned by Thomas Grange Simons in 1853. In 1926, the Olmstead brothers laid out the "General Plan for The Crescent" for the Wappoo Realty Company, which owned the property. The Crescent derives its name from the crescent-shaped land that embraced Wappoo Creek. Moreland, established in 1942 by William S. Means, was the site of the original farmhouse for Harrison Farms. Old Windermere, established in 1926 by the late J. S. Simmons, was the site of the first all-electric home in St. Andrew's Parish. The neighborhood was named for Windermere, England, as the property owners were of English ancestry. The old grand oak trees shading the neighborhood were planted when the neighborhood was originally developed. Bill Ackerman developed South Windermere in the early 1950s. The streets were named for Confederate personalities because of his interest in the Civil War. Westwood was originally surveyed as Byrnes Downs. Wappoo Heights was established in 1924 by George A. Nash and was part of the original Simons property. Immediately adjacent to Byrnes Downs going south on Savannah Highway is Coburg, owned by the Hanckel family. In 1921, Francis S. Hanckel Jr. and I. D. Auld established the dairy on Coburg; since that time, the dairy has played a strong role in the community. The cow and sign at the corner of Coburg Road and Savannah Highway is the reference point for the area, and the Cookhouse located on Coburg was a popular place for community events.

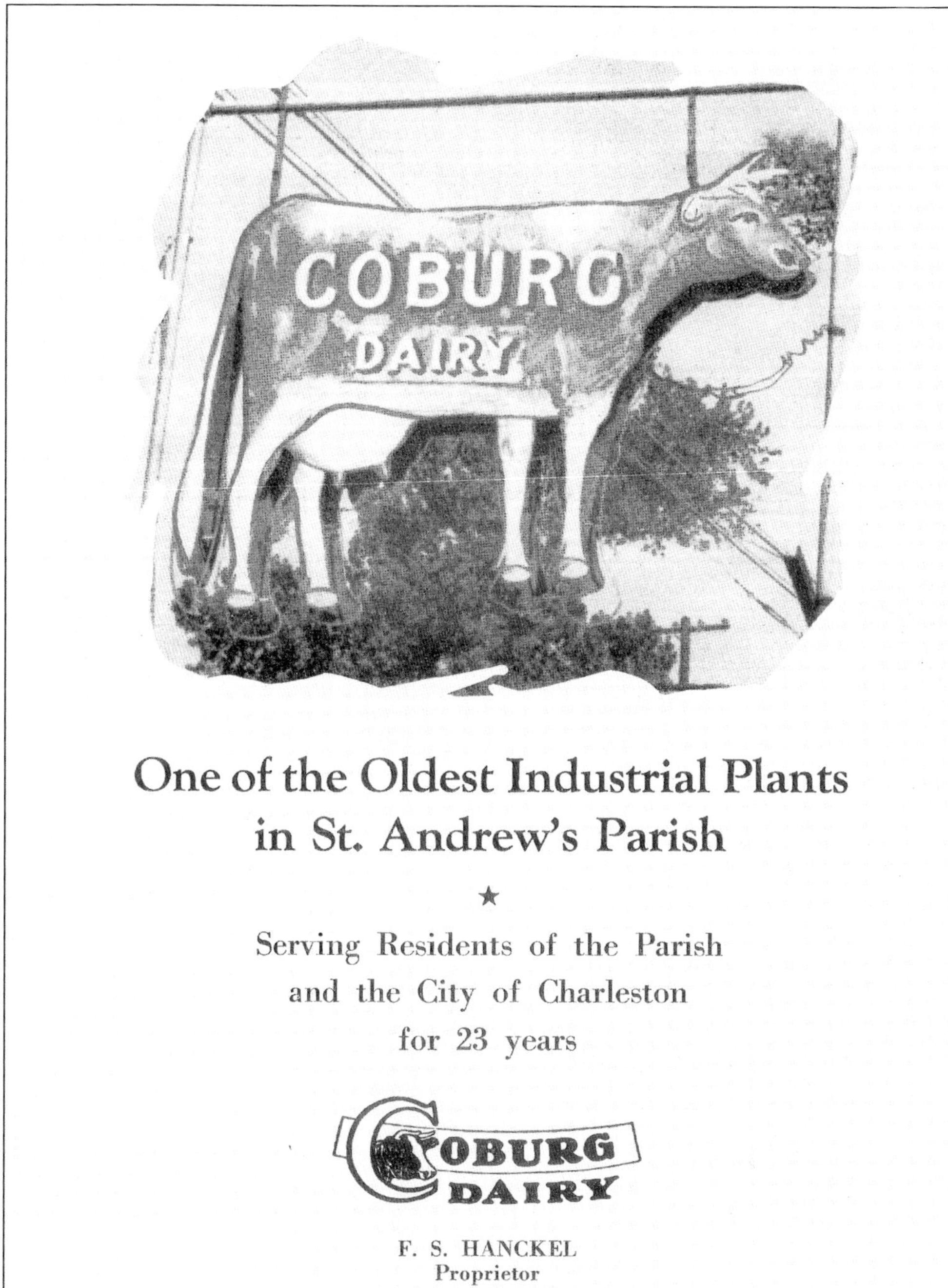

When giving directions directions to Byrnes Downs, people will say, "Do you know where the Coburg cow is?" or "If you've passed the cow, you've gone to far" or "When you pass the cow, take the next right." The Coburg Dairy cow proudly defines the beginning of Coburg Road and the southwest corner of the Byrnes Downs neighborhood and is the reference point for the area. This advertisement from the 1940s shows one of the original signs at the beginning of Coburg Road. Today this sign is a large structure with the trademark neon "C" and a rotating platform that displays a cow and a carton of milk. (Courtesy of Frank Hanckel and Charlotte Hanckel Hay.)

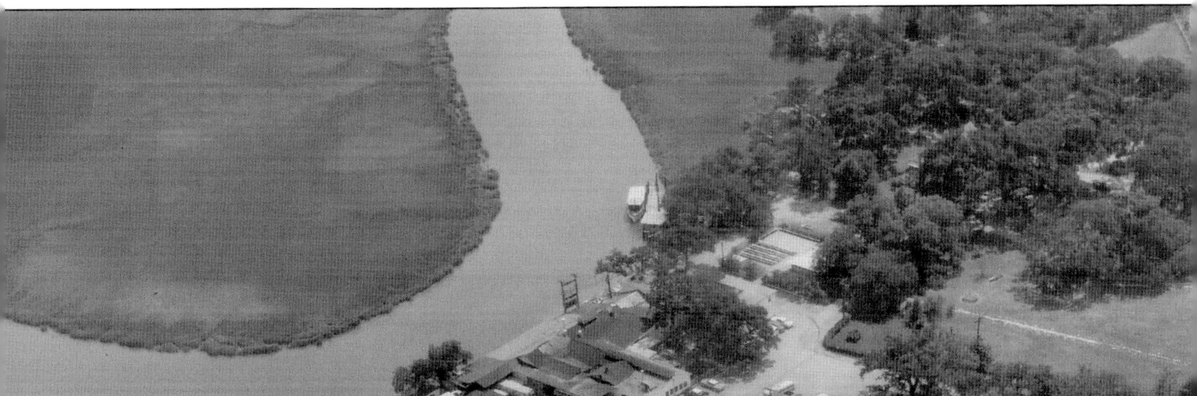

On January 29, 1921, an article appeared in the *News and Courier*, "Mr. Francis Stuart Hanckel, Jr. of Charleston and Mr. I. D. Auld of Mount Pleasant have announced the opening of their dairy farm." The article states that only Guernsey cows will be used and a purebred Guernsey bull had been purchased. They advertise that milk will be delivered within 24 hours of milking. With this passion for cows, community, and fun, Francis Hanckel developed Coburg into a successful dairy that has always played a strong role in the community. Ultimately the dairy outgrew the scenic waterfront property of Coburg and relocated to North Charleston in 1987. It was sold in 1998, ending 78 years of family operation. Today the old Coburg farm is still home to members of the Hanckel family. (Courtesy of Frank Hanckel and Charlotte Hanckel Hay.)

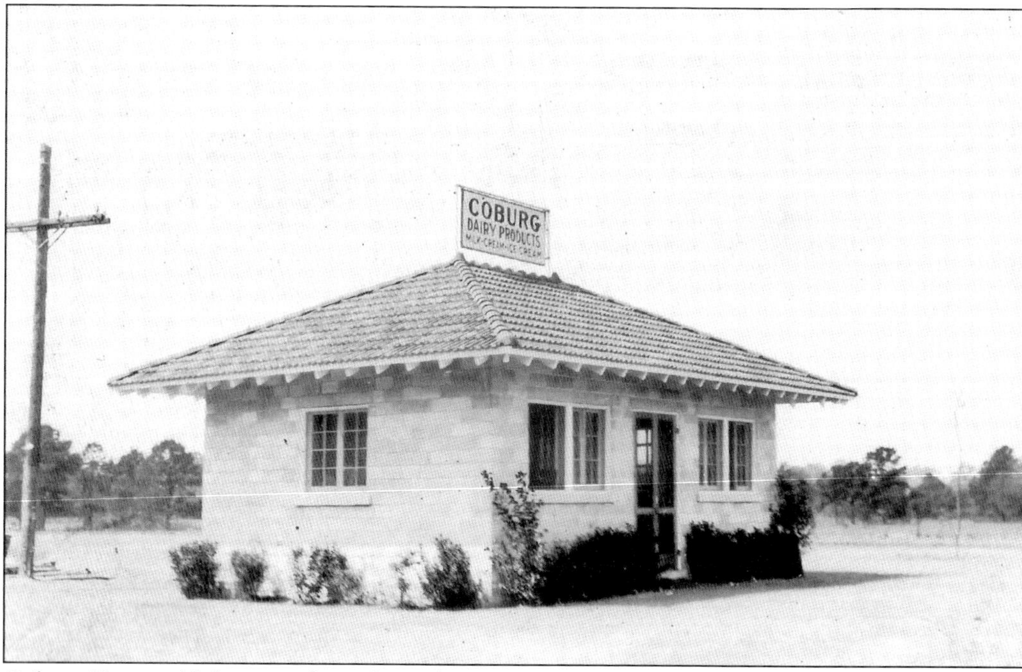

Coburg Dairy sold dairy products from this store on Savannah Highway. During World War II, the building was used as a draft board. Later this site would become the St. Andrew's Center. The Hanckel family lived at Coburg in addition to running the dairy from the property. Charlotte Hanckel Hay remembers having to get up for school in time to make it down the dirt road before the cows ambled their way down the road to the pasture past the railroad track (now the West Ashley Greenway) to Savannah Highway. As seen in the lower photograph, cows, trucks, and buildings all shared the property. (Both courtesy of Frank Hanckel and Charlotte Hanckel Hay.)

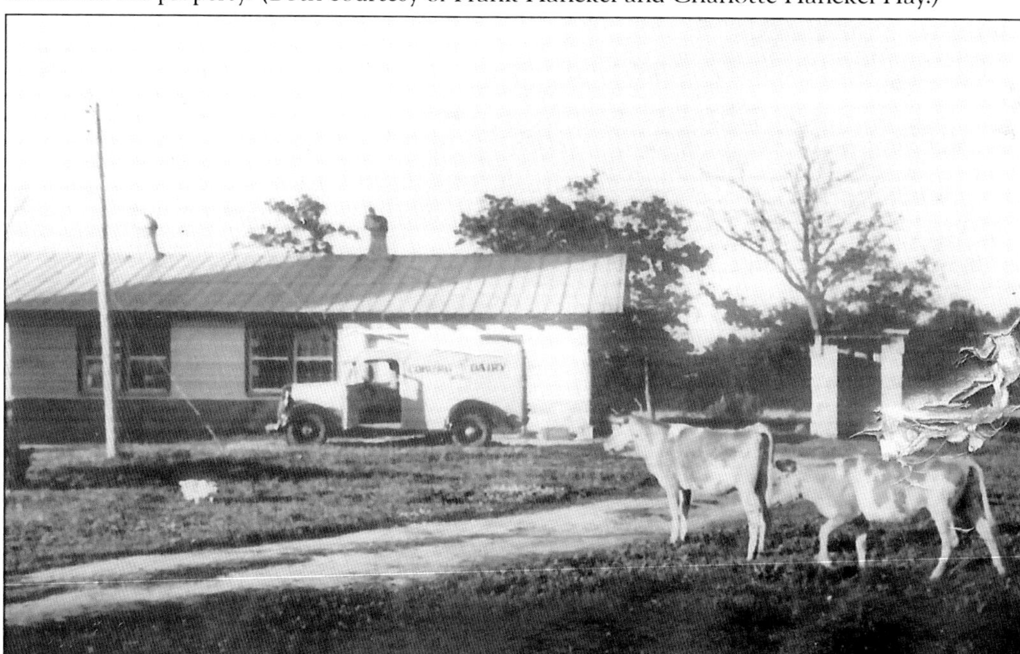

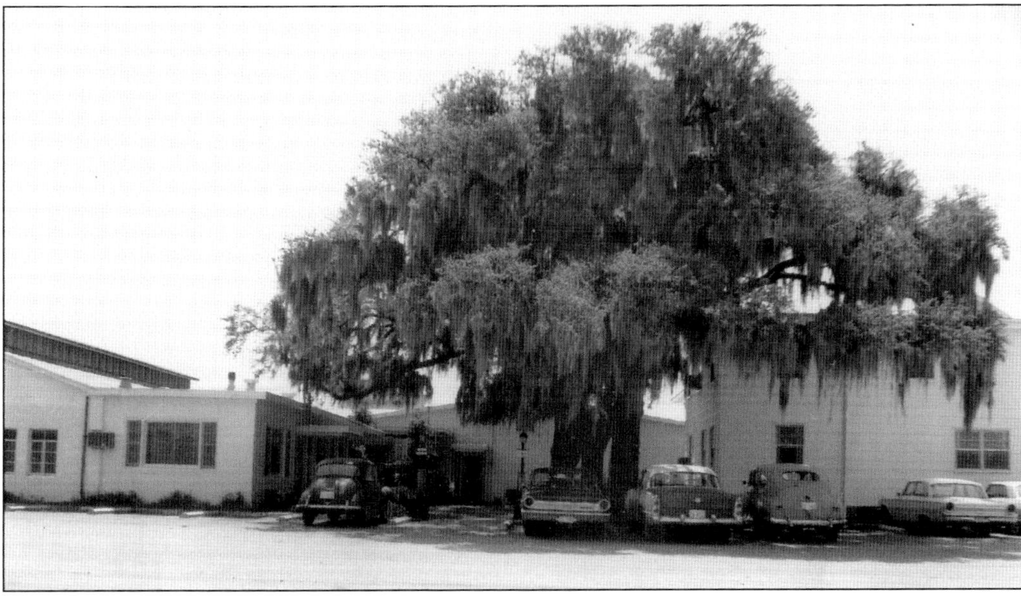

Francis Hanckel's wife, Polly, was always involved with community activities. She loved children, having seven of her own, and was very involved with the schools, church, and community programs. There were regular field trips from the local schools to tour the dairy buildings and see the cows. Many Charleston County schoolchildren of the 1940s and 1950s remember their field trip to "the dairy," highlighted by a carton of chocolate milk and a romp on the swings and slides on the playground under the big oak trees. On one of these tours, a child insisted on knowing which cow was the "chocolate milk cow." The Cookhouse at Coburg Dairy (pictured below) was a popular place for community events. The Hanckel family encouraged church groups, neighborhood groups, and the like to use the place for functions. On page 84 of *History Byrnes Downs Garden Club* is a newspaper article outlining the club's plan to have a benefit chicken supper on May 14 at Coburg. (Both courtesy of Frank Hanckel and Charlotte Hanckel Hay.)

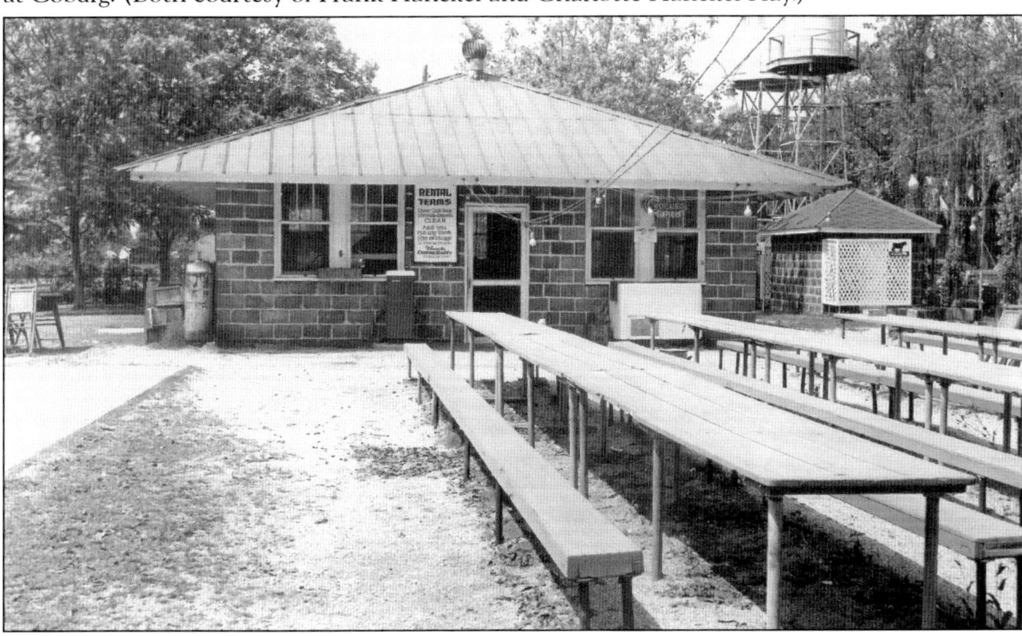

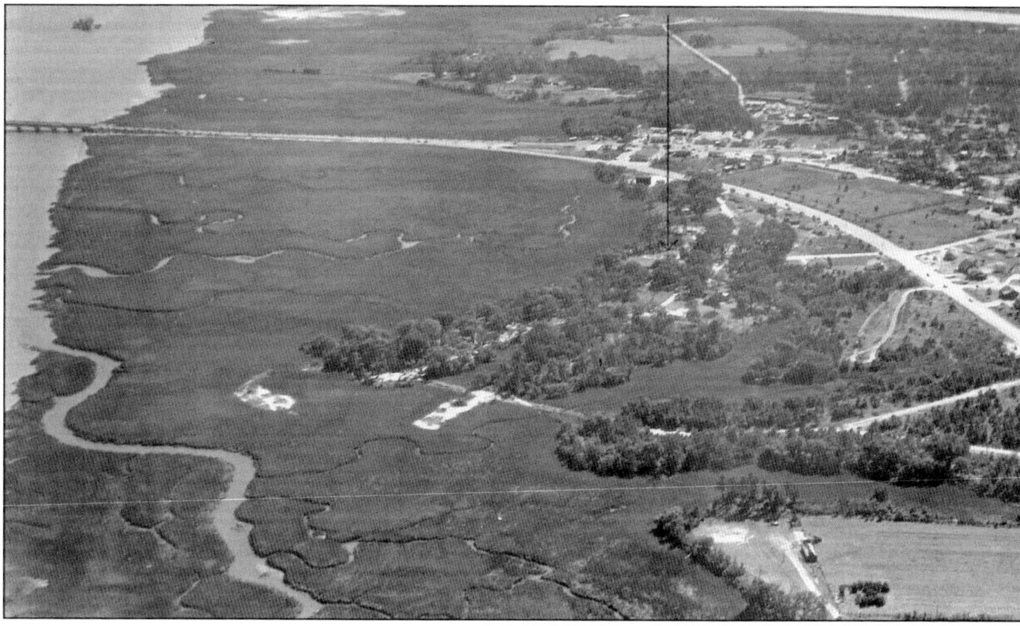

Albemarle Point is located on a piece of land along Wappoo Creek accessed by a causeway, graced by 10 homes, and embraced by the marsh along the west bank of the Ashley River. The residents recount with delight their childhood memories of growing up on Albemarle Point in the 1950s and 1960s. Riding horses, swinging in tire swings, walking along the railroad tracks to South Windermere Shopping Center, swimming in the man-made tidal canal, playing in the pea field that one day would become a tennis court and swimming pool, and exploring the surrounding farmland are among these memories. Today some of these same residents are bringing up the next generation in these original family homes. The West Ashley area surrounding Albemarle Point has boomed in the last 50 years, but the residents of Albemarle Point still feel the embrace of the marsh and the quiet solitude of the point. (Above courtesy of Cantey Hare; below courtesy of Sandra Marshall Foxworth.)

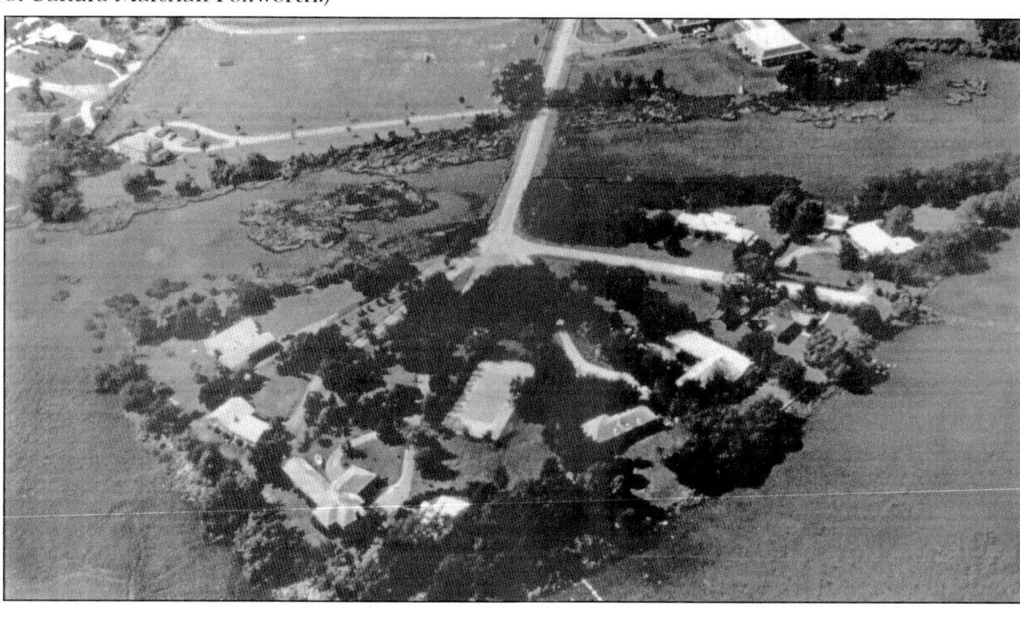

At 10 years of age, Sandra Marshall Foxworth received a Brownie Kodak camera for Christmas. It was the only item on her wish list. She immediately began documenting her life and the lives of her family on Albemarle Point. Her shadow decorates the photograph she took of her childhood home. Today she lives on the adjacent property that was once owned by her grandmother, Caroline Webb Marshall. (Courtesy of Sandra Marshall Foxworth.)

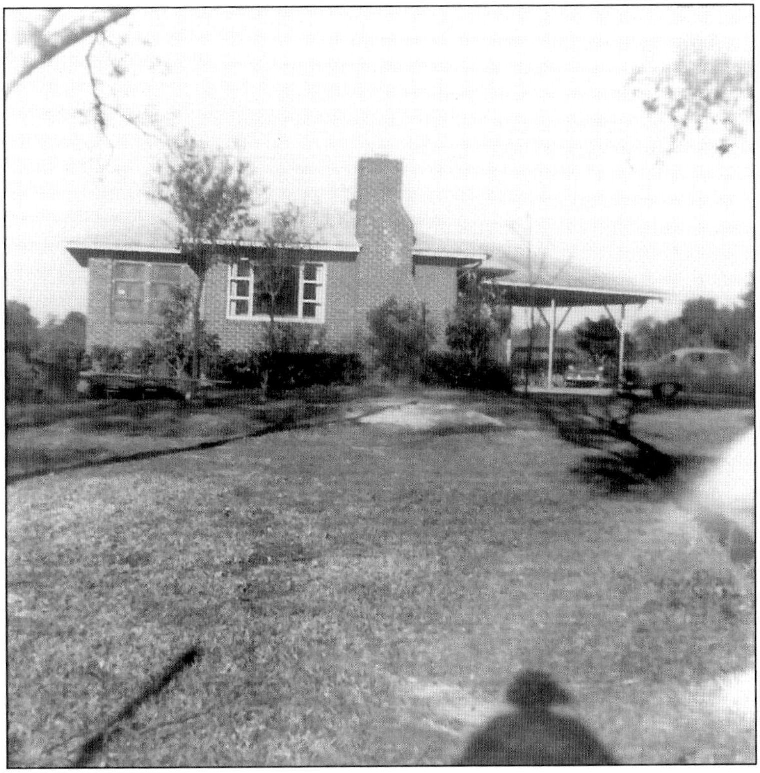

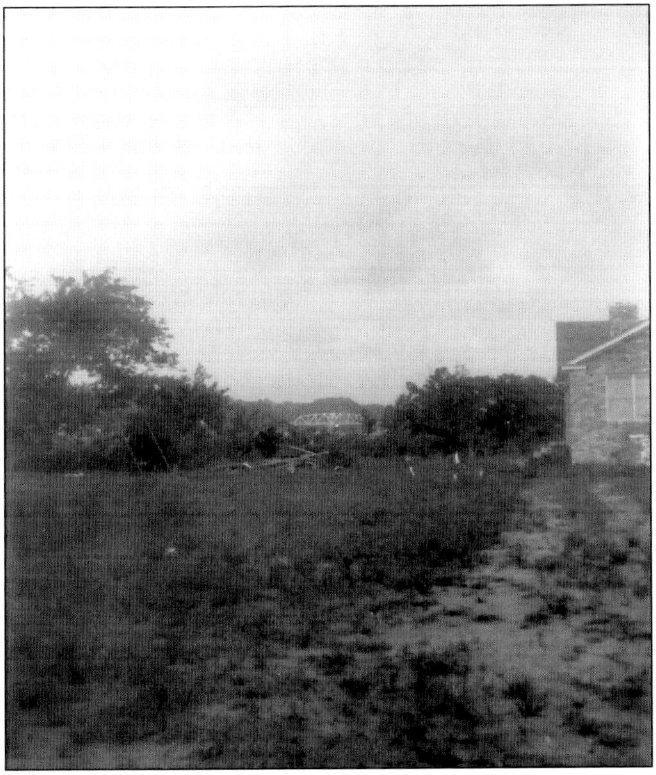

On January 6, 1947, Robert T. Ball purchased a lot on Albemarle Point from Thomas Stevenson for $1,800. He and his wife, Elizabeth Martin, were not quite ready to build their dream home, so they moved to 54 Campbell Drive in Byrnes Downs, where they resided from 1949 to 1954. When the Jenkins Orphanage on the peninsula of Charleston was torn down, Ball salvaged the bricks to build his home at 8 Albemarle Point. In the background of this photograph, note the structure of the original Wappoo Bridge. (Courtesy of Dr. Robert Ball.)

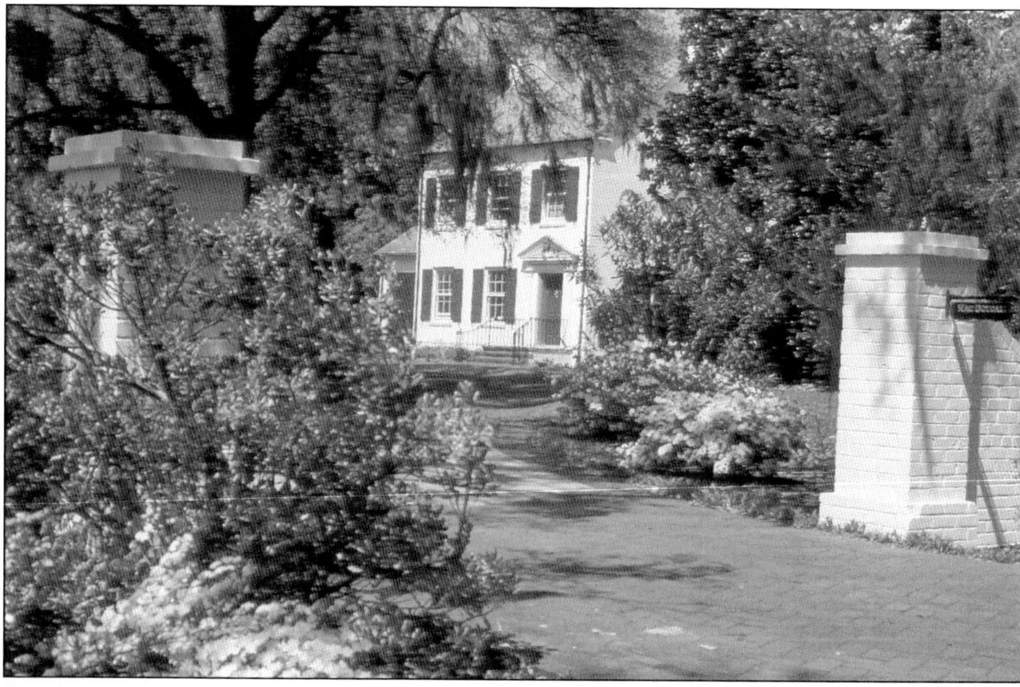

One New Town Lane is built on land believed to be the site of the Crescent Plantation house, although no evidence of the structure exists today. Thomas Grange Simons purchased the 235 acres that included the area now known as The Crescent in 1853. The property conveyed in 1901, again in 1909, and in 1920, the Wappoo Realty Company purchased the property and commissioned the Olmstead brothers to design the neighborhood described as "The Battery of the Suburbs" in a 1943 advertisement. When the MacDougals excavated the well on this property, they found a penny dated 1853. (Courtesy of Jan MacDougal.)

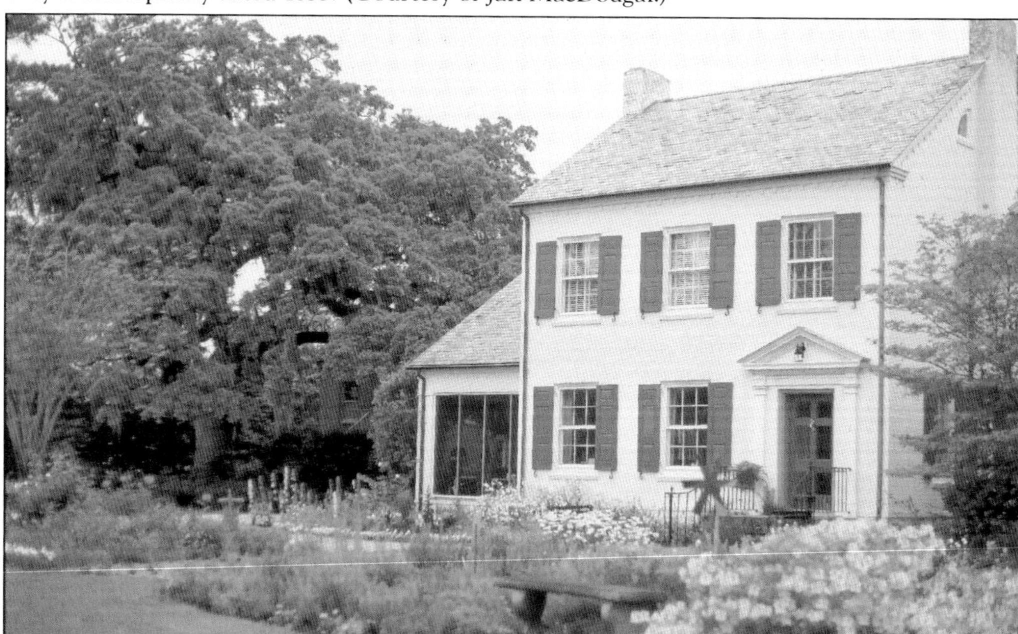

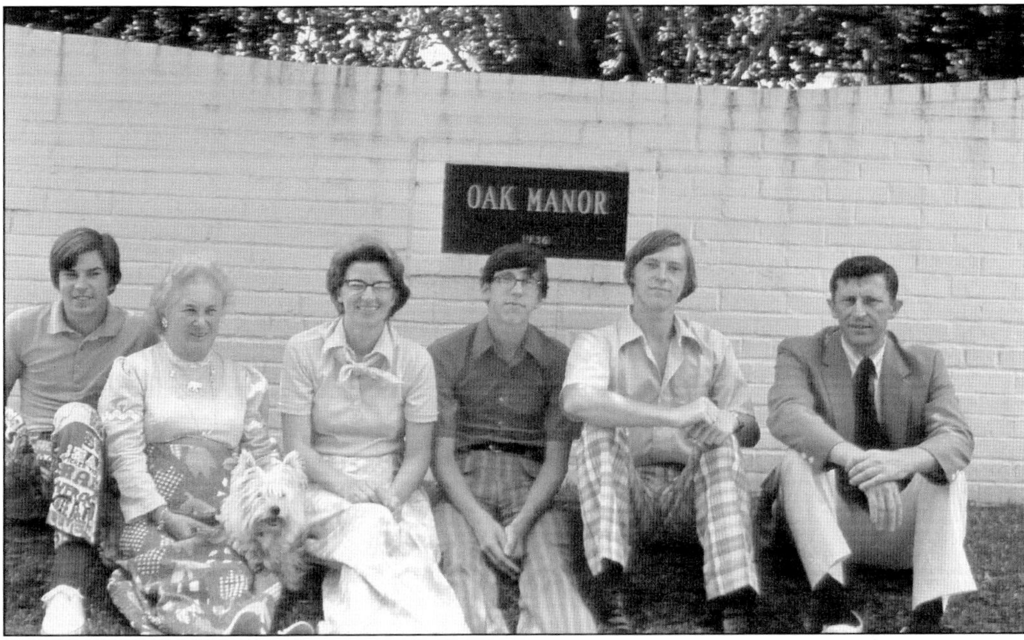

Rouette Mochrie, John MacDougal's maternal aunt, came to Charleston from New York for a visit. The MacDougal family took the opportunity for a family photograph. Pictured from left to right along the property wall of 1 New Town Lane, from left to right, are Paul, Rouette, Jan, Kent, John, John, and the family Westie named Candy. (Courtesy of Jan MacDougal.)

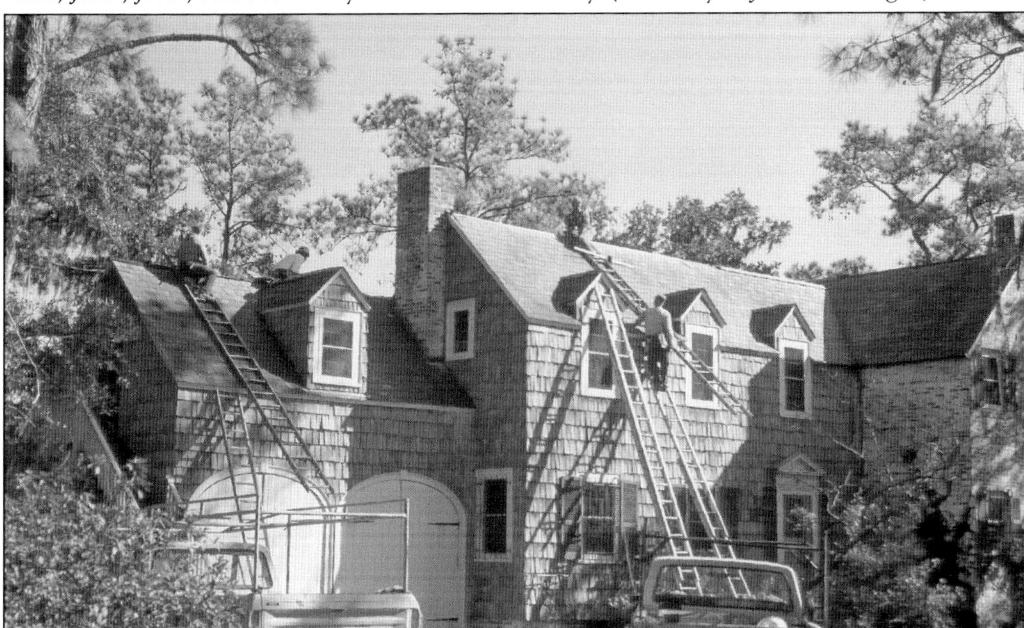

Two New Town Lane, also known as Siskaya, is located in The Crescent. Alexander Sprunt Jr. built Siskaya. Alexander was a noted ornithologist and in 1934 was hired as the southern representative of the National Audubon Society. During the construction of his home, Alexander extensively documented the land, construction, plants, birds, and other wildlife in his personal journal. This exquisite book conveys with the home to each new owner. (Courtesy of Jan MacDougal.)

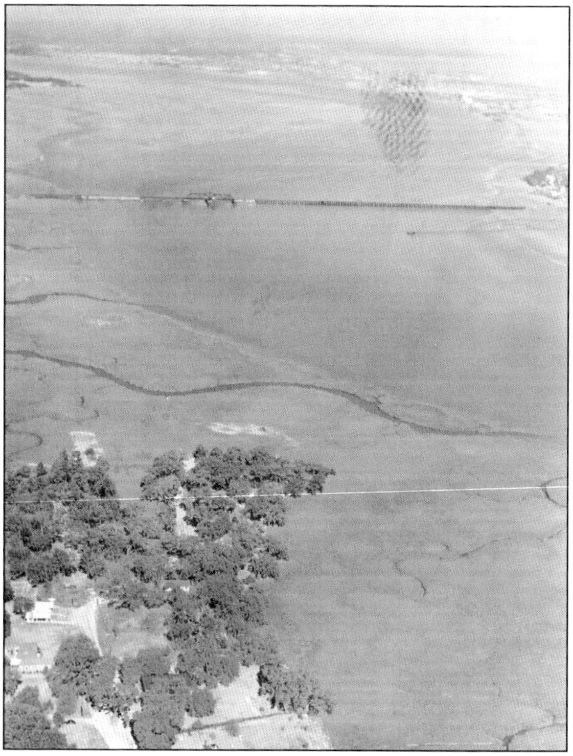

This aerial shows a tip of land in the Moreland subdivision that was once part of J. M. Harrison's farmland. In 1916, Rene Ravenel prepared a map of 330.8 acres of the "Crafts Tract" for J. M. Harrison. Joseph Harrison, pictured below in his cornfield, became known in St. Andrew's Parish as a prominent planter. The corn, cabbage, potato, and green bean fields as well as the magnificent fields of narcissus decorated a large section of St. Andrew's Parish. His second wife, Mamie Santos Harrison, used the narcissus fields as her source of income, selling the flowers to local florists. The cabbage field south of Savannah Highway adjacent to the Hanckel property would one day be plowed under, sold, and turned into the community of Byrnes Downs. (Left courtesy of Cantey Hare; below courtesy of Irene Burk Tezza and Ruth Burk Gay.)

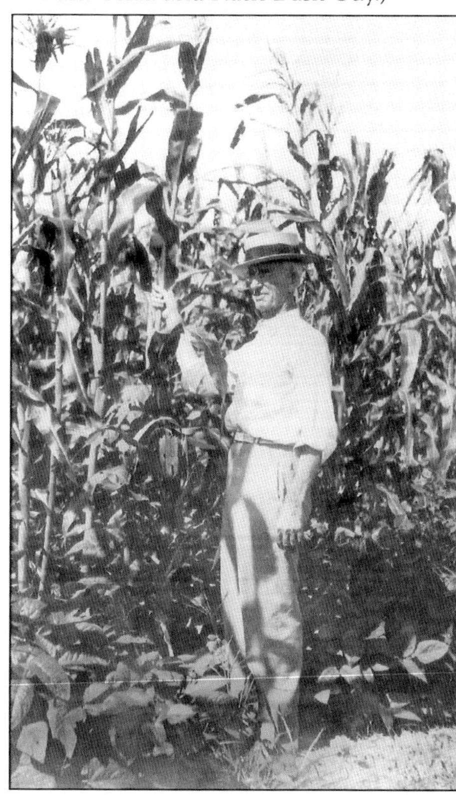

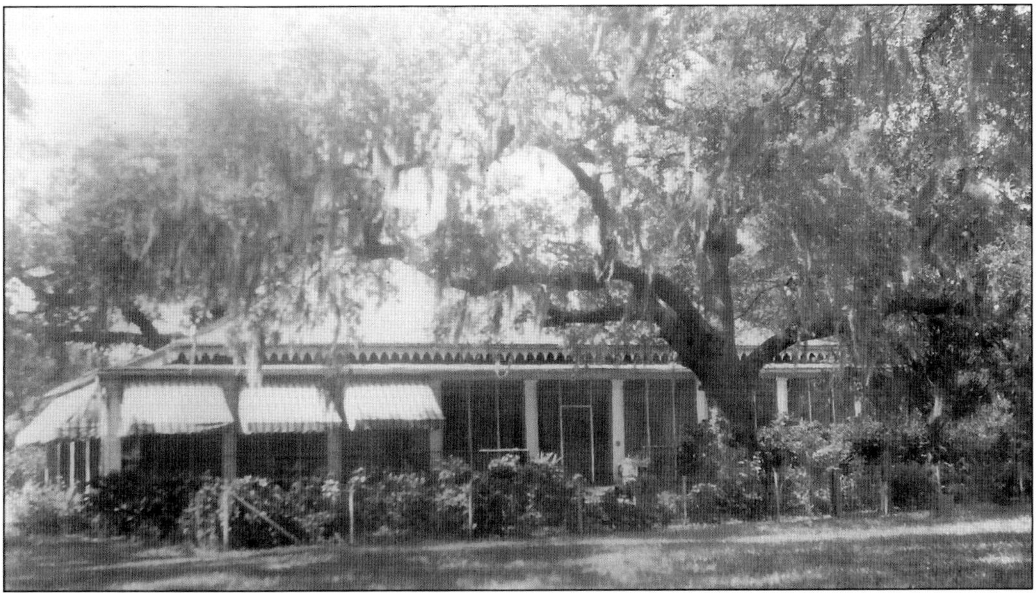

Joseph's second wife, Mamie Santos Harrison, had five nieces from her sister Irene Santos Burk. Two of them, Irene Burk Tezza and Ruth Burk Gay, have vivid stories of walking from their home at 65 Pitt Street across the "Ashley River" or "New" bridge to their uncle Joe's farm at 752 Woodward Road to get milk and vegetables and maybe take a horseback ride to the Flood home. Gus Flood was Joe's caretaker and lived on Harrison farmland south on Savannah Highway at what is now the end of Betsy Road. Joe and Mamie's house on Woodward Road was built in 1845 and was originally a dance hall before Joe converted it to his residence. Their home remains today as part of the neighborhood and has a magnificent view of the Ashley River. (Courtesy of Irene Burk Tezza and Ruth Burk Gay.)

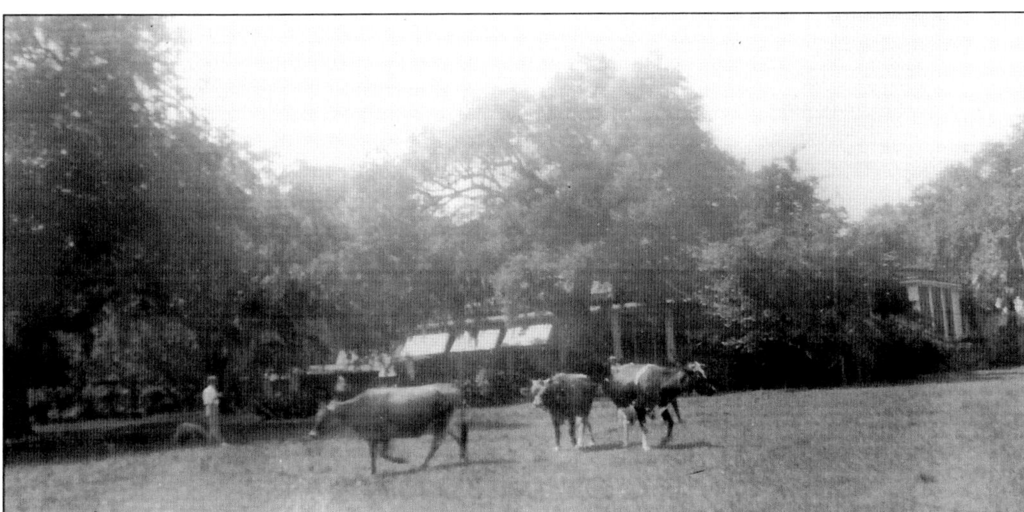

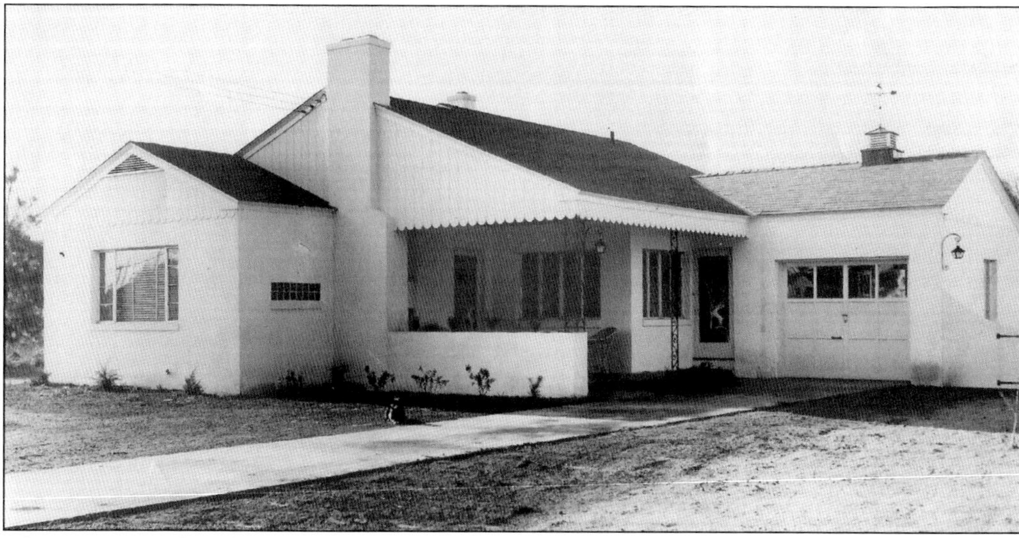

Christmas 1950 found the Bohne family moving into their new home at 10 Harrison Road. Later this address would change to 711 West Harrison Road. Peggy Bohne (below) grew up in Moreland. She learned to ride her bicycle in the streets of Moreland, attended the Blessed Sacrament School and Church, and has been the president of the Moreland Neighborhood Association. Her stories of growing up in Moreland have been a valuable resource. (Courtesy of Peggy Bohne.)

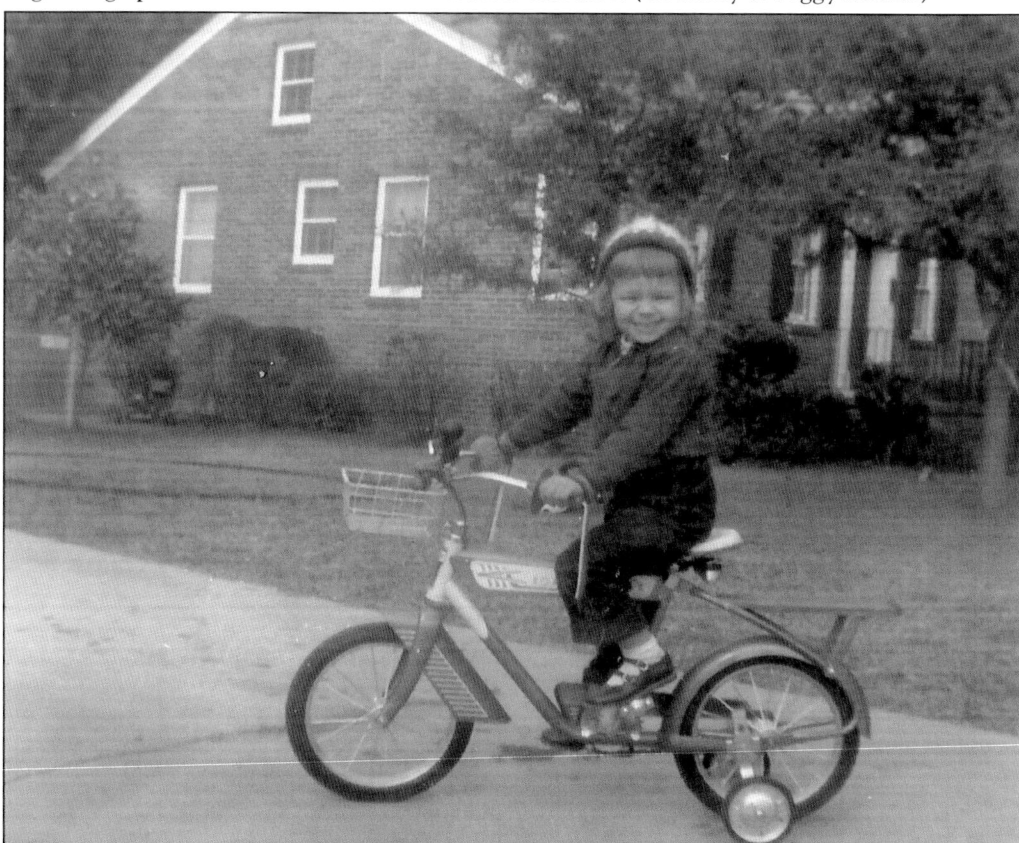

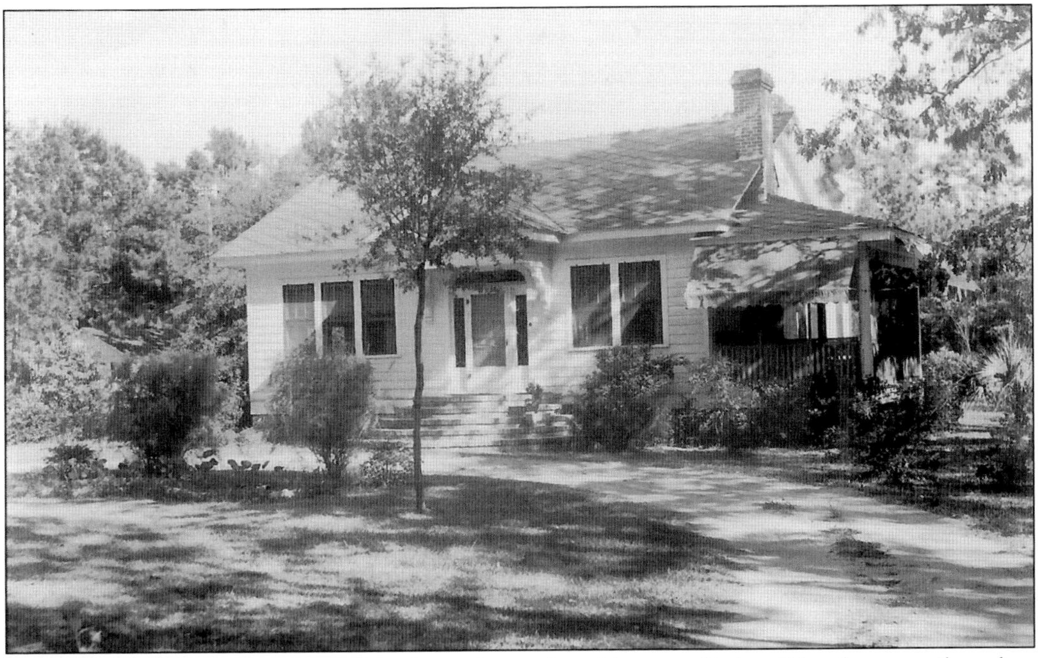

The Wallace home in Wappoo Heights is located on Formosa Drive. The dates attributed to these two photographs are 1937 (above) and 1977 (below). Interestingly the shingles are original to the home even though it has gone through several renovations. Formosa Drive was originally known as Azalea Drive. In 1963, many streets in Charleston County needed to be renamed to eliminate duplication. Streets with the same names were causing confusion to the fire and police departments, the postal service, and the populace in general. Formosa is the type of azalea common in the neighborhood and decorating the Wallace front yard. (Courtesy of Bill Wallace.)

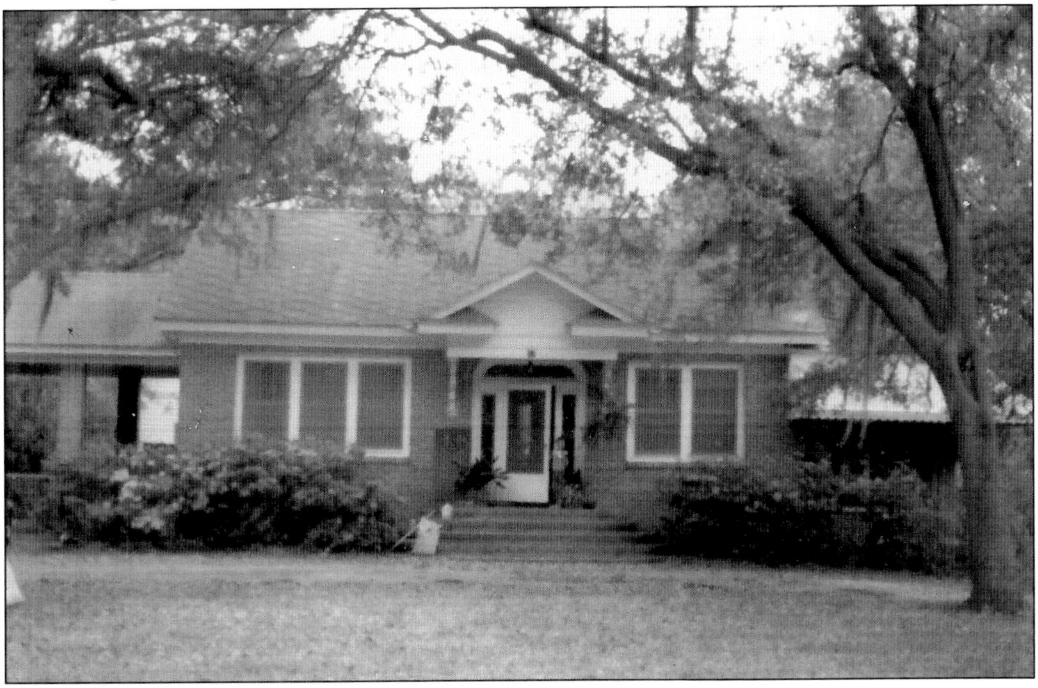

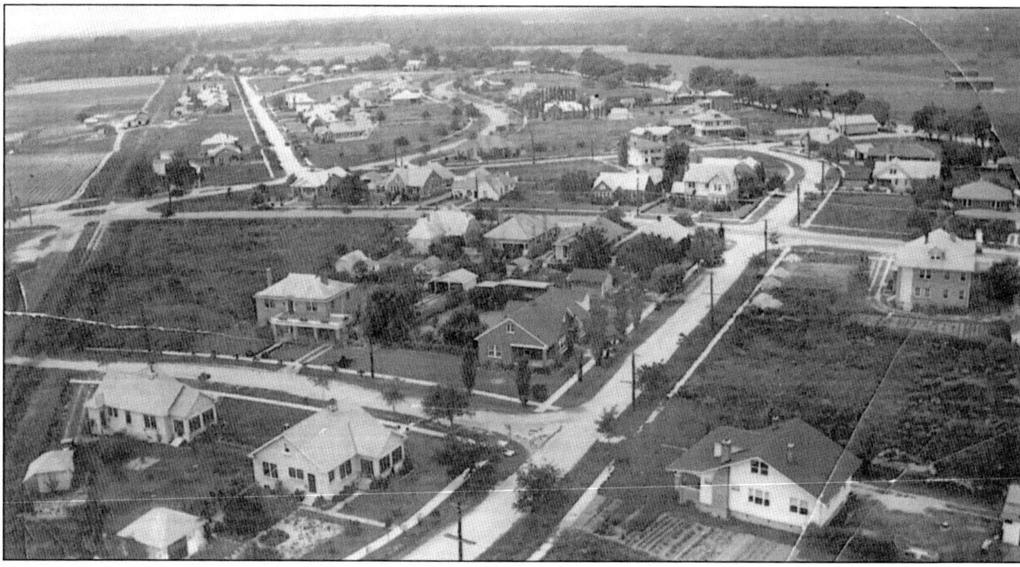

At 12:30 p.m. on May 5, 1935, an unidentified shutterbug climbed the water tower located near the Windermere neighborhood and took this photograph. The 70-plus-year-old perspective is amazing, for it only took 15 years for the area to develop as seen in the previous aerials. People like the Dandridge family were anxious to have their own home. Tom Dandridge, the maternal grandfather of Margaret Thorne Seidler, built the house seen below at 6 Fenwick Drive in 1928. (Above courtesy of Carolee Williams; below courtesy of Margaret Thorne Seidler.)

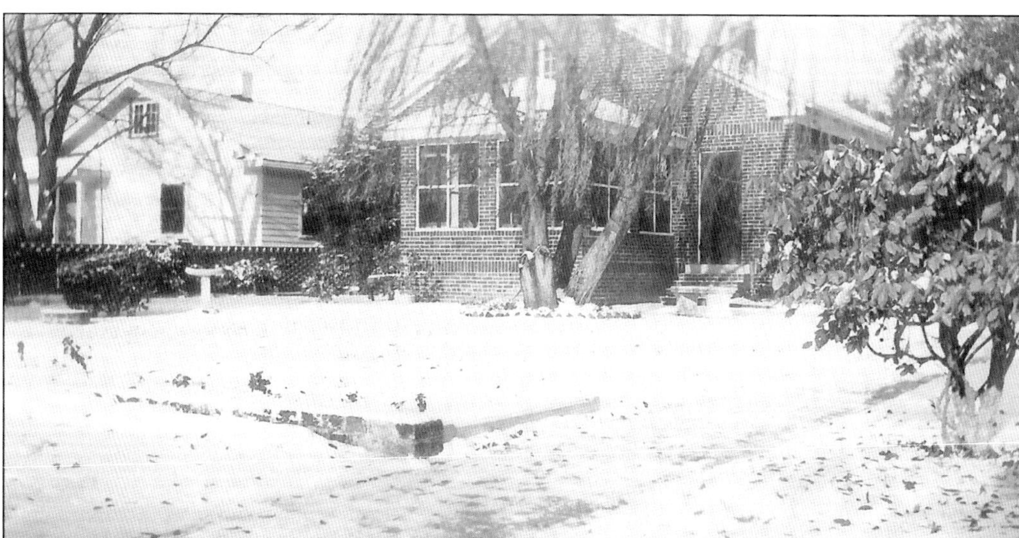

Mamie Louise Dandridge (right) lived in Windermere in the house on Fenwick Drive. She married Robert Thomas in the mid-1930s and raised two children. Mamie (or "Aunt Mamie" as she was known not only to family, but also to friends) was the life of every party. Her laughter was infectious, and she loved to describe the food at the party as "gogeous." Mamie (right), her father, Tom Dandridge (center), and her sister June (Dandridge Thorne) relax at the family home on Fenwick Drive while entertaining their children, Jeanne Thomas (seated) and Lynda Thorne (standing) with a swimming pool. (Courtesy of Margaret Thorne Seidler.)

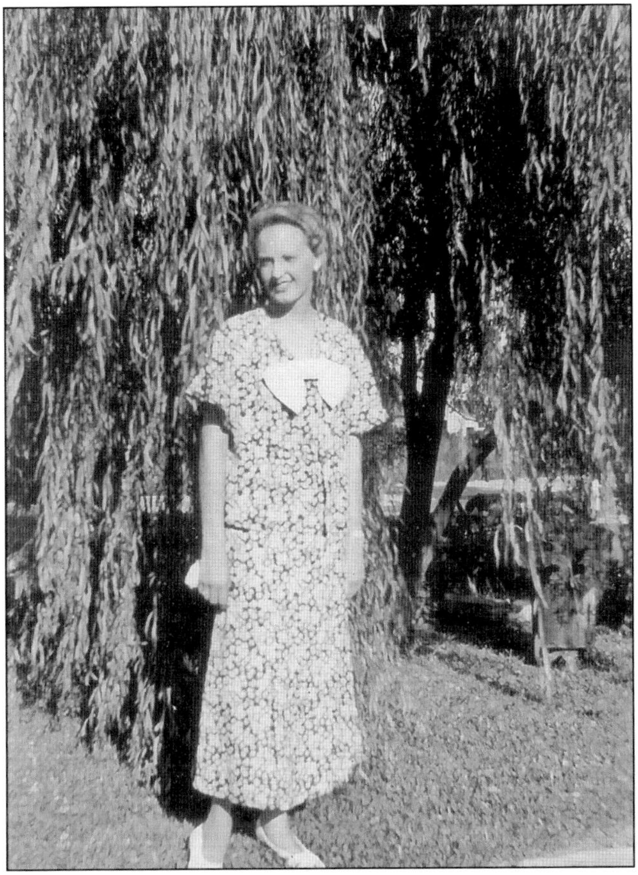

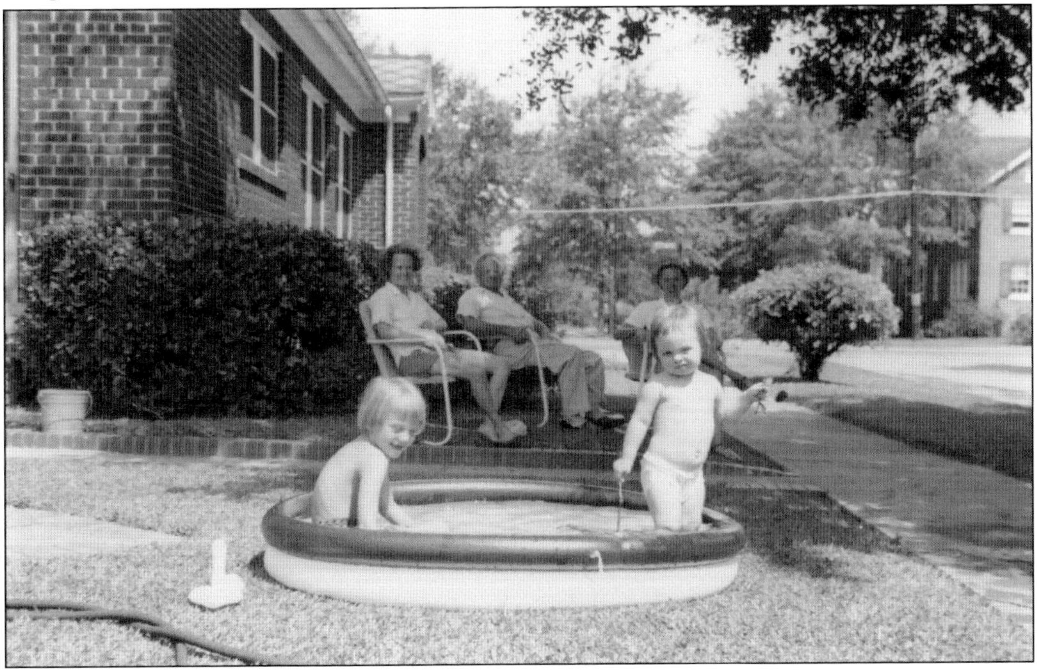

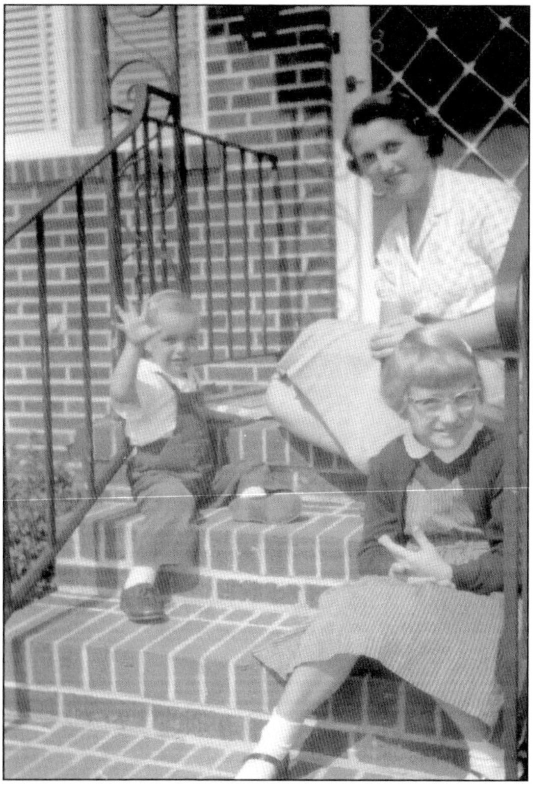

In 1953, Julian and Barbara Kiel purchased a lot in South Windermere where the streets were not paved and one had to walk to a central location (now the site of the Charleston County Library in the South Windermere Shopping Center) for the mail. W. L. Riggs built the home, and they moved into their home in May 1954. Barbara is shown sitting on her front porch with their children Barbara Ann and Chris. (Courtesy of Barbara and Julian Kiel.)

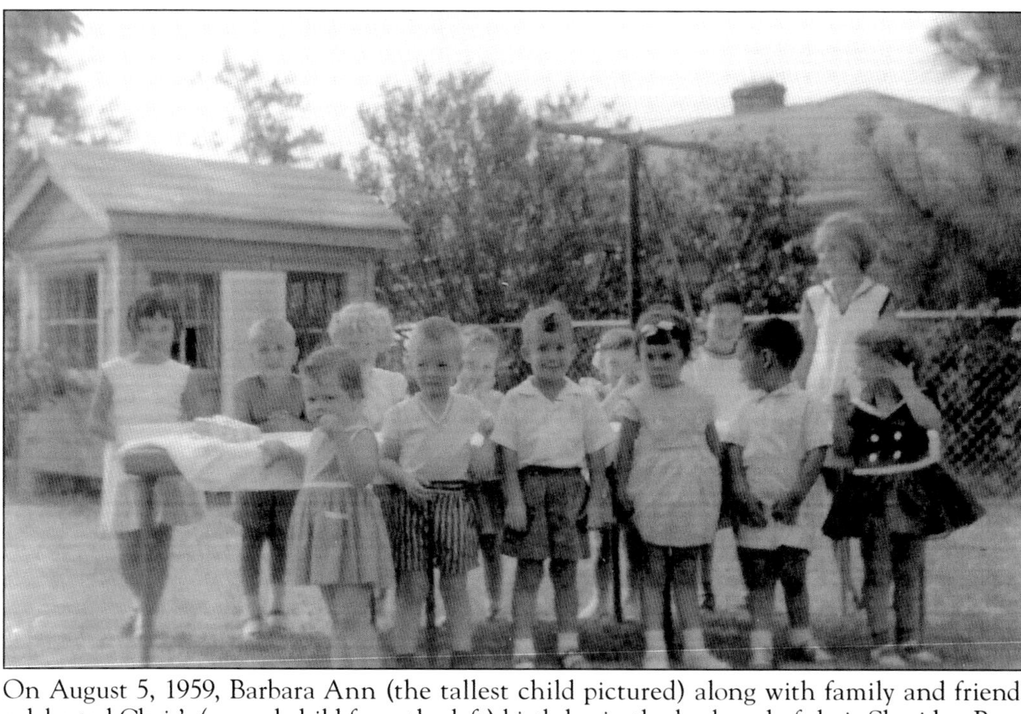

On August 5, 1959, Barbara Ann (the tallest child pictured) along with family and friends celebrated Chris's (second child from the left) birthday in the backyard of their Sheridan Road home. (Courtesy of Barbara and Julian Kiel.)

Barbara proudly shows off her garden at her Sheridan home. Today the Kiel home is accented by landscaping that has been cultivated by years of attention. Barbara and Julian Kiel have stayed active in the community. Julian served as president of the South Windermere Neighborhood Association and has a continued interest in the history of the area. He conducted several interviews with Bill Ackerman about the development of South Windermere and the shopping center. (Courtesy of Barbara and Julian Kiel.)

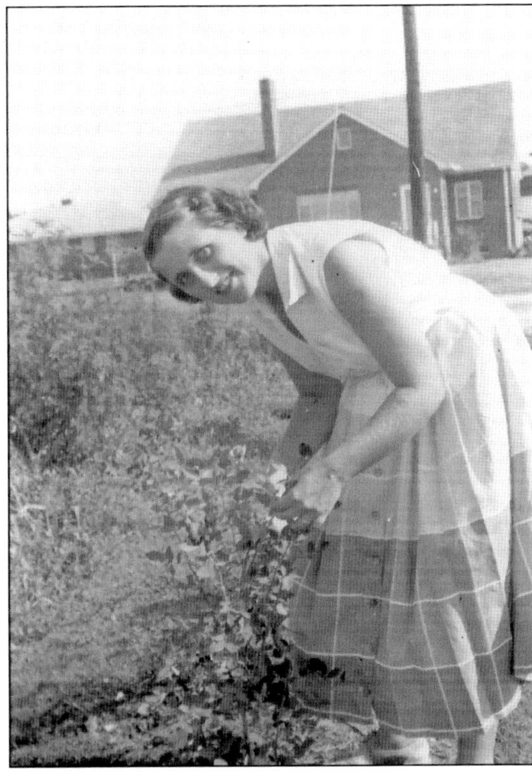

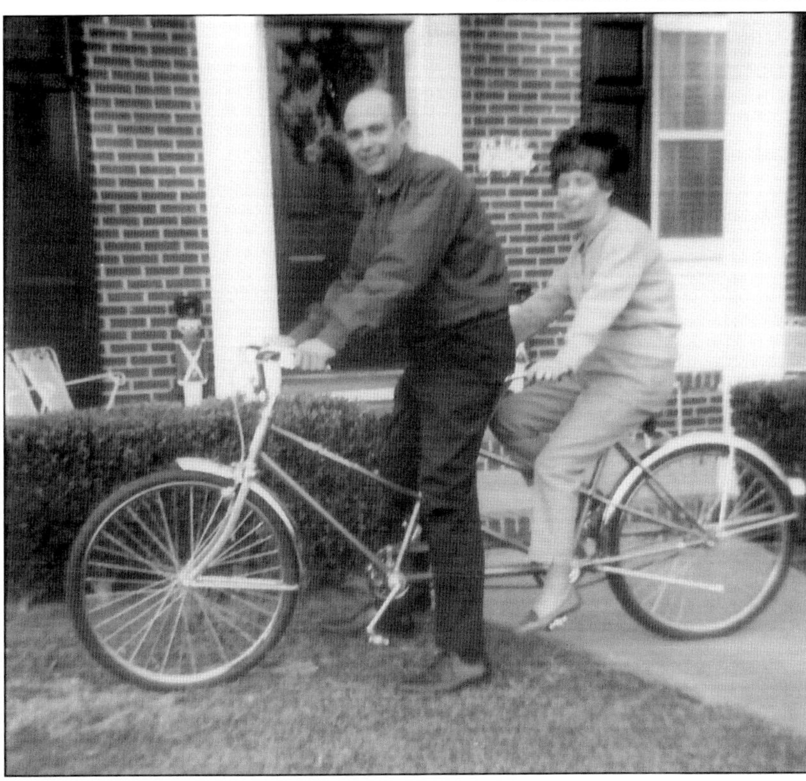

Santa Claus brought Peggy and Ed Rugheimer of 18 Sheridan Road a bicycle built for two for Christmas. When South Windermere was developed in the 1950s, the home at 18 Sheridan Road served as the model home and was owned by Howard Sears, the manager for Charleston County. (Courtesy of Barbara and Julian Kiel.)

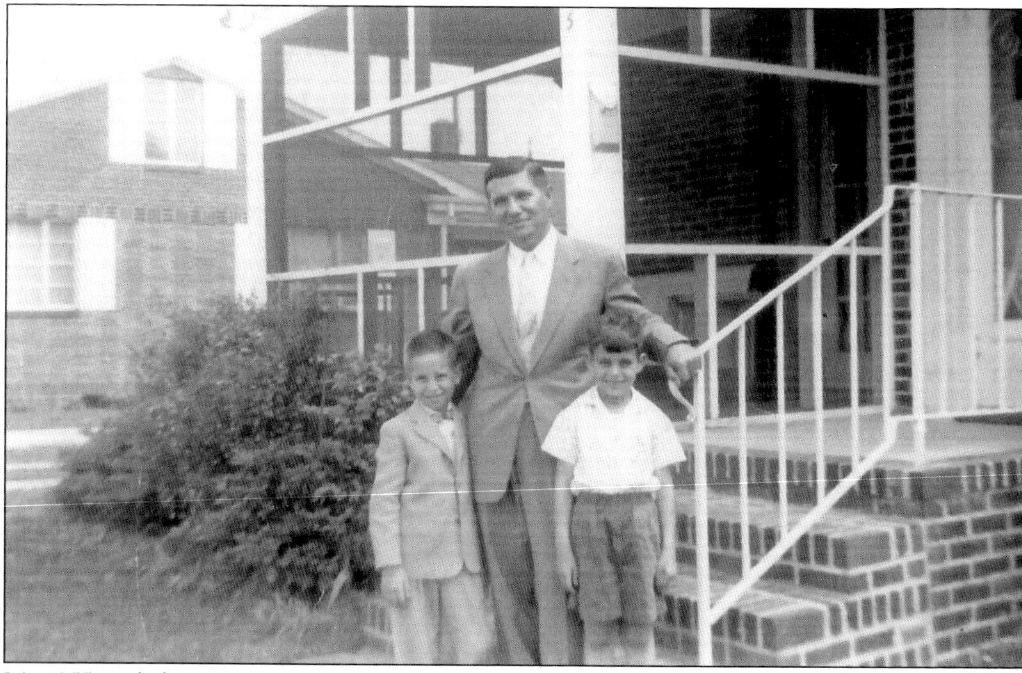

It's 1955 and the Dimitri family is living on Morton Avenue in Westwood. Interestingly, in April 1947, Morton Avenue appears on a survey labeled "Blocks A thru F Byrnes Downs." The survey is attributed to the John McGrady Company. As yet, there is no information as to why the neighborhood was developed differently from the survey and named Westwood. However, in *History Byrnes Downs Garden Club* are newspaper articles and programs that describe the First Annual Spring Flower Show hosted by Byrnes Downs and Westwood Garden Clubs in April 1952. The upper photograph shows John (left), his father, Mitchell, and brother Jimmy at their home on Morton Avenue. Below, John and his friend pose before taking off on their bicycles to points unknown. (Both courtesy of John Dimitri.)

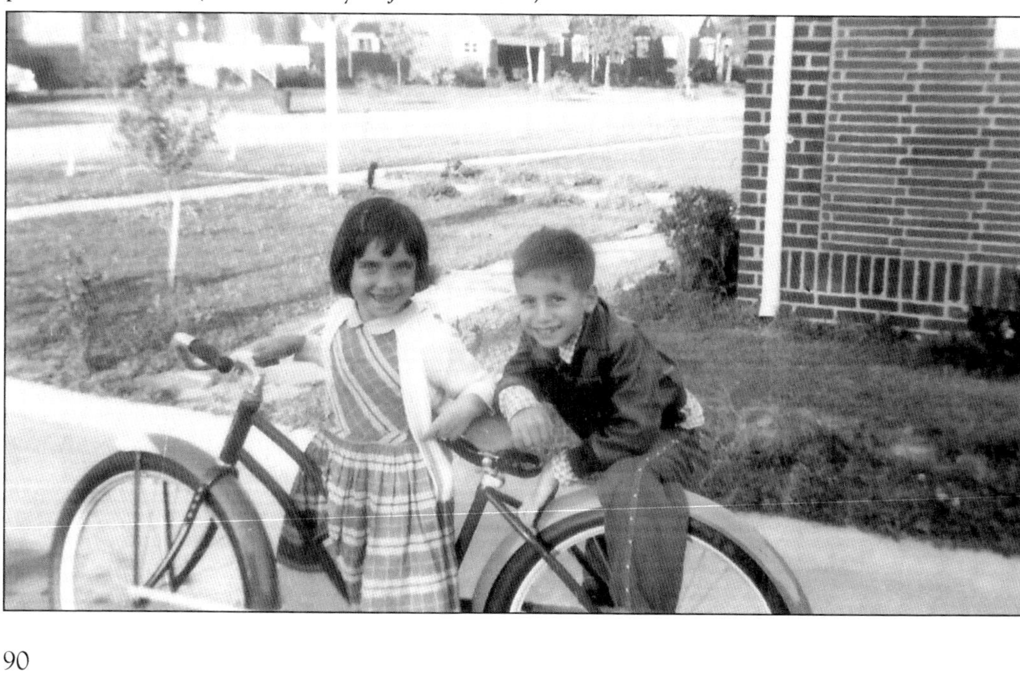

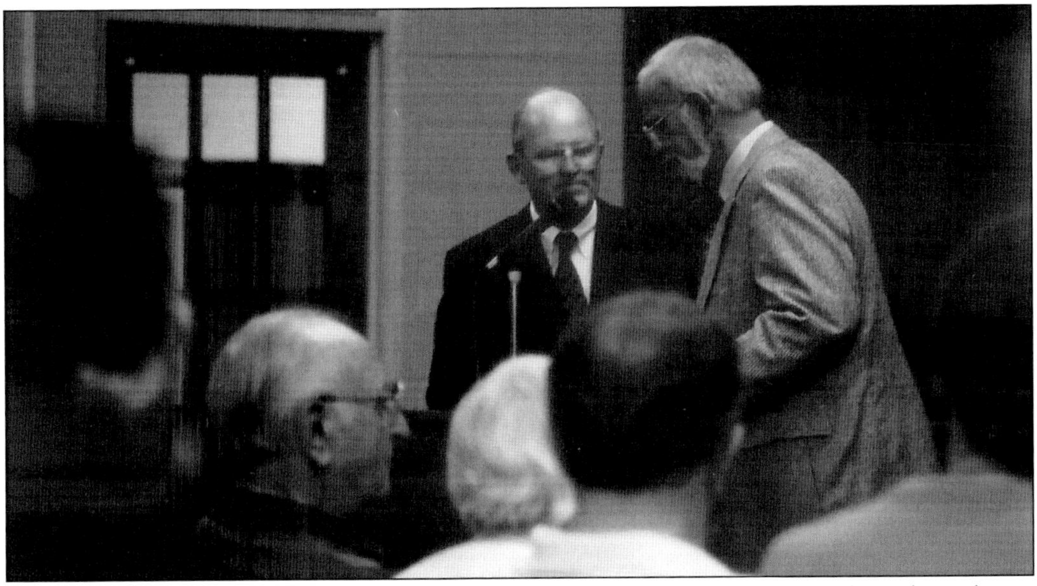

In 1993, the building at the corner of Wesley Drive and St. Andrews Boulevard was being considered for use by the Charleston County Substance Abuse Commission's administrative offices, detox unit, and medical center. The neighbors were quite uncomfortable with this proposition and organized a vocal opposition to this plan. They were successful in their efforts, and the building was ultimately torn down and replaced by the Moreland Medical Building. Bill Regan (above, left), attorney for the City of Charleston, and Bill Lawrence (above, right) lead a discussion group at St. Andrew's Elementary School. Included in the lower picture in front of the building are some of the people who were active in the protest: Micky Willis, Polly Lady, Toi Estes, Ethel Nepveux, John Graham Altman, (District 119's representative to the South Carolina House of Representatives) Leslie Infinger, Ledlie Bell, Bill Lawrence, Charles Karesh, Frank Loftin, and Dana Nettles. Not pictured is Dick Mappus. He was active in this protest as his house was adjacent to the controversial site. (Both courtesy of Ethel Nepveux.)

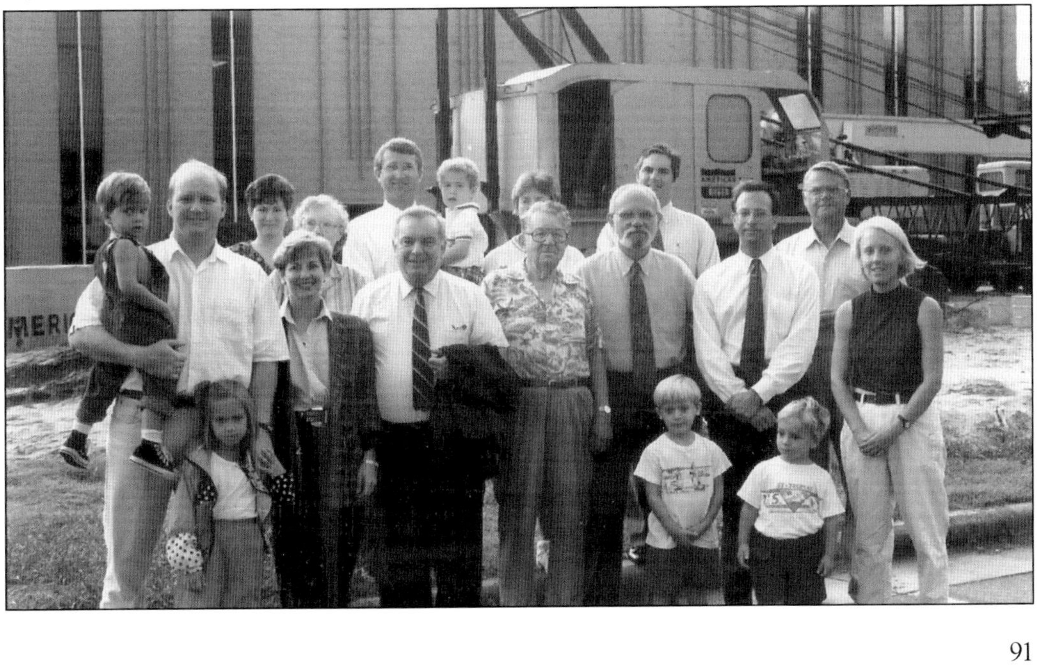

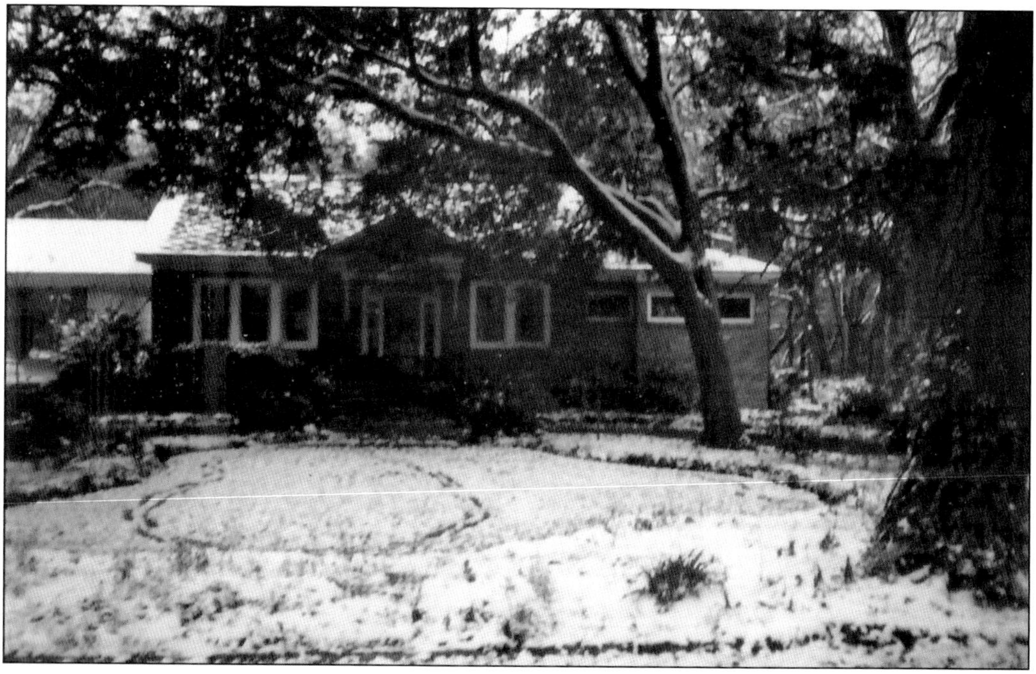

The Wallace home in the Wappoo Heights subdivision (above) and the Kiel home in the South Windermere subdivision (below) are shown after the Christmas snowstorm of 1989. Snow is a rare and fleeting event in the Lowcountry and usually commands that a photograph or two be taken to document the event. Even in its beauty, the snow was tough on the community, coming on the heels of Hurricane Hugo. (Above courtesy of Bill and Sally Wallace; below courtesy of Julian and Barbara Kiel.)

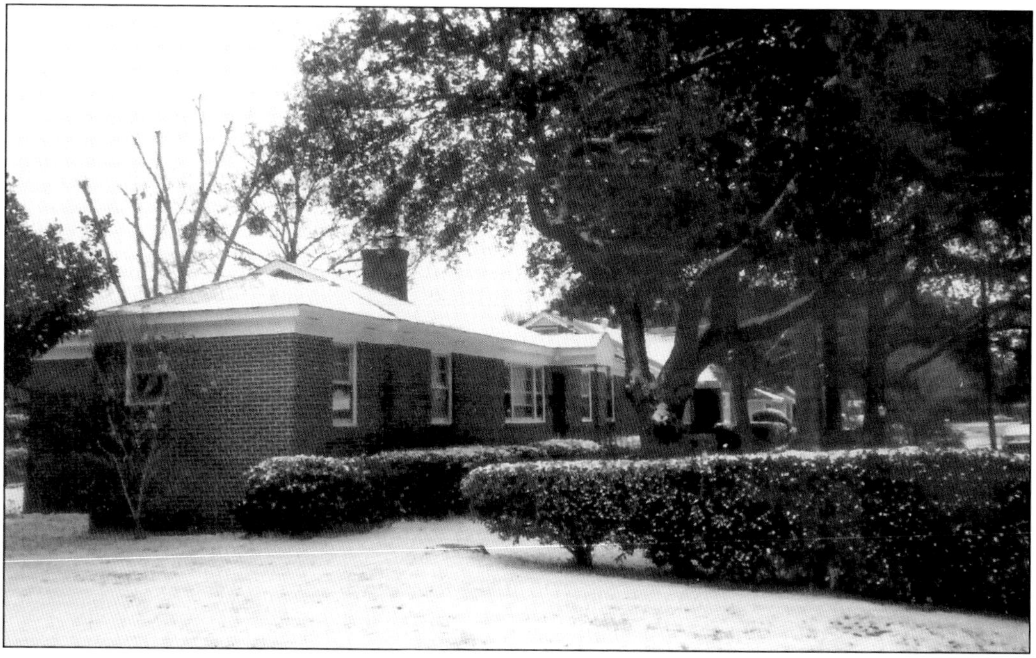

Five

Wind and Snow

Windstorms and snowstorms were great reasons for residents of Byrnes Downs and the surrounding area to get out the camera and record a terrific weather event. Unless there was a real shutterbug in the family, this might be one of the few times the camera came out besides holidays, birthdays, and weddings. Hurricanes are common occurrences for the coast, and the Charleston area has had several brushes with hurricanes and the tornados spawned from them. Particularly, three names come to the minds of current West Ashley residents when hurricanes are being discussed: Gracie, Donna, and Hugo. All three of these hurricanes impacted the area in September of their respective years: 1959, 1960, and 1989. Gracie formed in late September and was the strongest hurricane of the season at a Category 3. It made landfall near Beaufort, South Carolina, but most of the monetary damage was experienced in the Charleston area. Donna formed in early September and developed into a dangerous Category 5. It has a reputation for impacting all states along the Atlantic Coast as it spun parallel to the coast from the Caribbean to New England, where it made landfall. Hugo, also at a Category 5, has the reputation for being the most intense storm to strike the United States north of Florida since Hazel in 1954. An unexpected and rarer phenomenon, snow, has been known to catch us off guard, so much so that even a dusting like confectioner's sugar on a pound cake will keep everyone off the roads and at home making and throwing snowballs. On a couple of occasions, the snow and ice have been more "Northern" in nature. In February 1973, the *Charleston Evening Post* of the *News and Courier* (now the *Post and Courier*) ran a special pictorial edition—"Snow of the Century." Then, to add insult to injury, on Christmas Eve in the year that Hugo damaged almost every house in the greater Charleston area, a significant snowstorm left many in the area again without water. The pipes froze and burst. Many homes were still uninhabitable as a result of Hugo, so when the pipes thawed, the resulting unattended leaks caused the water pressure to drop significantly.

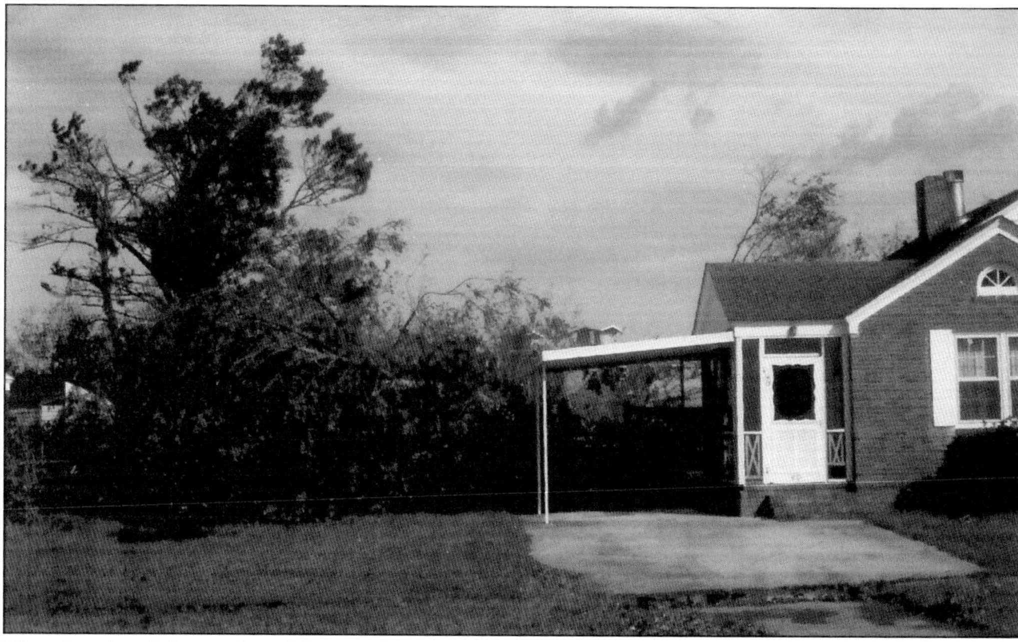

The details of the night of September 21, 1989, are permanently etched into the minds of the people who experienced Hurricane Hugo. The Blessed Sacrament Church located on Savannah Highway originally had two steeples until that night. If one looks carefully, the "steepleless" church can be seen in the background of the above photograph, taken from Lyttleton Avenue looking north. In addition, numerous trees were uprooted, and many residents found them littering their yards and lying on their rooftops, as did the Feldmans of Moreland. Leon and Marilyn Feldman built this home (below) on Sheldon Road in 1956. (Above courtesy of Bob and Karen Thames; below courtesy of Leon and Margaret Feldman.)

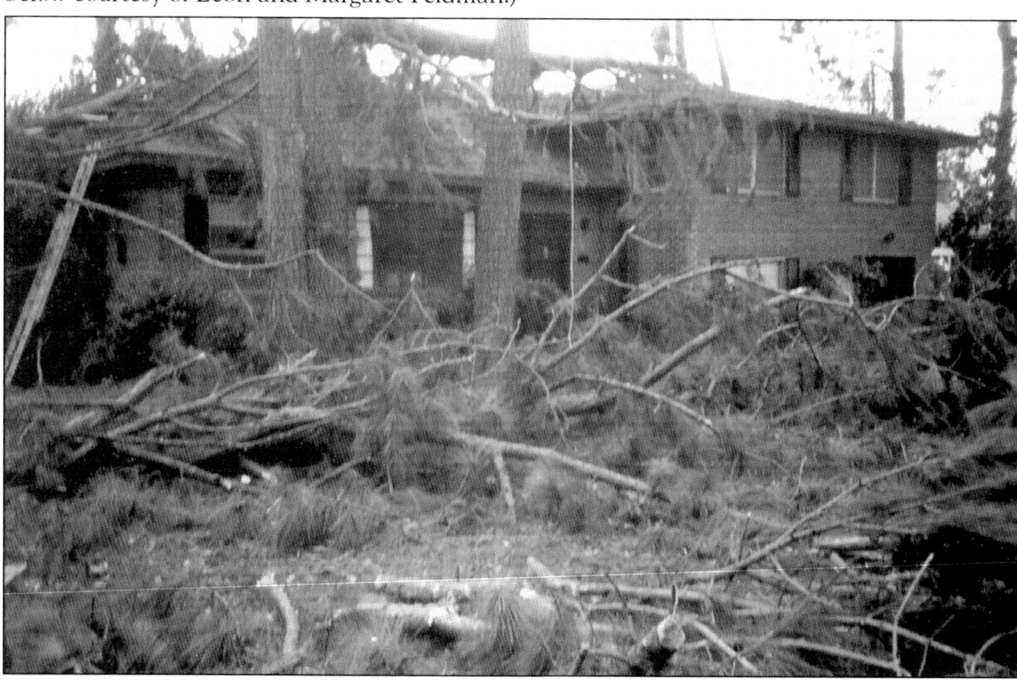

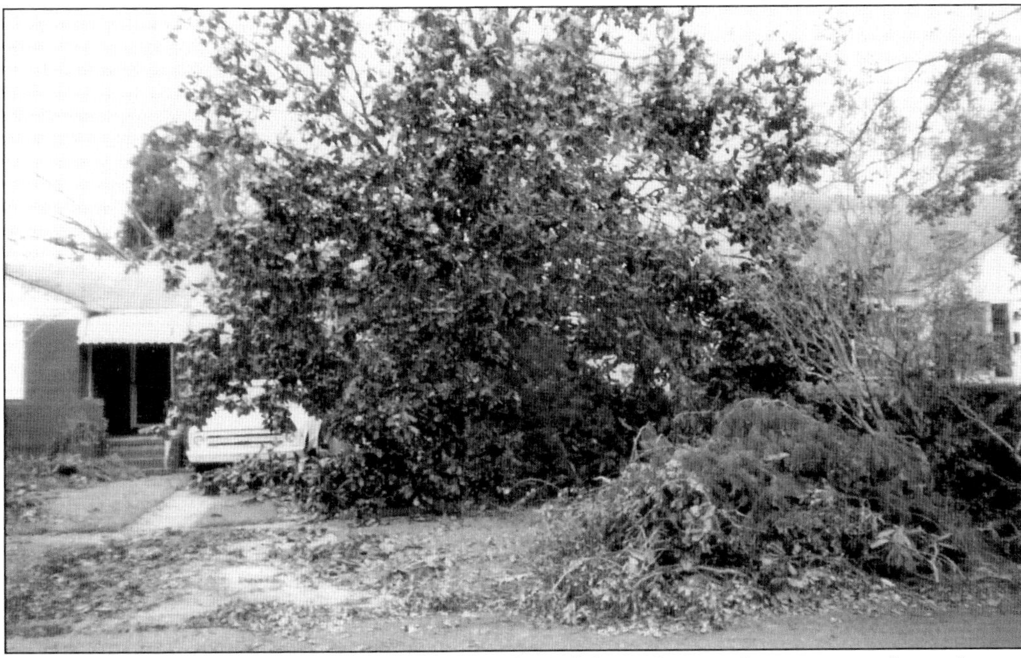

Even though the West Ashley area did not take the full fury of Hugo, there was significant damage and enough debris to keep everyone busy with cleanup for several months. The Corvettes' house on Campbell Drive is almost hidden from view by the large oak tree that fell in their yard (above). The neighborhood was fortunate in that most of the trees survived the terrific winds. Rutledge Corvette shared the below photograph looking up Campbell Drive toward Savannah Highway. It illustrates the daunting task ahead for the residents. For months after Hugo, one could barely see the houses from the street thanks to large piles of debris stacked along the road. (Both courtesy of Rutledge and Margaret Corvette.)

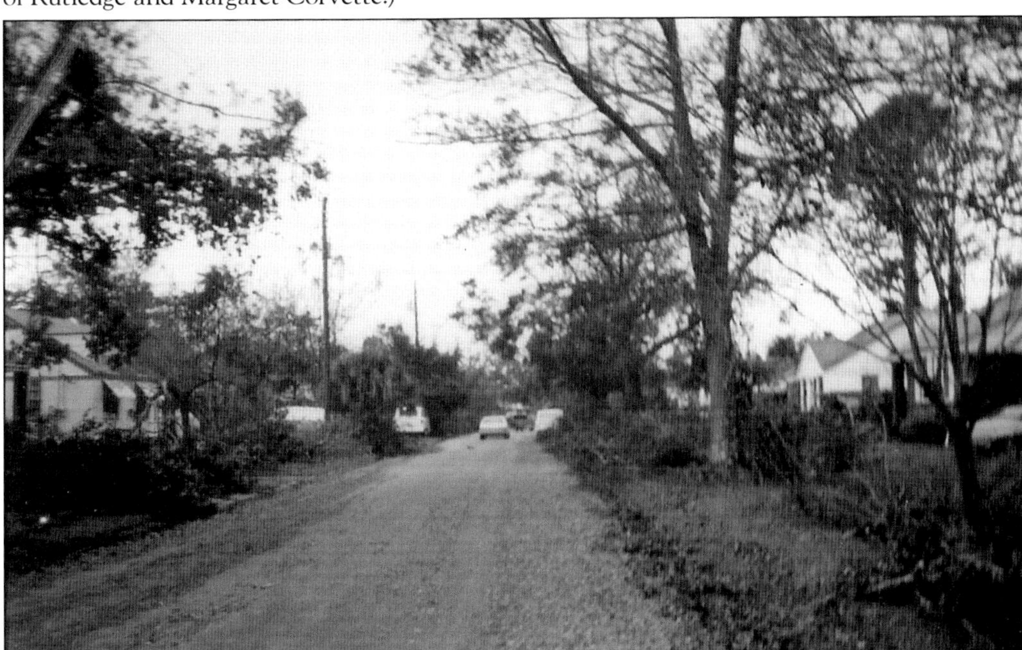

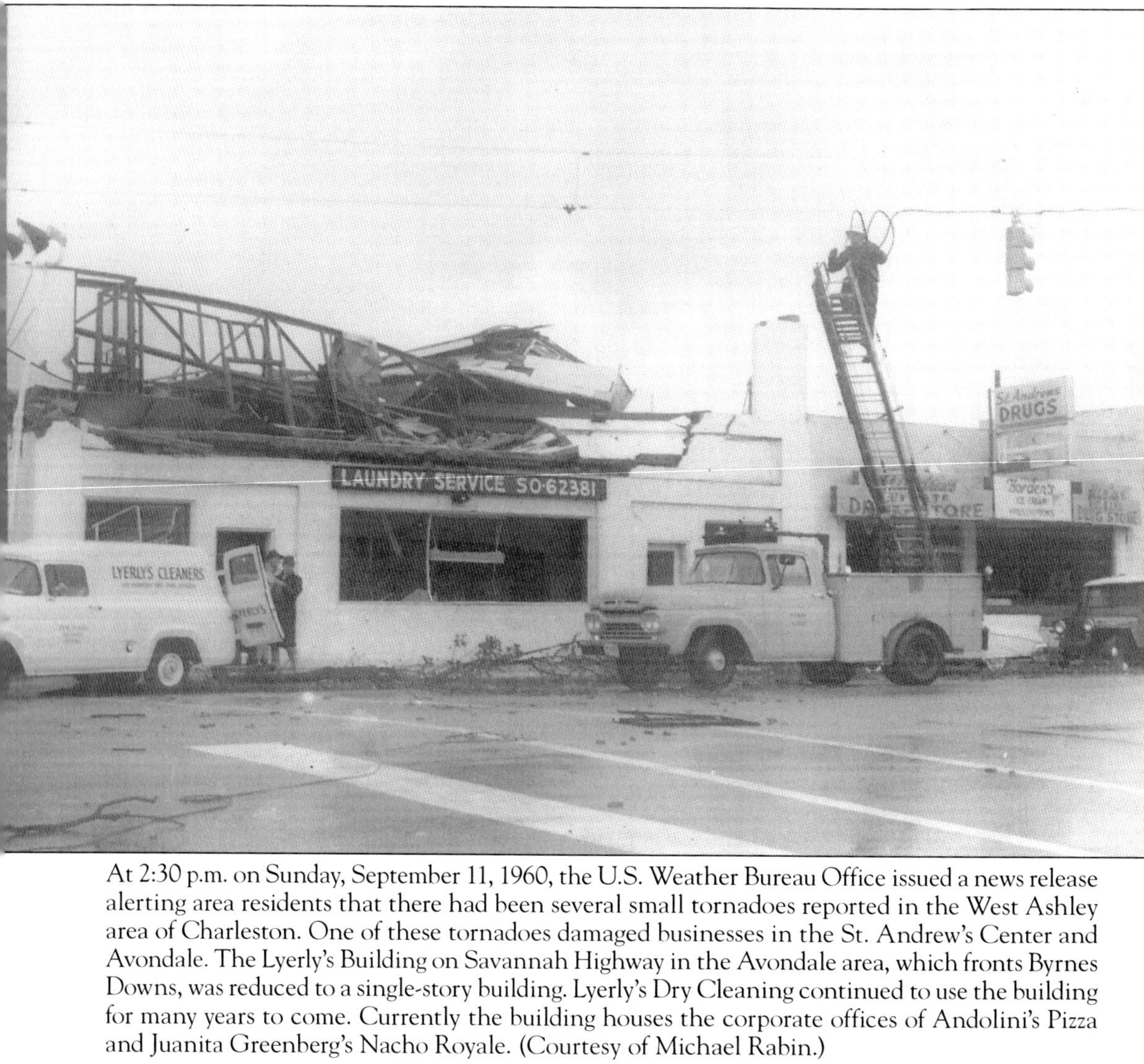

At 2:30 p.m. on Sunday, September 11, 1960, the U.S. Weather Bureau Office issued a news release alerting area residents that there had been several small tornadoes reported in the West Ashley area of Charleston. One of these tornadoes damaged businesses in the St. Andrew's Center and Avondale. The Lyerly's Building on Savannah Highway in the Avondale area, which fronts Byrnes Downs, was reduced to a single-story building. Lyerly's Dry Cleaning continued to use the building for many years to come. Currently the building houses the corporate offices of Andolini's Pizza and Juanita Greenberg's Nacho Royale. (Courtesy of Michael Rabin.)

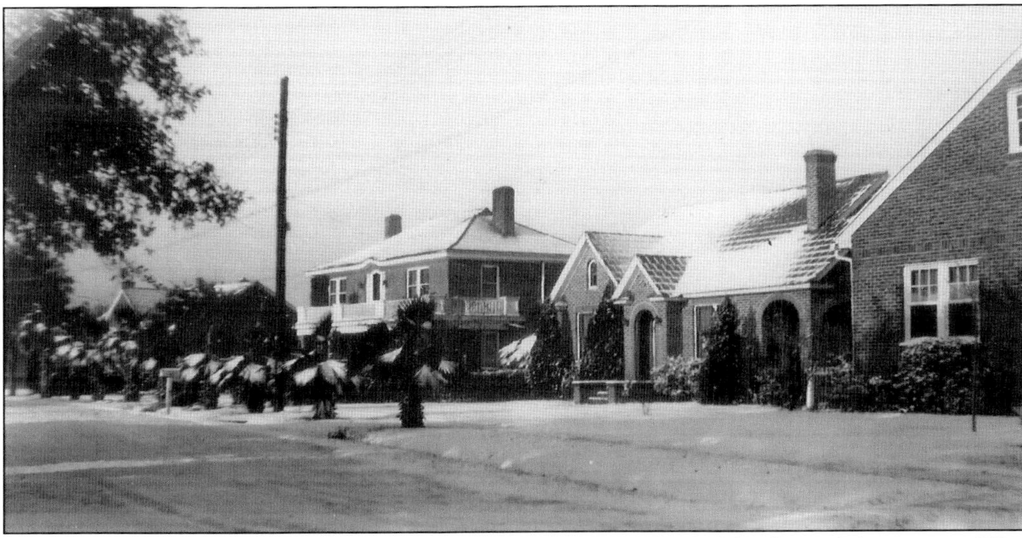

It's snowing! Windermere, now called Old Windermere, was one of the first subdivisions in West Ashley. Tom Dandridge built the family home in Windermere with an address of 6 Fenwick Drive, although the house faced Folly Road. The Dandridges captured the houses and palmetto trees along Fenwick Drive dusted with a snow that occurred in 1943. (Courtesy of Margaret Thorne Seidler.)

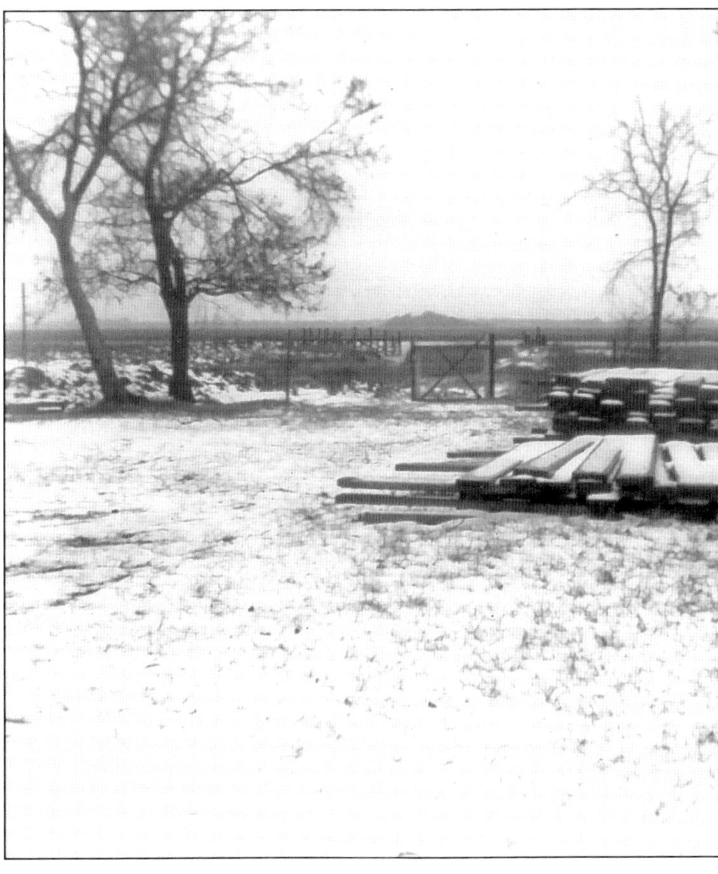

Snow falls on Albemarle Point—but not quite enough for a fort or a snowman. The fence guards access to the causeway and canal to Wappoo Creek. In warmer weather, the children would swim in the canal, sail in the creek, and fly kites while standing along the causeway. (Courtesy of Sandra Foxworth.)

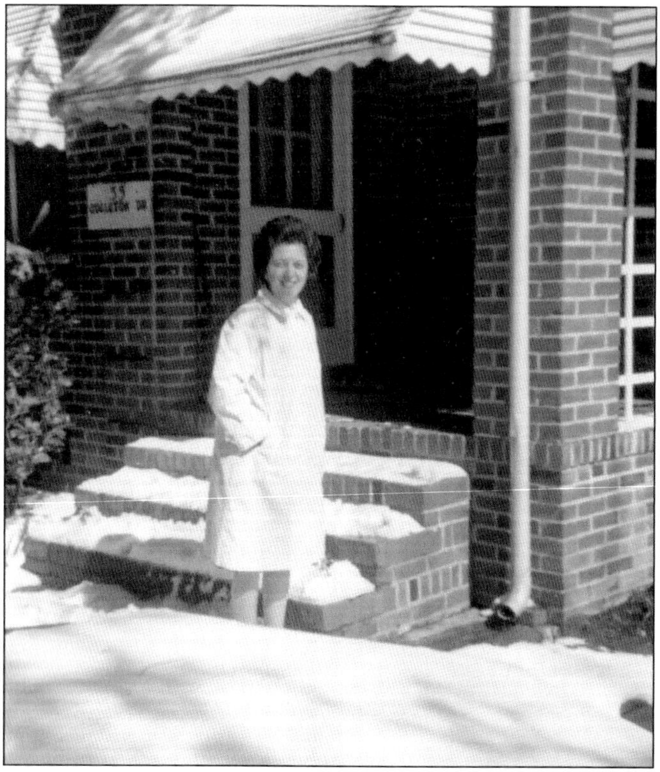

The Snow of the Century, February 9–11, 1973, as defined by the *Charleston Evening Post* edition of the *News and Courier*, was a freak meteorological storm that blanketed the eastern portion of South Carolina but not the mountains and Piedmont area that usually experiences snow. It was a record snowfall for Charleston, 7.1 inches. The previous record was set in February 1899 at 4.4 inches. At left, Virginia Caldwell stands bravely by her front porch on Colleton Drive so Mendel can capture the depth of the snowfall on film. Across the street (below), Sara Calas (left) and Camilla Blanton waste no time in making snowballs and engaging in a friendly snowball fight. (Left courtesy of the Caldwell family; below courtesy of Camilla Blanton.)

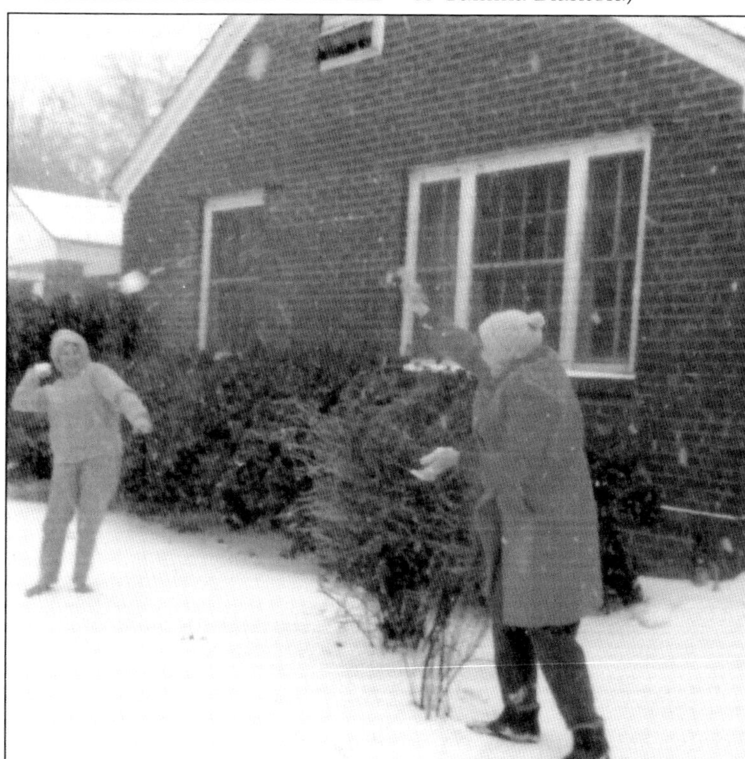

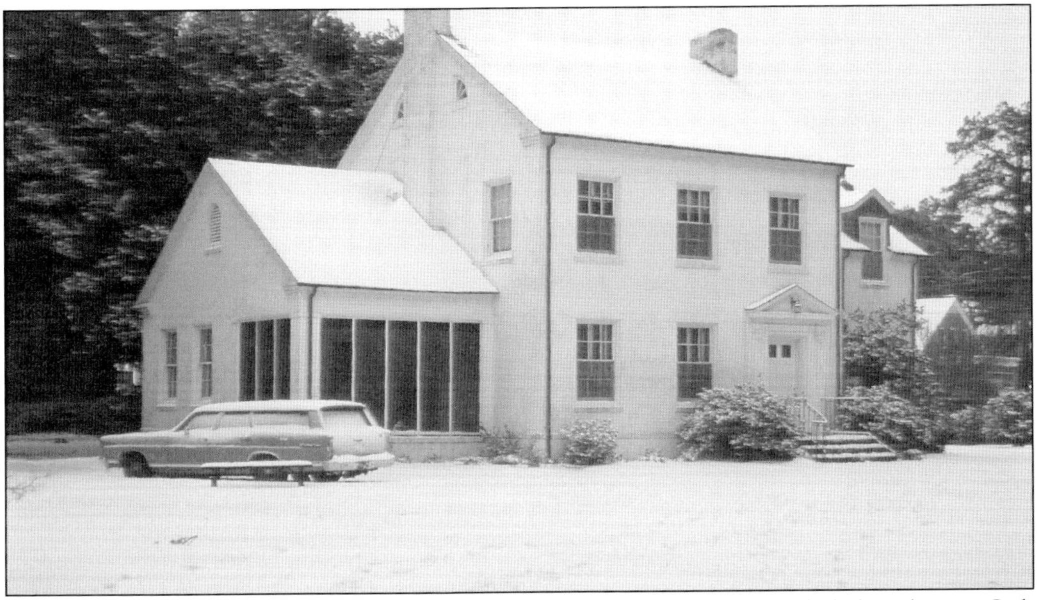

In The Crescent subdivision, the MacDougal family shutterbug recorded their home, Oak Manor at 1 New Town Lane, after the February 1973 "Snow of the Century." (Courtesy of Jan MacDougal.)

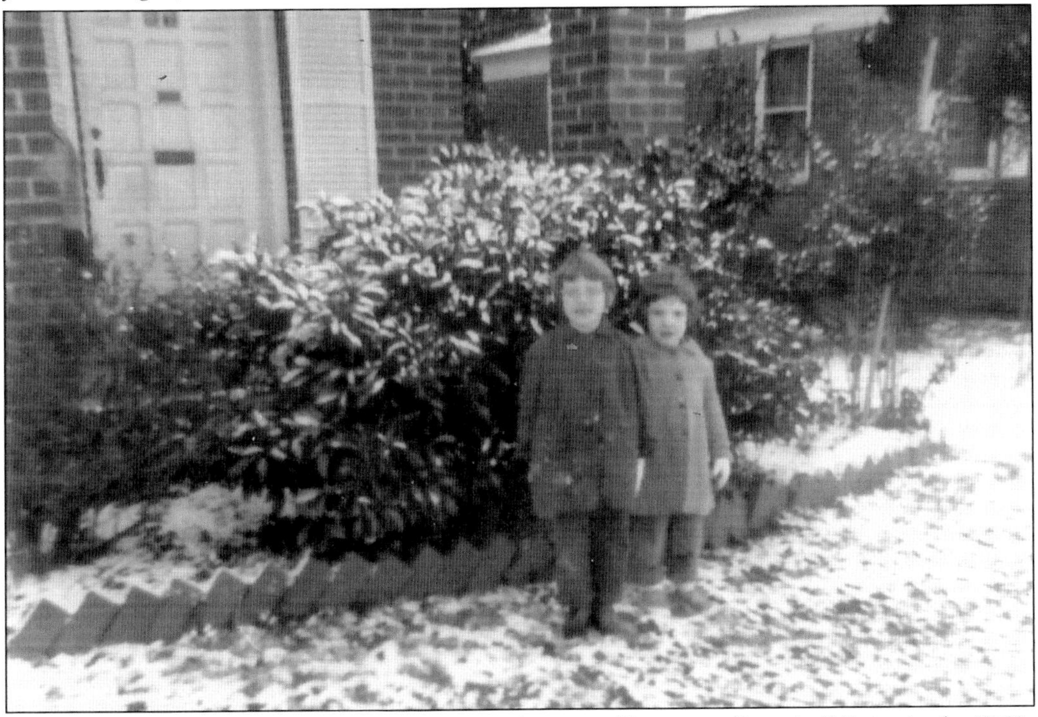

Joe and Frances (Melfi) Roy moved into Frances's parents' home on Campbell Drive in the 1960s and raised three children: Joseph, Debbie, and Frances. The family delivered the newspapers in the neighborhood for many years. Of course, when it snowed, out came the camera to capture Debbie (left) and Frances posing on the snow-dusted lawn in front of their home on Campbell Drive. (Courtesy of Frances and Joe Roy.)

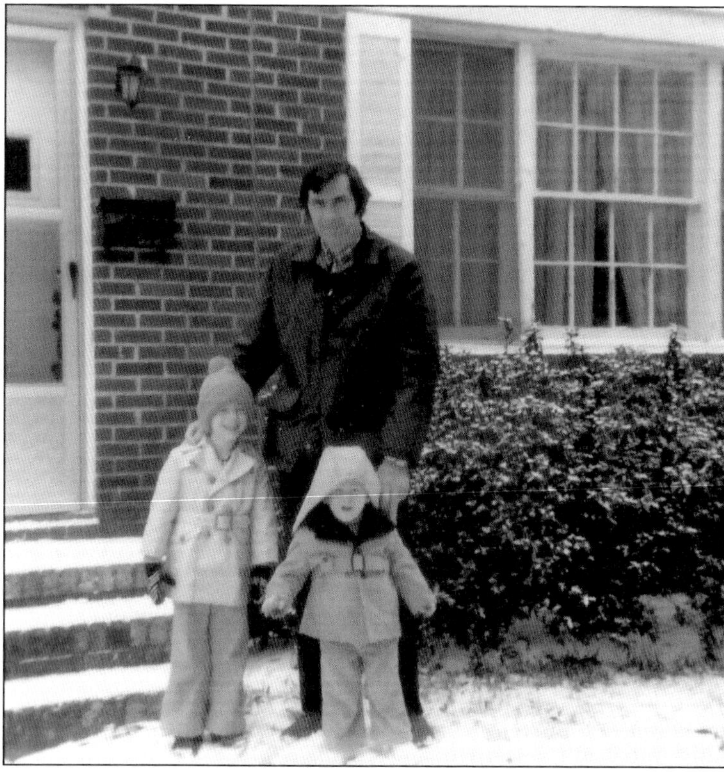

Jim and Saundra Austin lived on Yeadon Avenue with their sons Shane and Aaron when this snow occurred in 1980. It didn't take long for the guys to don coats, hats, and mittens. First Shane (left), Jim (center), and Aaron pose for Saundra, then watch out! In the picture below, Shane (left) and Aaron practice the art of snowball making. When Jim and Saundra returned to the Lowcountry, they moved back to Byrnes Downs, this time to live on Craven Avenue, where they share a fence with the Jacobs family. (Both courtesy of Jim and Saundra Austin.)

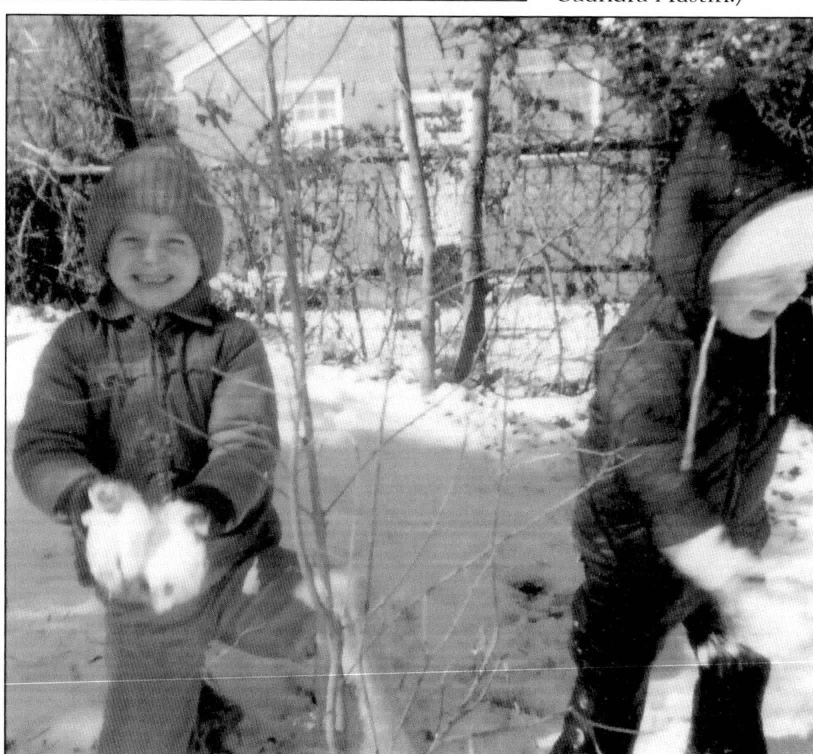

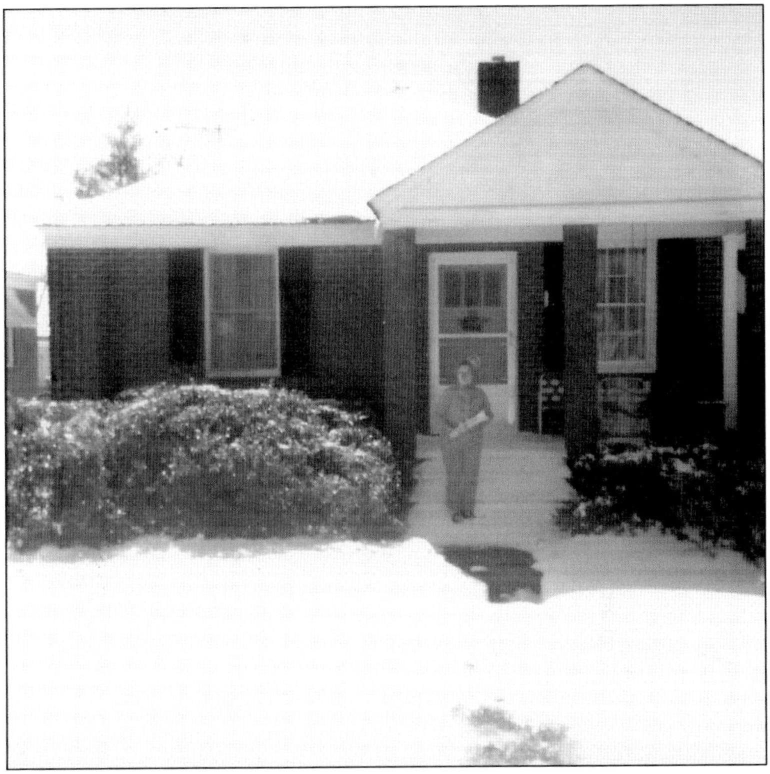

Everyone wanted to document the "Snow of the Century" in February 1973. Carrie L. Weathers stands on the steps of her Savannah Highway home where she had lived since 1945. The sidewalk has been cleared, so one can get a perspective on the depth of the snowfall. The bright sun of the day would soon make puddles of this beautiful white blanket. In addition, Weathers remembered the eerie winds of the tornado that touched down in West Ashley spawned from Hurricane Donna. (Courtesy of William H. Barron Jr.)

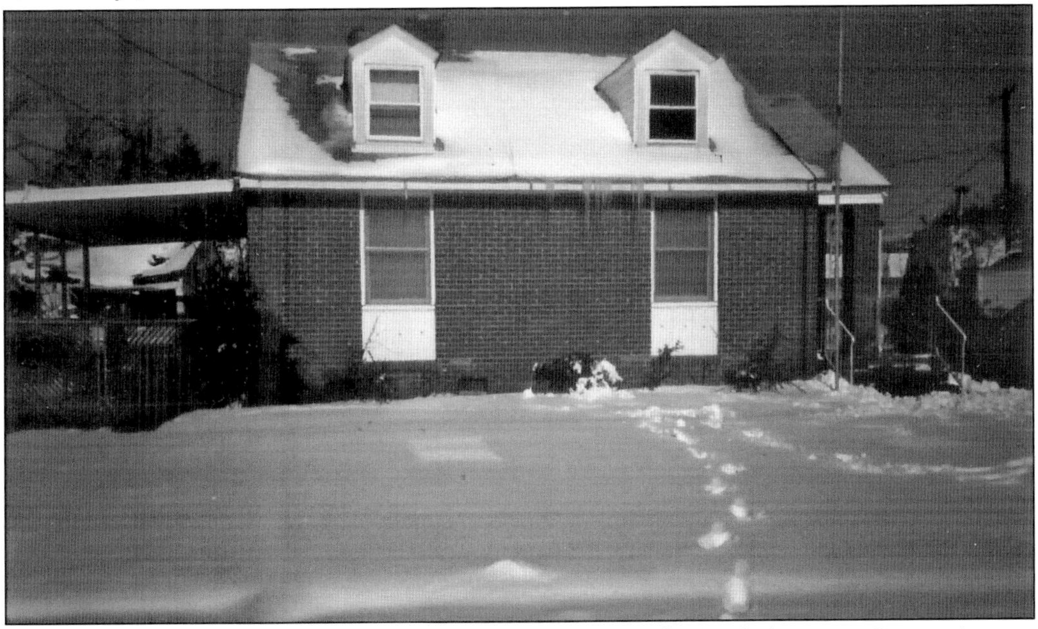

Christmas and snow are a rare combination for Charleston. The Jacobs home on Craven Avenue had only minor damage from Hugo, and Byrnes Downs was also lucky to quickly have electricity and water restored to most of the homes. The snow, however, was another story; it was a few days before the city was able to restore pressure to the water system. This picturesque day tells a different story.

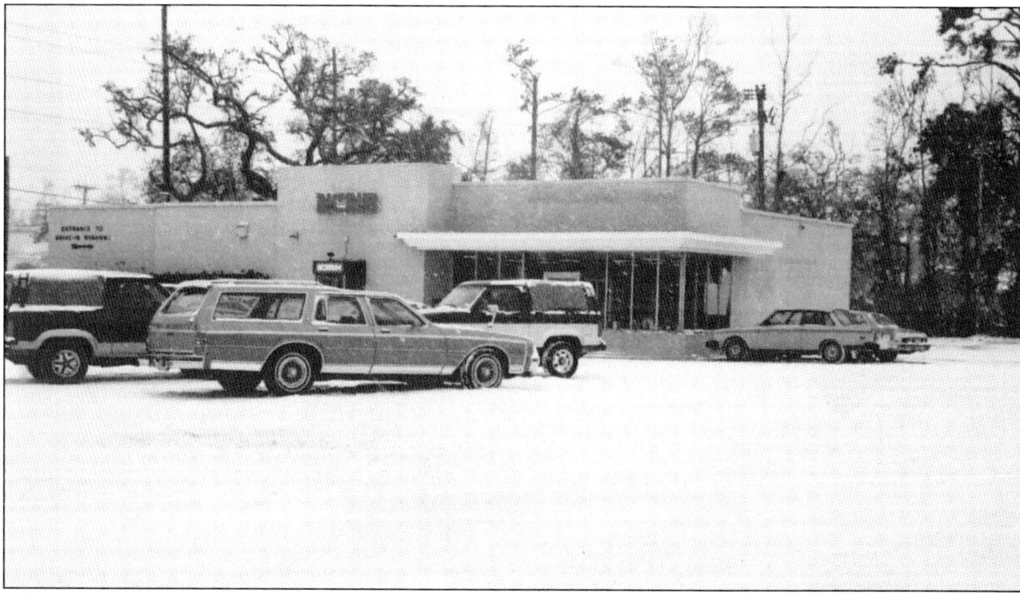

The parking lot of the South Windermere Shopping Center with the NCNB Bank (currently the site of the Osaka Restaurant) in the background is blanketed with snow. Missy Cohen Gold shared this photograph as well as a story for a sunny day. She and Harriet Rittenberg Steinert would walk from South Windermere to Zinn's Deli (now Med Bistro) in the shopping center and share french fries and TruAde. (Courtesy of Missy Cohen Gold.)

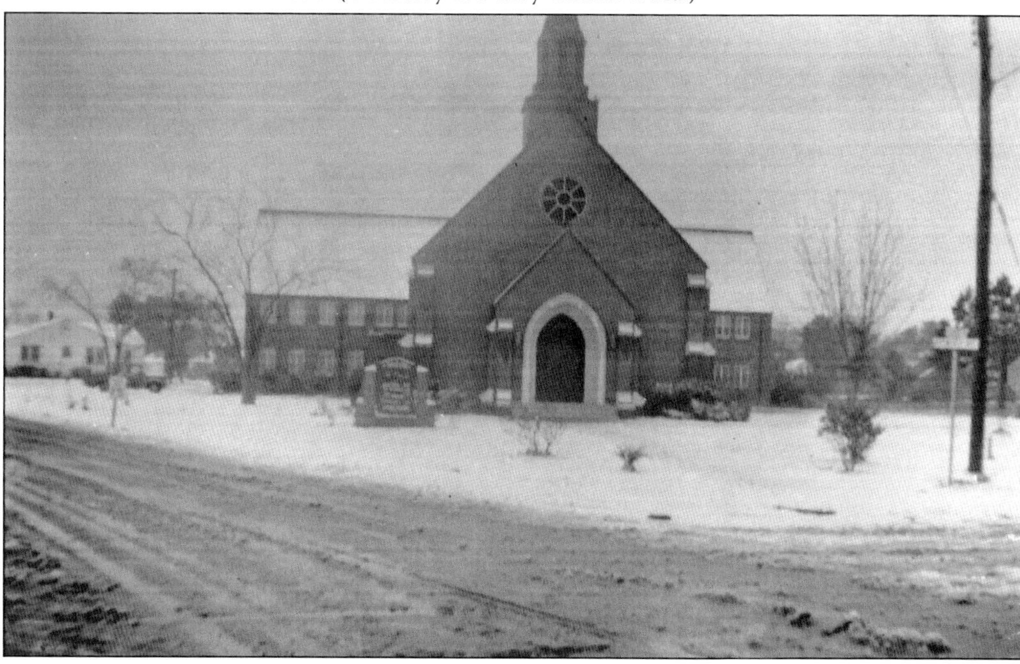

The Redeemer Lutheran Church is located in the Avondale neighborhood at the fork of Riverdale Drive and Avondale Avenue. The church was organized by Rev. Milton J. Bieber, D.D., on May 2, 1943, with 113 names appearing on the charter roll. Rev. Everette Lineberger became the pastor of the church on September 1, 1958, and captured the church while the snow was falling in 1959. (Courtesy of Everette and Ann Lineberger.)

Six

SANCTUARIES, SCHOOLS, AND SHOPS

No community would be complete without places to worship, learn, and shop. Four church steeples grace the area as well as the synagogue minyan house. St. Andrew's Elementary School, Porter Gaud School, and Blessed Sacrament School provide educational opportunities for the area. The West Ashley Library opened on April 20, 1964. The library was constructed on property donated to Charleston County by South Windermere Realtors through William H. Ackerman and provides a gathering place for the greater community. South Windermere is often described as the first shopping center in the state of South Carolina. A recent renovation to South Windermere Boulevard has made the thriving center more pedestrian friendly. Avondale Pointe has been the home to many shops dating back to the late 1940s and early 1950s. In *History Byrnes Downs Garden Club*, the construction of Rodenberg's Grocery Store as well as some of the other commercial buildings is documented. In recent times, there has been a renaissance in Avondale Pointe. Gene's Haufbrau has been returned to its 1950s look and is a popular neighborhood bar. Poe Studio, Avondale Wine and Cheese, Lava Salon, Culture Vultures, Consigning Women, Reinvented, Moondrops, the Beadery, Lola Salon, Twiggs and Ivy, and Charleston Antique Mall advertise themselves as the unique shopping destination of Avondale. Moreland Shopping Center is home to the famous Ye Olde Fashioned Café and Ice Cream Parlor. If you want to get people drooling, strike up a conversation about Roy Hart's, Red and Bertha's Drive In, Fountain Inn, Bootles, Holly House Dairy Bar Restaurant, or Seven Seas Grill. A half an hour discussion on hamburgers, hotdogs, french fries, or barbecue will occur. No photographs of these establishments emerged for this book, but the memories and stories are delicious.

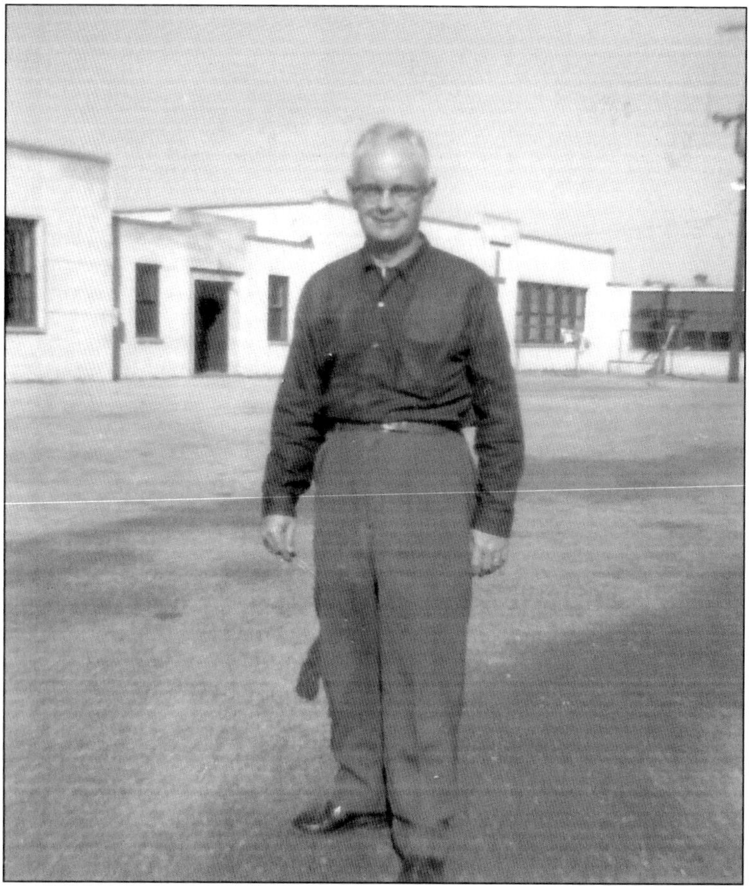

Joseph William Bohne stands with the Blessed Sacrament Church buildings in the background. Msgr. John J. McCarthy was named the first pastor of Blessed Sacrament Parish on December 4, 1944. The parish began with 40 members, and its first chapel and rectory were located at 149 Savannah Highway in Byrnes Downs. On May 13, 1965, the dedication was held for the present church sanctuary. The grotto pictured in the lower photograph is in front of the school. Blessed Sacrament School opened in September 1948, and the ground breaking for this building was on June 15, 1952. (Both courtesy of Peggy Bohne.)

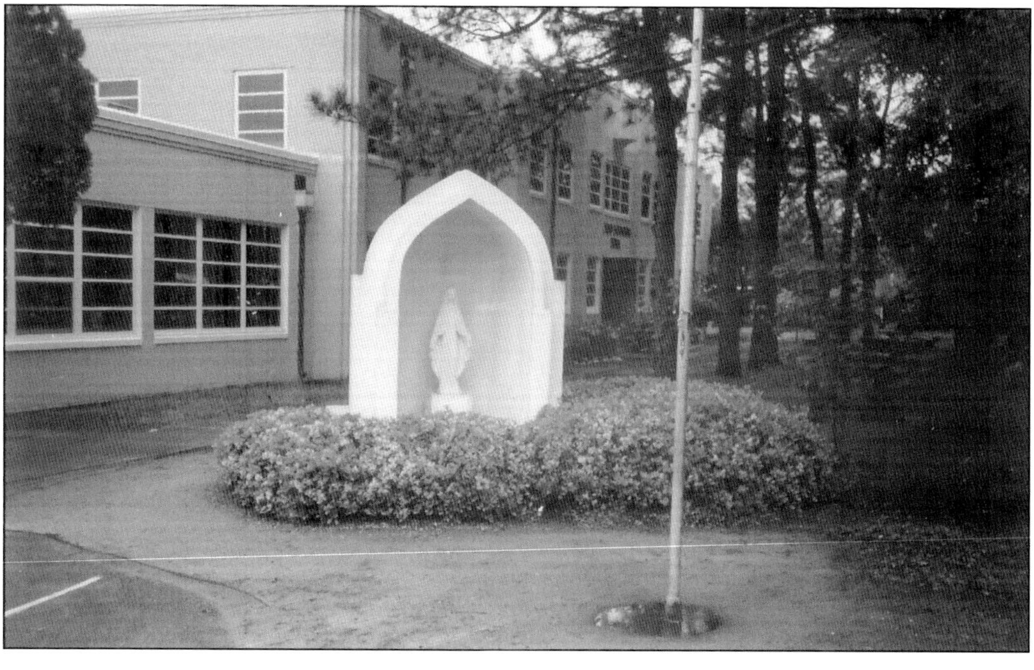

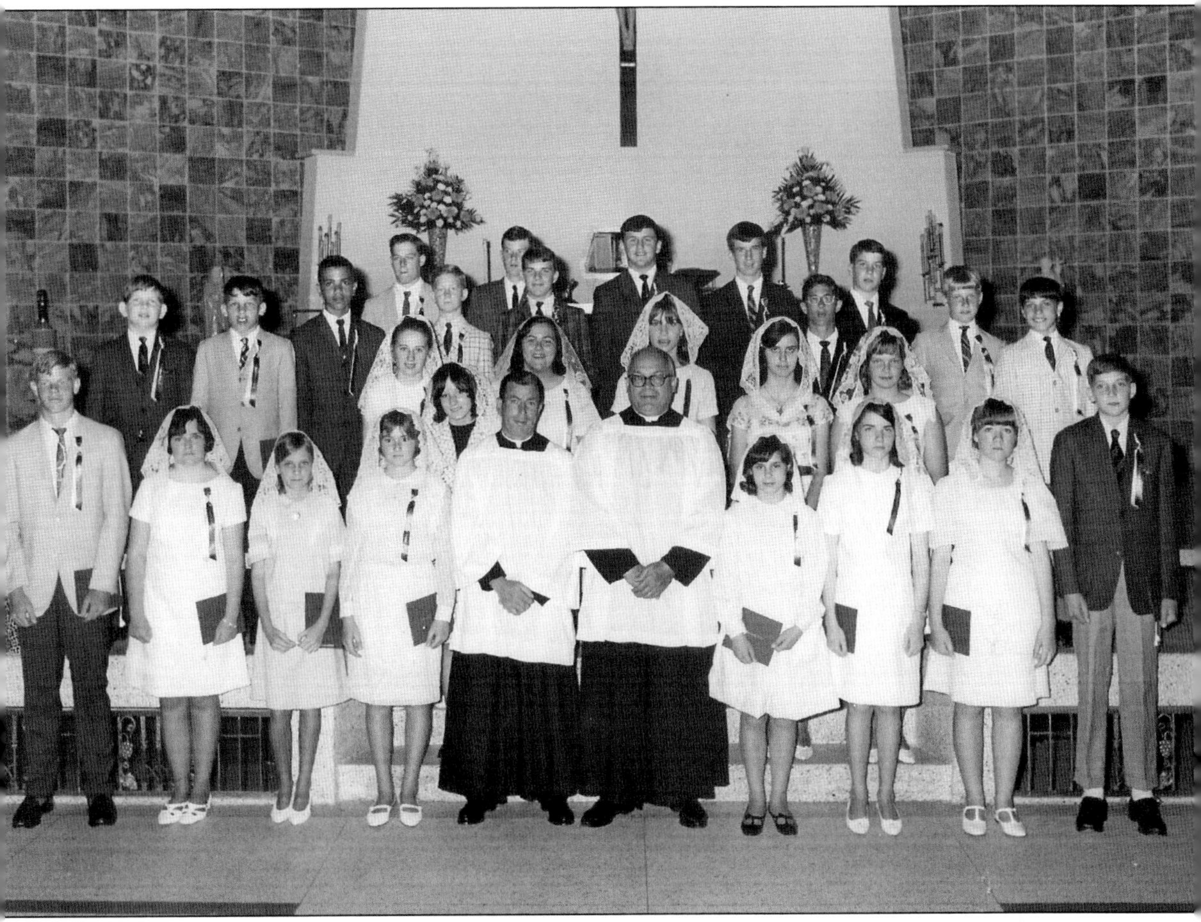

Blessed Sacrament's eighth-grade class of 1967 graduated in May. The class picture was taken at the altar in the sanctuary of Blessed Sacrament Church. The graduates are, from left to right, as follows: (first row) Chris Cannon, Patti Luhrs, Patti Baldessari, Martha Montgomery, Sydney Lighthart, Mary McAllan, Claudia Blyth, and Tom Magee; (second row, in veils) Alexandra Gressette, Sandi Berry, Debbie Heuer, Jean Roe, Francois Noe, and Peggy Bohne; (third row) Bernie Molony, Tom Finnerty, John Brown, Paul Ferrara, Paul Cantwell, Thomas George, Mark Smith, Lamar Brabham, Michael Fentress, Glenn Bridgeman, Bruce Austin, Hank Roland, and Michael Holmes. Fathers Maher and Huback are pictured with the graduates. (Courtesy of Peggy Bohne.)

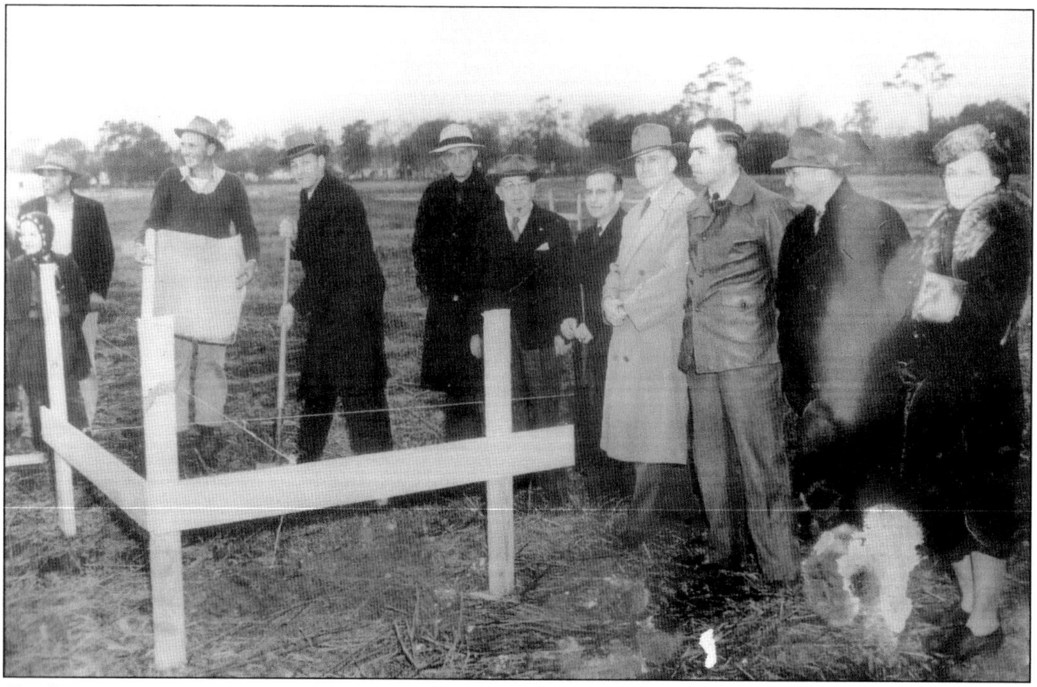

On January 10, 1946, ground was broken for the John Wesley Methodist Church Educational Building. Present for the occasion were, from left to right, "Ruth Watkins, R. R. Blocker, Henry Sauls, Dist. Supt. Shuler (Reverend H. L. F. Shuler), Lawyer M. L. McCrae, Architect Thomas, J. G. Altman, Rev. R. B. Shumaker (2nd Pastor), H. E. Blocker, George Seignious, and Mrs. W. R. Richardson." The area's postwar housing boom resulted in many new members attending service. Thus the congregation decided in April 1950 to build a sanctuary for 600. An amount of $55,000 was borrowed for the sanctuary construction, and on July 1, 1950, the cornerstone for the sanctuary was placed. The steeple framework is shown below. (Both ourtesy of DeeDee Webb Luff.)

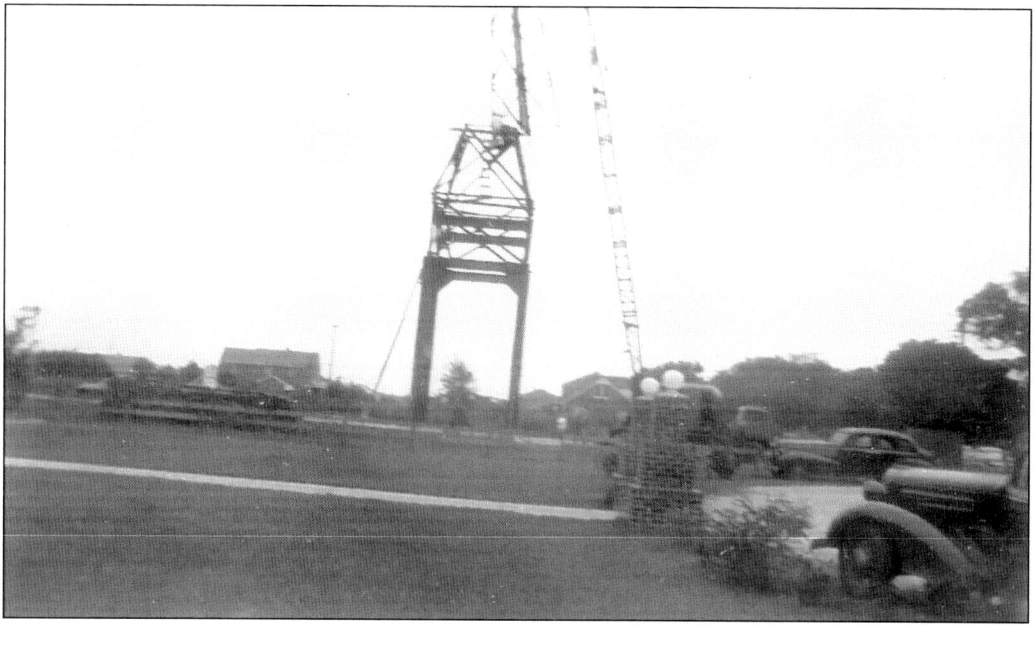

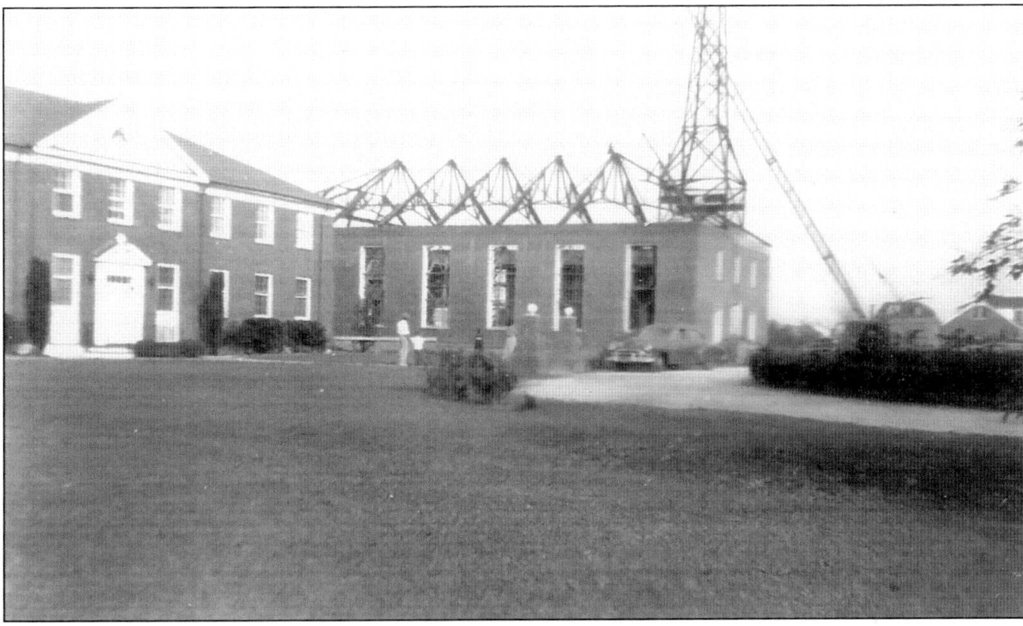

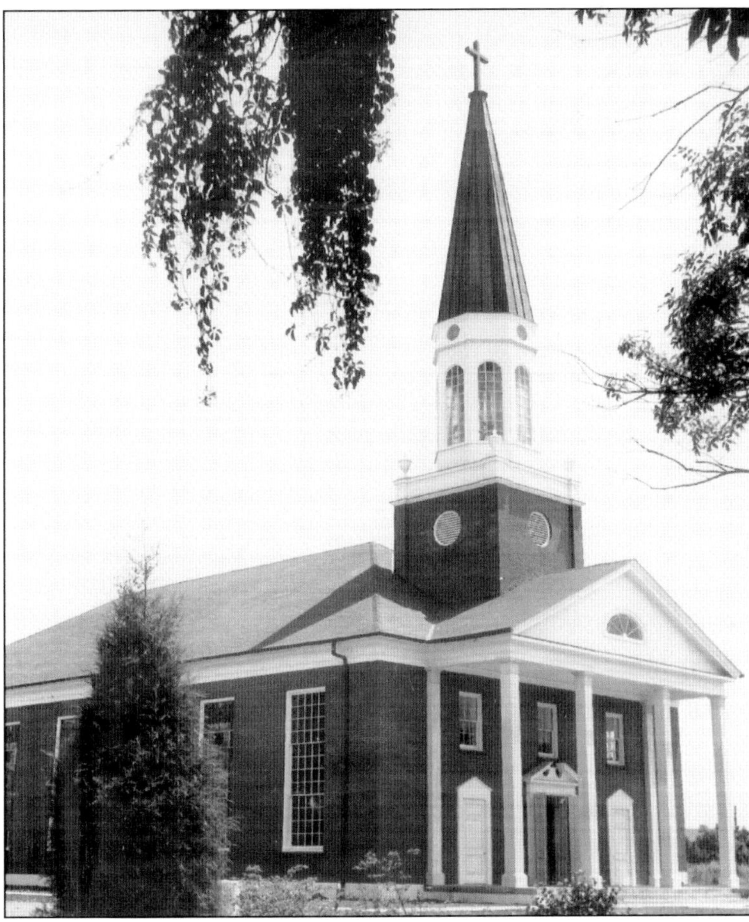

From the original 34 people who attended worship service at the Exchange Club building on June 18, 1944, through the sanctuary construction and completion, John Wesley Methodist Church has been a prominent landmark in the West Ashley community. Some of the residents of Byrnes Downs were active charter members of the church. On July 22, 1951, Rev. Ralph Shumaker conducted the first service in the new sanctuary. Rev. Ralph Shumaker performed the first wedding ceremony on September 15, 1951, for Herman M. Staubes Jr. and Hazel Myers. (Both courtesy of DeeDee Webb Luff.)

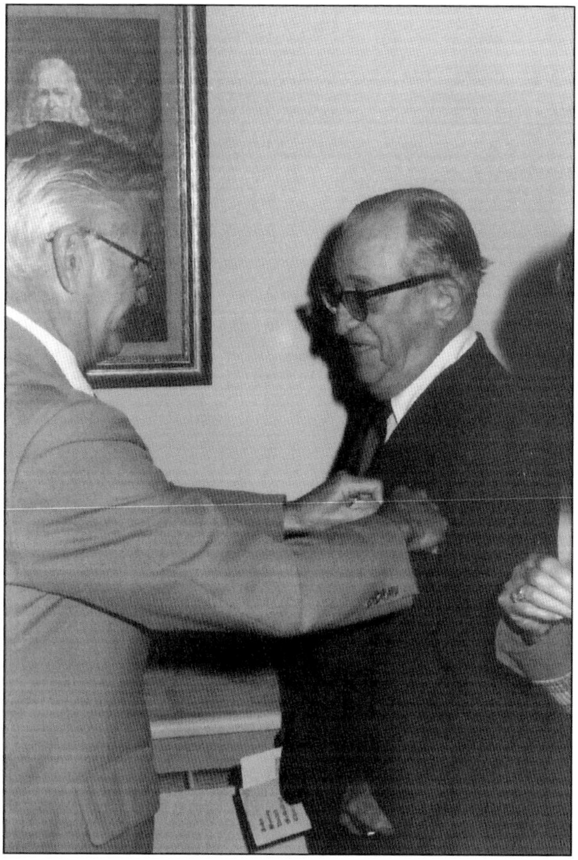

Charles H. Webb Jr., pictured at left in the dark jacket, was listed as one of John Wesley's charter members. Webb and his family lived on Campbell Drive in Byrnes Downs. Their yard was selected as the Garden of the Month at one point and was featured in the newspaper. Webb not only lived and worshipped in the area, but he also worked for Francis Hanckel at Coburg Dairy. Today his daughter DeeDee is the historian for the John Wesley Methodist Church. Before DeeDee became the historian, she was a participant in the Spring Festival held on May 4, 1950. DeeDee stands in the first row proudly holding her flowers below. (Both courtesy of DeeDee Webb Luff.)

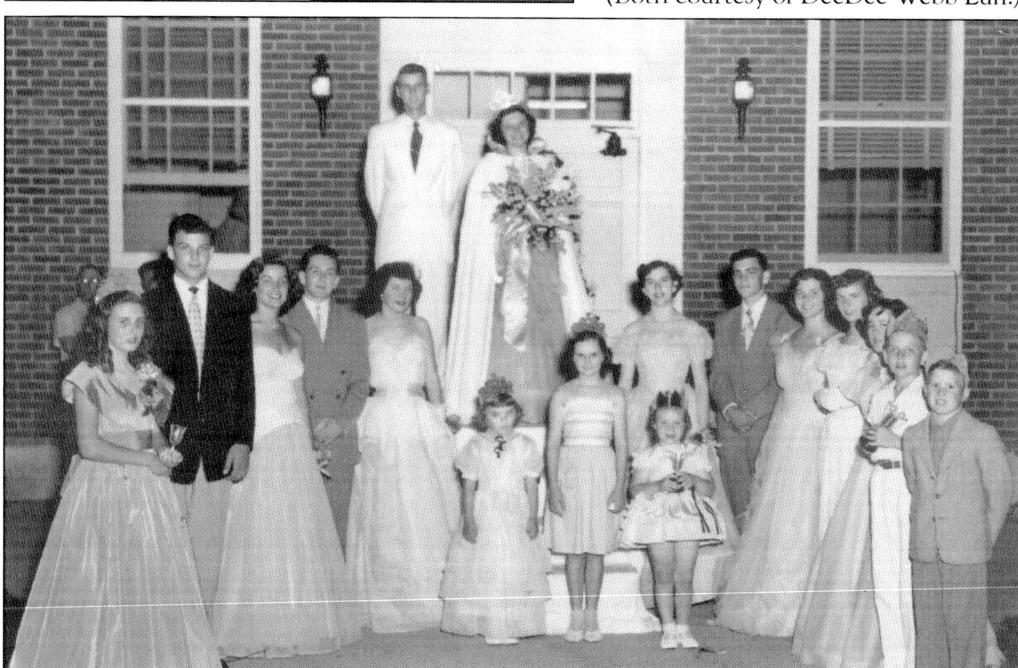

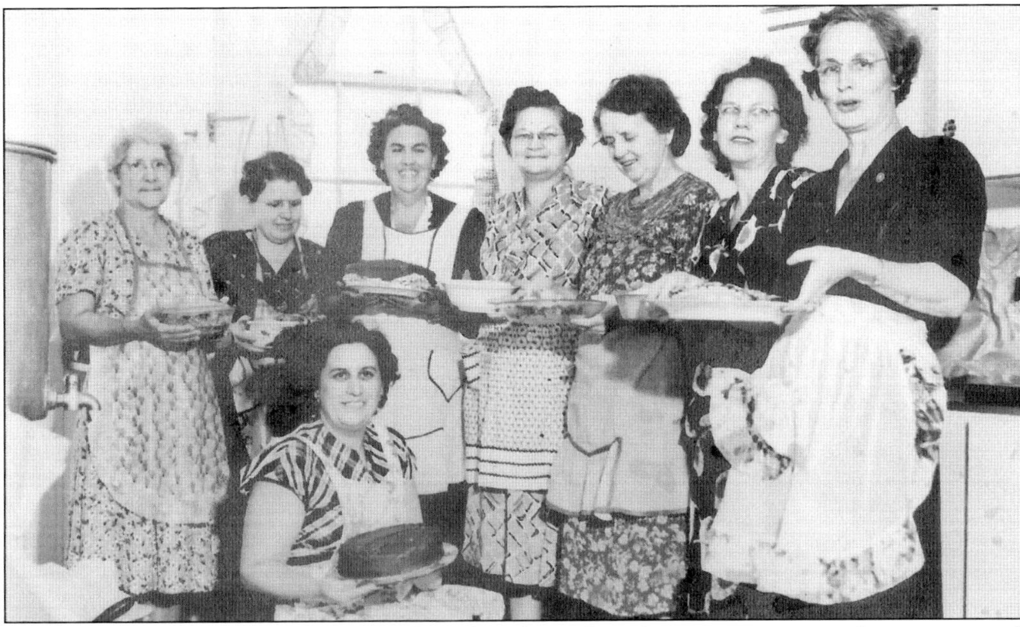

The ladies of the John Wesley Methodist Church Kitchen Committee pose in their aprons with a delicious assortment of cakes and pies on the day the Sunday School Building was dedicated. Pictured from left to right are Mrs. A. M. Riser, Mrs. J. B. Williams, Mrs. T. M. Limehouse, Mrs. J. E. Corvette, Mrs. J. T. Dempsey, Mrs. W. E. Mosley, and Mrs. W. R. Richardson. Seated in the center is Janie Mattoon. Mrs. J. E. Corvette also lived on Campbell Drive in Byrnes Downs, as did her son Rutledge and his wife, Margaret. (Courtesy of DeeDee Webb Luff.)

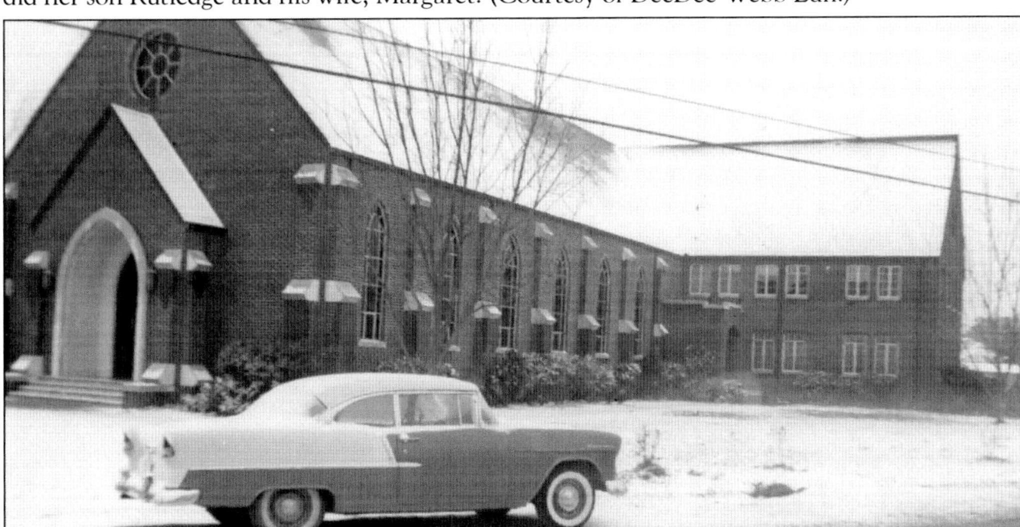

Rev. Milton J. Bieber organized the Evangelical Lutheran Church of the Redeemer in Avondale in May 1943. The present sanctuary was built in 1955. In 1958, Rev. Everette Lineberger became the pastor. Reverend Lineberger purchased the 1953 Chevrolet Model 210 pictured in the snow in front of the church on June 13, 1953, prior to marrying his wife, Ann, on August 16, 1953. They drove the car to Miami for their honeymoon. On their 50th wedding anniversary, they drove it to the reception. The car remains in Reverend Lineberger's possession, and the odometer reads over 300,000 miles. (Courtesy of Everette and Ann Lineberger.)

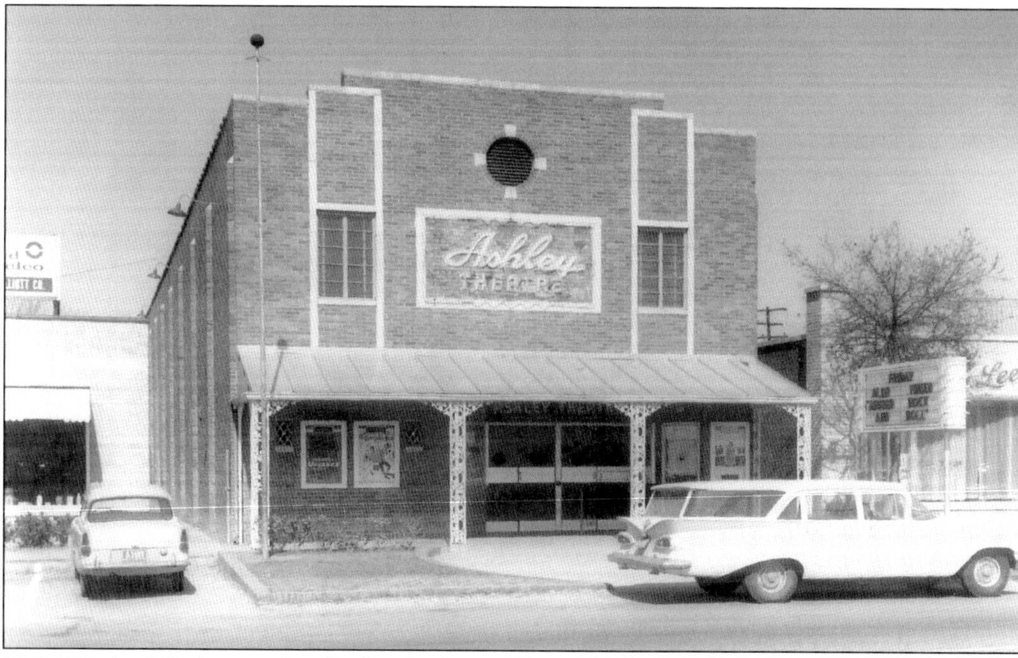

Holy Trinity Mission, under the leadership of Rev. Marshall E. Travers, gathered for its first worship service at the Ashley Theater on Magnolia Road in Avondale (seen above). Reverend Travers had resigned from St. Philip's Church to establish a church in the Windermere section of West Ashley. The 1957 Diocesan Convention accepted the church as a mission under the auspices of Old St. Andrew's Church. Mr. and Mrs. Charles Dwight (Harriet Travers's family) made available a beautiful site on Folly Road. Ted Boinest of Boinest Construction Company oversaw the construction. In the fall of 1957, the parishioners were excited about the completion of the church building on Folly Road (below). (Both courtesy of Martha Rodgers.)

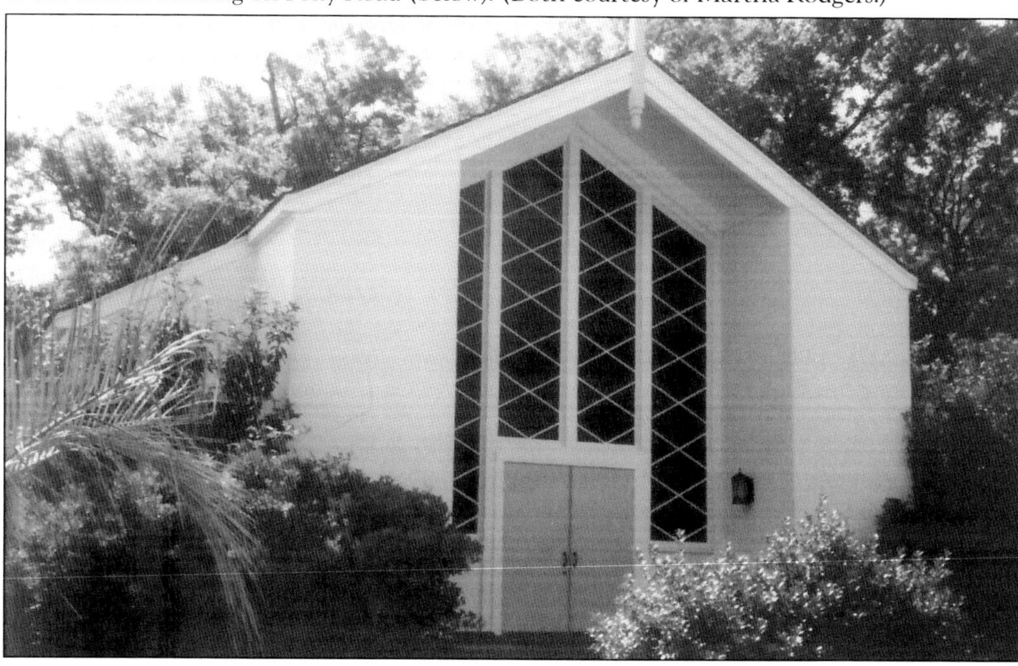

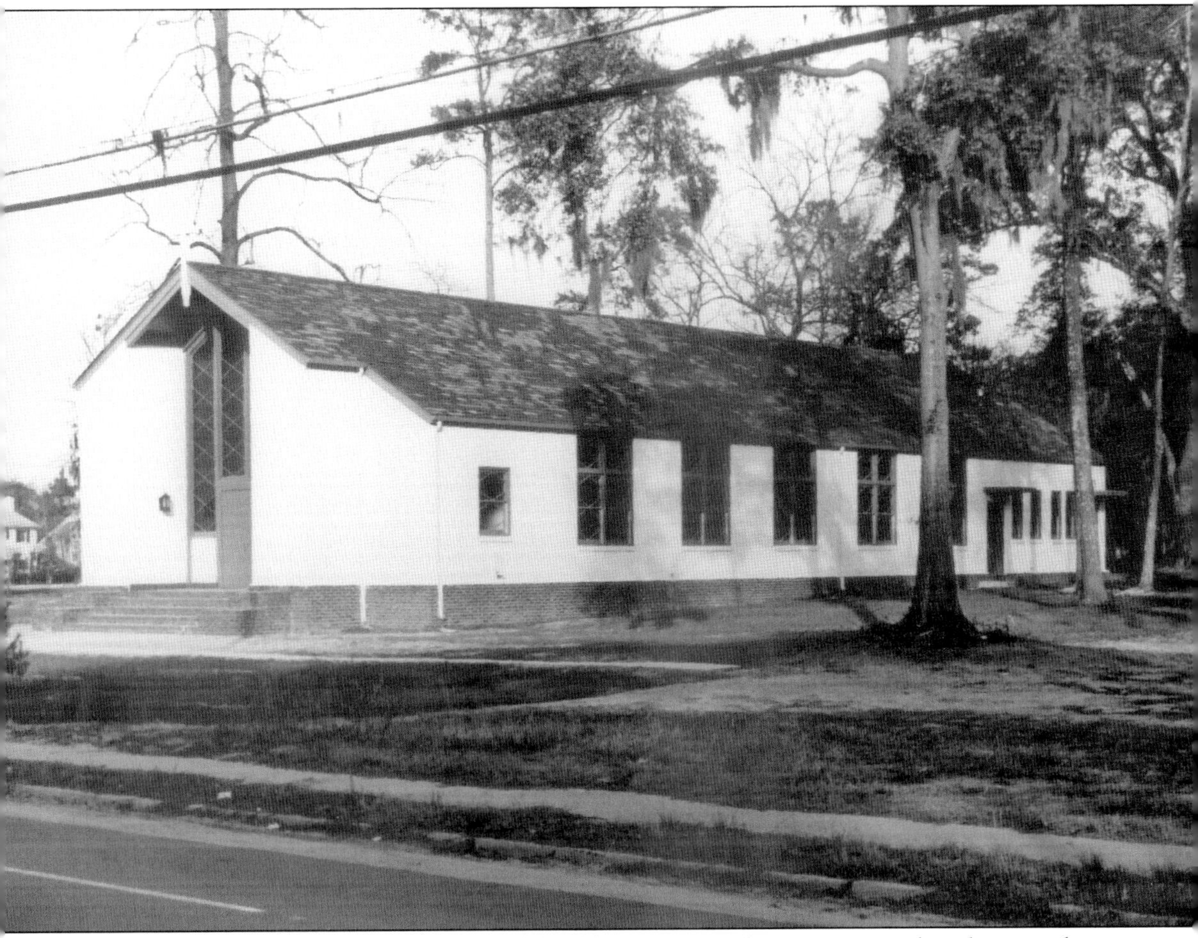

The construction of the Holy Trinity church building was complete, as seen in this photograph, but there were details to be finished. The Hartnett family of Byrnes Downs was active as members of Holy Trinity. Doris Hartnett was known for her sewing skills, and she handmade the first altar hangings for the new Holy Trinity Church and the linens for the altar. Stewart Shehee built the altar and carved the altar figures. The pulpit, eagle lectern, and altar rail were acquired when the old Merchant Seaman's Chapel closed. According to the Garden Club records, the Shehee family also lived in Byrnes Downs, on Sothel Avenue. (Courtesy of Martha Rodgers.)

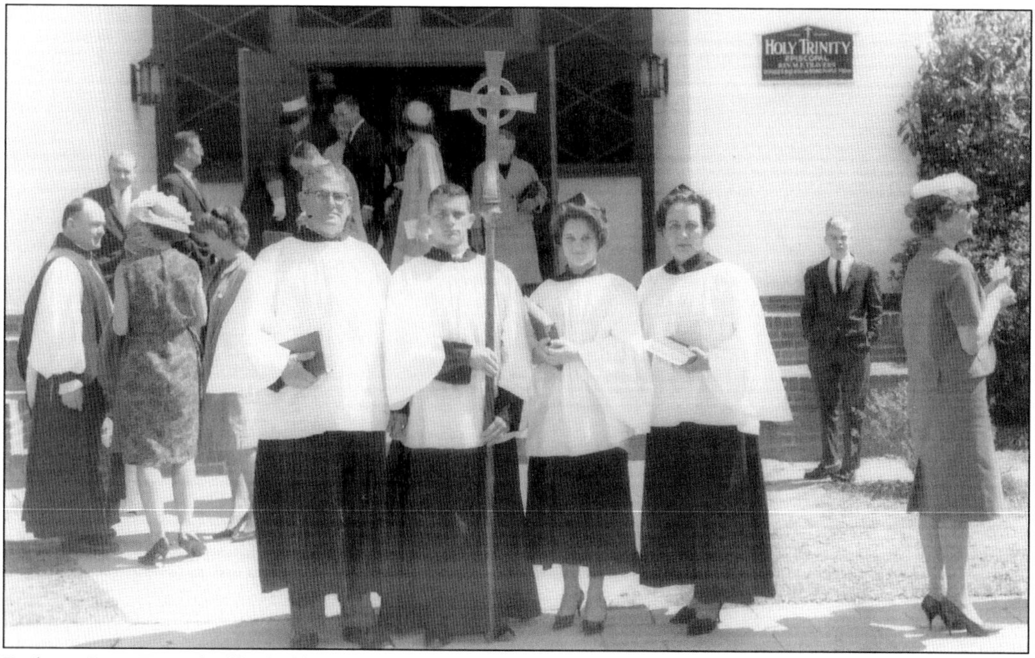

Bishop Gray Temple (far left) was among the worship assistants pictured in front of the new Holy Trinity Church building. Holy Trinity occupies the site on Folly Road adjacent to The Crescent. (Courtesy of Martha Rodgers.)

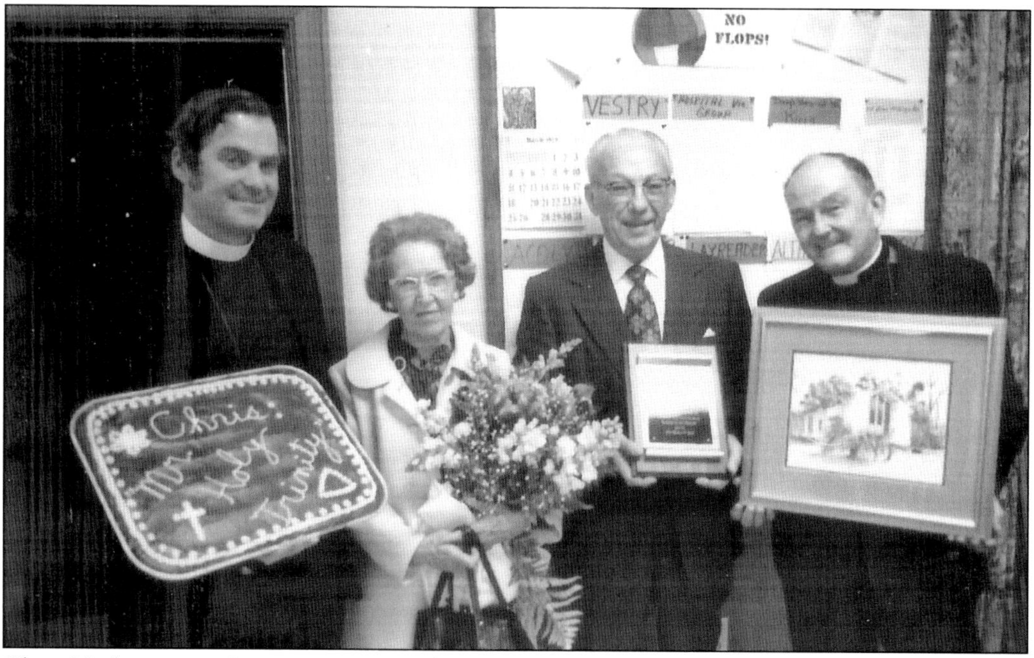

Chris Mathewes was known as "Mr. Holy Trinity." Therefore, it was only fitting that when the parish hall was renovated in 1978, it was dedicated Mathewes Hall in his honor. Mathewes was instrumental in the maintenance of the church building and grounds. Pictured at the dedication are, from left to right, Fr. William Skilton, Ruth and Chris Mathewes, and Bishop Gray Temple. (Courtesy of Martha Rodgers.)

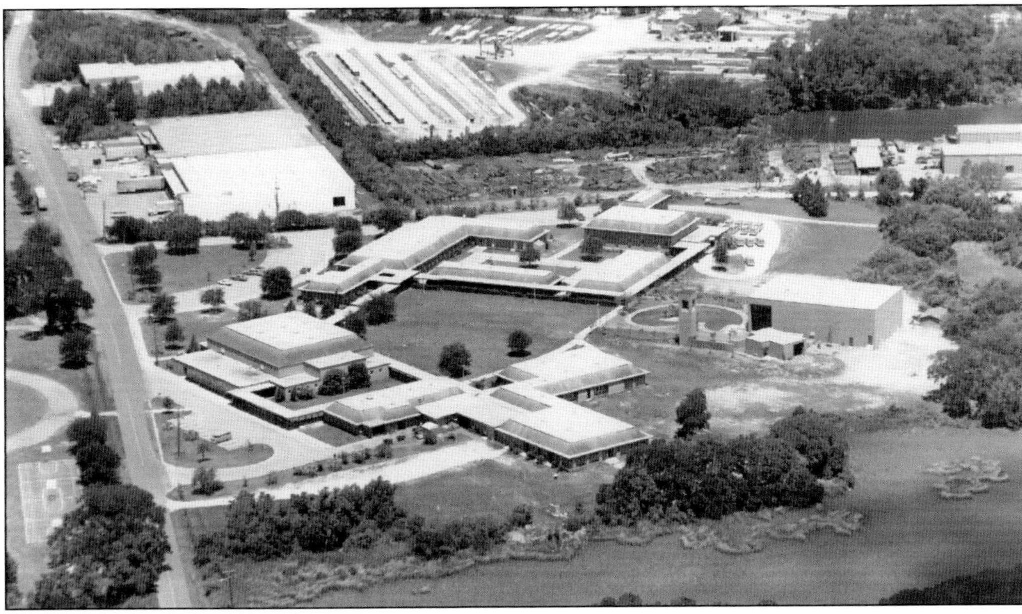

Porter-Gaud School has a long, rich history involving three individual schools: Porter Military Academy, Gaud School, and Watts School, all merged in 1963. Berkeley Grimball, a 1940 graduate of Porter Military Academy, was the headmaster of the Gaud School in 1963 and was named headmaster of the new Porter-Gaud School on July 1, 1964. Land that had originally been property of the Atlantic Coastline Railroad became the site for the new campus. In 1965, the student body, staff, and teachers moved to the new campus on Albemarle Road shown in this aerial. The Porter Military Academy chapel cornerstone carries the following inscription: "Established December 9, 1867 Corner Bee and Ashley Moved to Present Site September 1, 1965." (Courtesy of Dr. Tom Horton, Porter-Gaud School.)

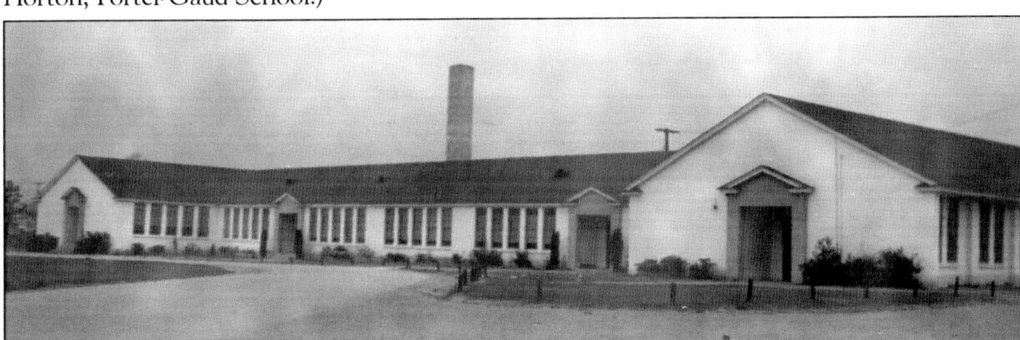

This photograph shows the St. Andrew's Elementary School with its original stucco facade. If one looks closely at the aerial on pages 20 and 21, one can see the school in the upper corner of the large field that would soon become the South Windermere subdivision. On October 11, 1949, school officials discussed the location of the new elementary school building on the property acquired from the estate of James S. Simmons. On December 20, 1949, school officials accepted the construction bid for $109,457 from Kinghorn Building and Supply Company of Beaufort. On March 20, 1950, St. Andrew's Parish Constituent Board approved the name of St. Andrew's Elementary School. V. M. Lomas, formerly of Albemarle School, was selected as the first principal. The Byrnes Downs Garden Club became involved and supplied the foundation plants around the newly constructed school building. The 1950–1951 school year listed 13 teachers and an enrollment of 464 students. (Courtesy of Tricia Peacock, St. Andrew's Elementary School.)

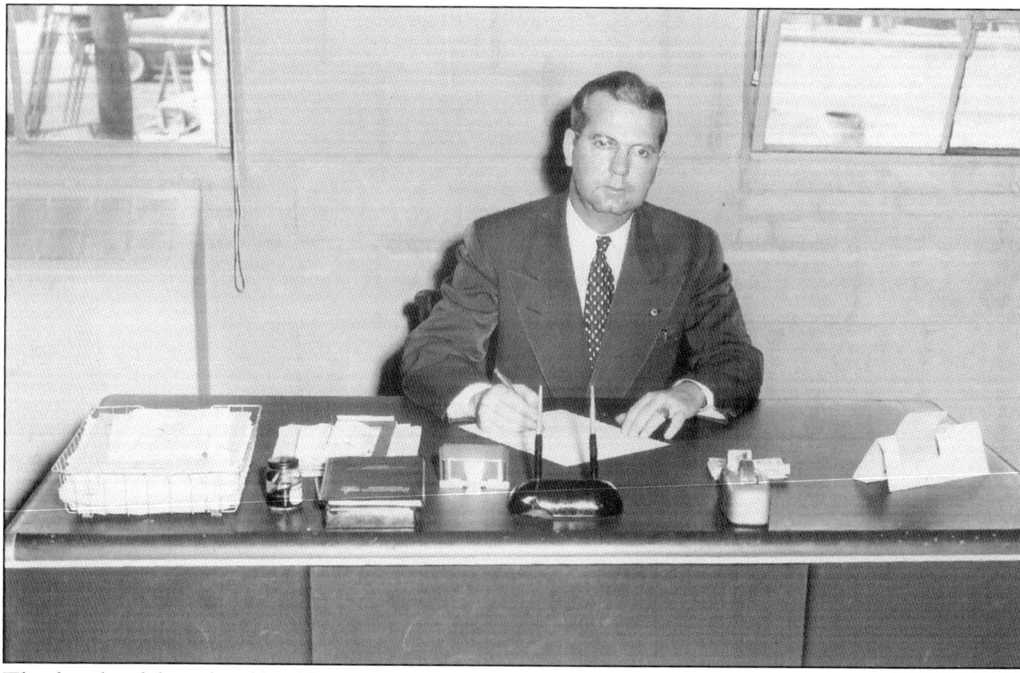

The facade of the school building and the principal were soon changed. White stucco was replaced with brick, and in 1953, Charles B. Culbertson became the principal. A 1954–1955 directory of St. Andrew's Parish Schools listed 19 teachers at the elementary school, 5 of whom lived in Byrnes Downs. Culbertson lived at 35 Campbell Drive. Walking to school was easy for both students and teachers. Culbertson served as principal until 1982. The closing of the connector road adjacent to the school was controversial. When it was moved and reopened, the road was named in his honor. The Byrnes Downs Neighborhood Association has won several awards planting trees along this road. (Both courtesy of Tricia Peacock, St. Andrew's Elementary School.)

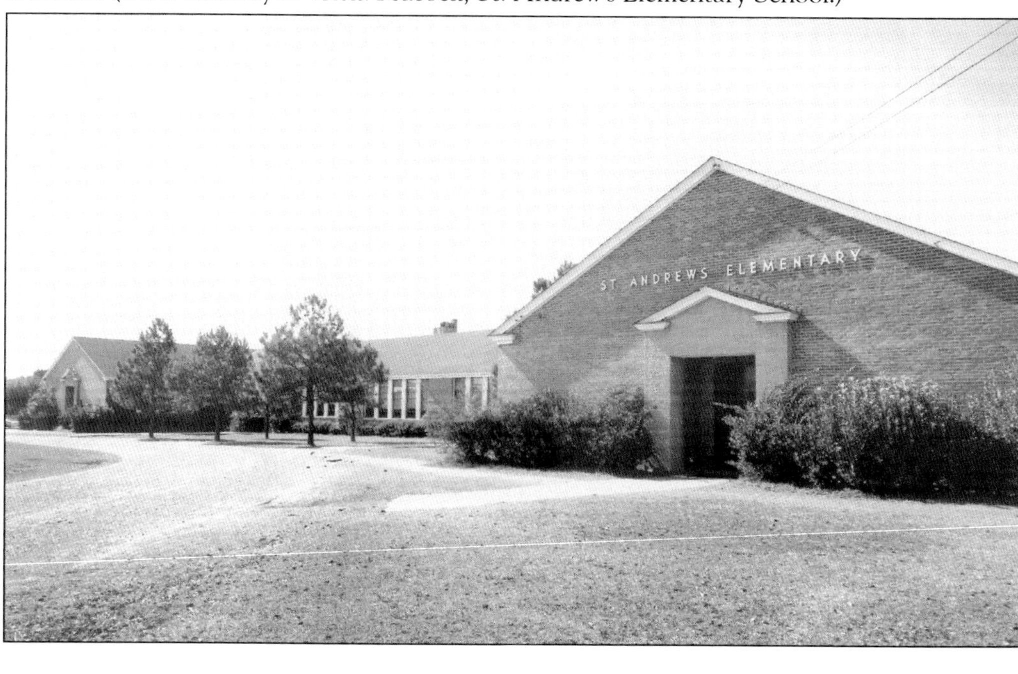

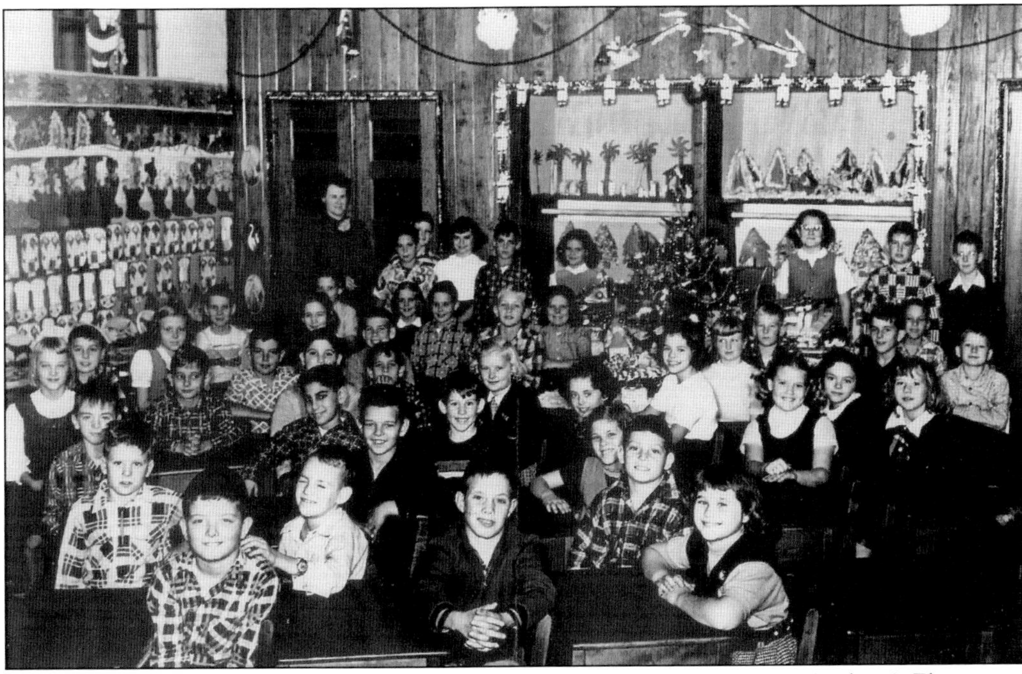

The children are all smiles in this early photograph of a classroom at St. Andrew's Elementary School. The room is elaborately decorated for Christmas, so maybe it is almost time for the holiday break from school. Perhaps they were excited about the upcoming Christmas program held in late December in the school cafeteria. Photographs of several generations of Christmas programs are in the care of the school. In the photograph below, there is a large choir in the foreground and a nativity scene set on the stage. Everyone is in a festive mood. (Both courtesy of Tricia Peacock, St. Andrew's Elementary School.)

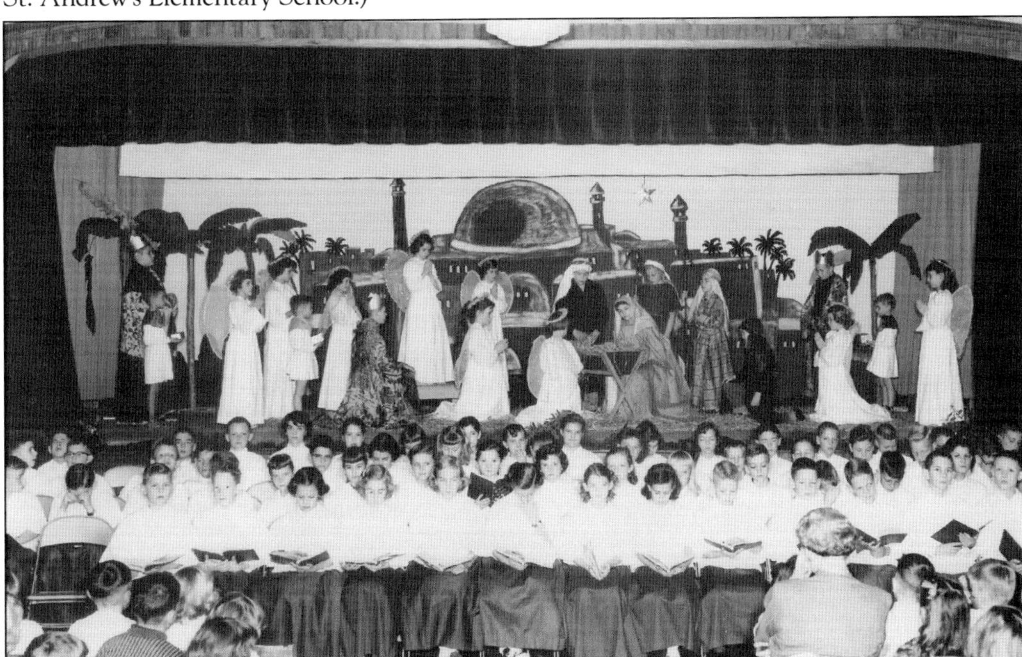

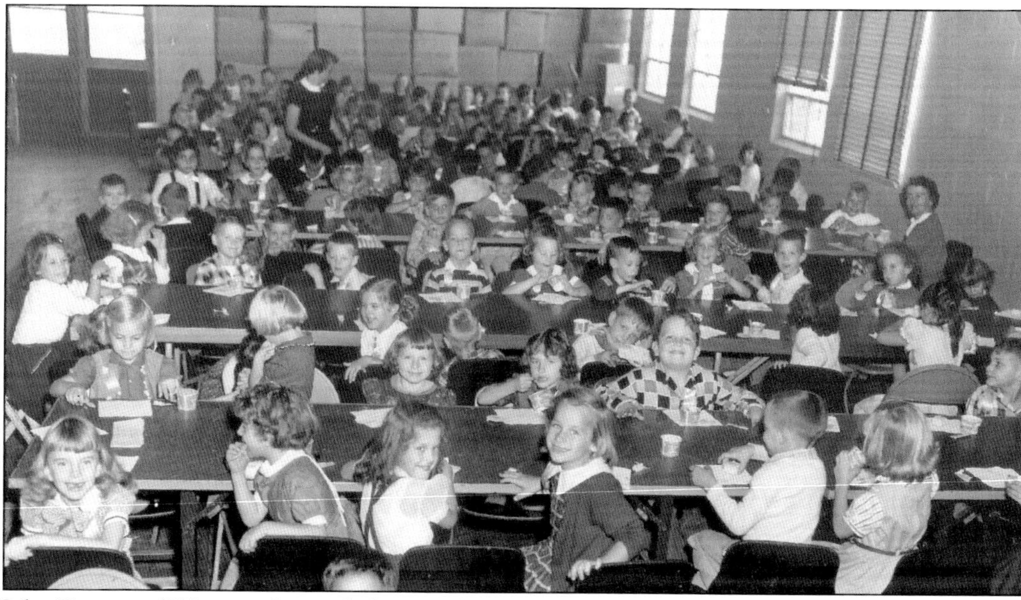

John Dimitri of Westwood attended St. Andrew's Elementary School. He recounts that he learned to hate spinach in this school cafeteria. These children seem to be enjoying their lunch break. In addition to serving its primary purpose of being a school cafeteria, this room serves as a gathering place for the community. St. Andrews fourth and fifth precincts vote at this location, neighborhood associations conduct meetings here, and public hearings are also held here. (Courtesy of Tricia Peacock, St. Andrew's Elementary School.)

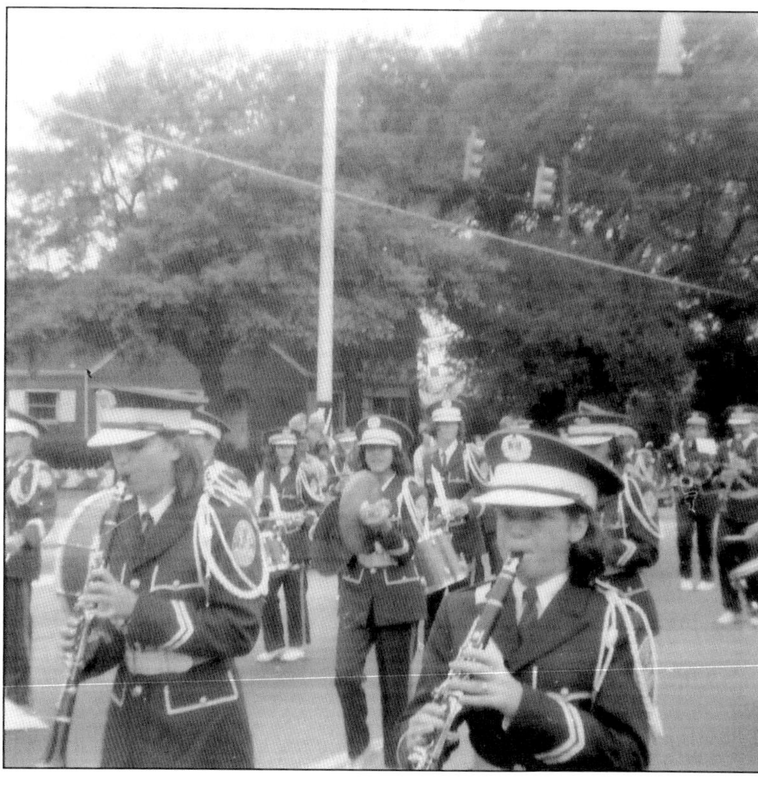

The Bishop England Band marches in the West Ashley Christmas Parade, a seasonal highlight for several years during the 1960s. The parade featured Santa and his reindeer and floats decorated by both the area businesses and the West Ashley Jaycees. In this mid-1960s photograph, the clarinet player on the left is Fay Nolen, whose family lived on Sothel Avenue in Byrnes Downs. (Courtesy of Peggy Bohne.)

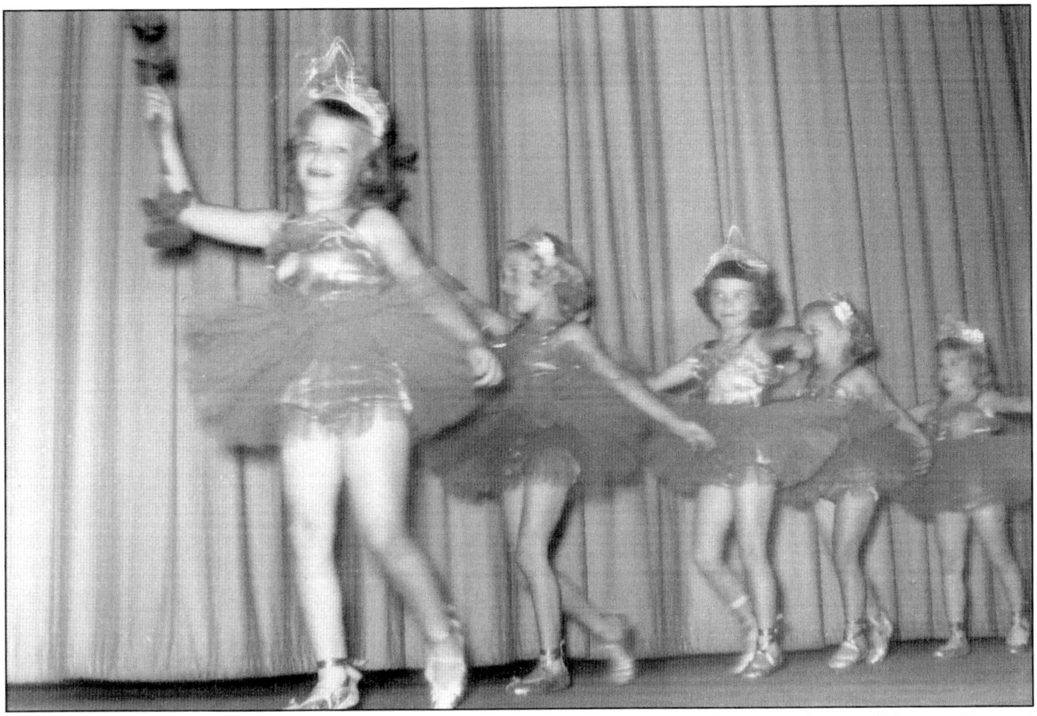

Peggy Bohne leads the dance line for the "Petite Ballerinas" during the 1958 Annual Dance Recital for Bette E. Saxton's School of Dance Arts. The recitals were held at Memminger Auditorium and culminated the year of dance instructions for the area girls. Bette E. Saxton's School of Dance Arts was located on Magnolia Road. Today Voodoo Tiki Bar and Lounge occupies the site. (Courtesy of Peggy Bohne.)

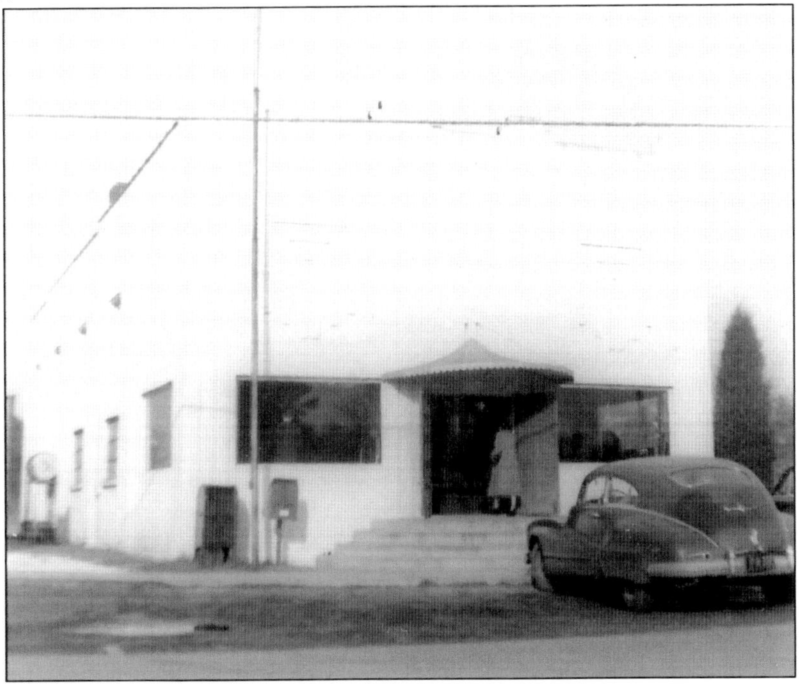

History Byrnes Downs Garden Club on page 66 features photographs of the new developments in the Byrnes Downs/Avondale business district. This photograph is of the new post office building. This building no longer exists in the Avondale area. (Courtesy of Margaret Thorne Seidler.)

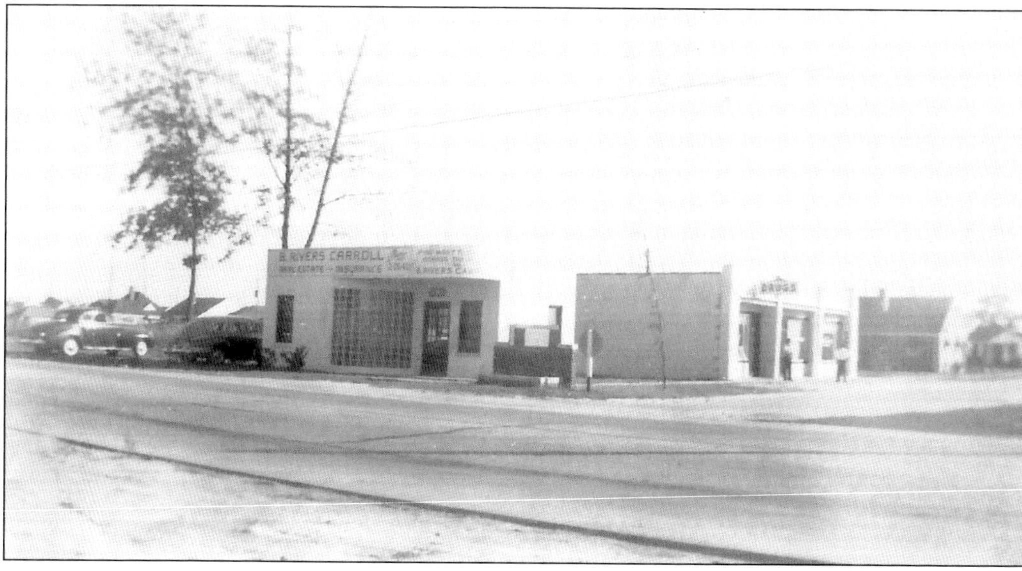

The ladies of the Garden Club were fastidious in their documentation of the development of not only the neighborhood, but also the businesses. The upper photograph shows the empty site next to B. Rivers Carroll's building where soon construction would begin on Rodenberg's. The Rodenberg family built a grocery store along Savannah Highway close to the corner of Daniel Street. The story is told that the Rodenbergs purchased the homes on Craven Avenue directly behind the store. The plan was to tear the homes down to make room for a larger parking lot. This plan was met with opposition from residents. Instead most of the backyards were transformed to pavement. This is the reason Alycia Alley is wider at the south end and that several homes at the south end of Craven Avenue have high fences and petite backyards. (Both courtesy of Margaret Thorne Seidler.)

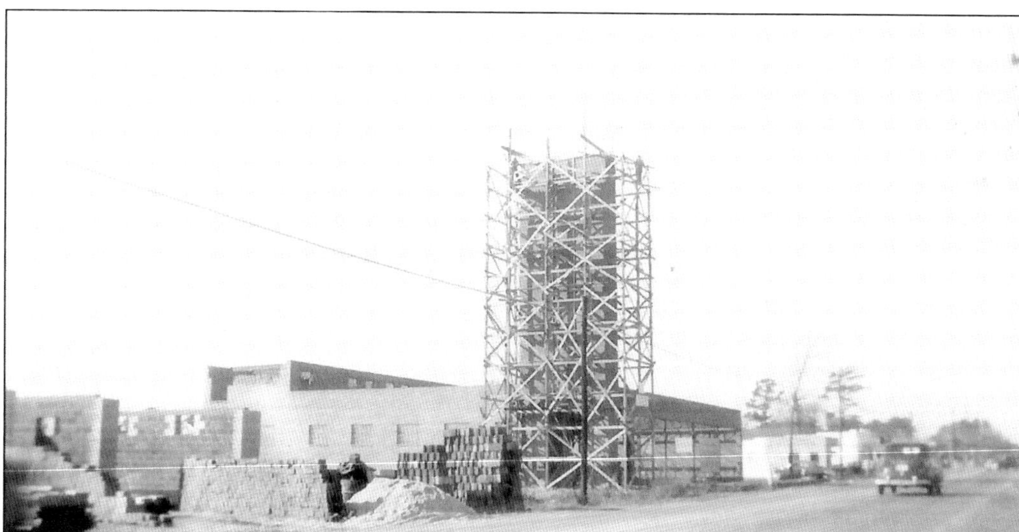

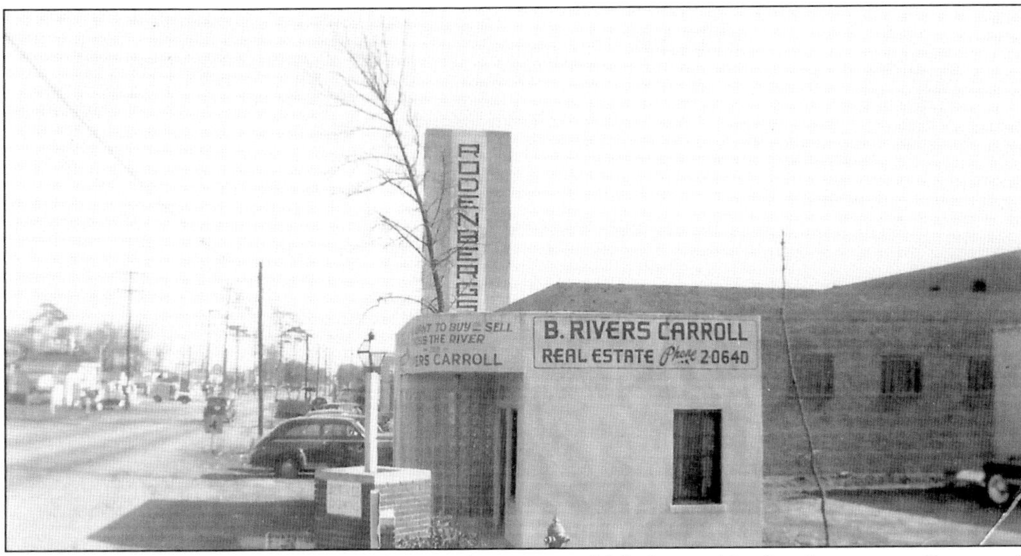

Looking north from the corner of Daniel Street and Highway 17, also known as Savannah Highway, one sees a two-lane highway, the Esso gas station, and cars parked in front of the new Rodenberg's grocery store. Featured prominently in the foreground is one of the brick columns that defined the street entrances to the neighborhood. Notice the gas lantern in the center of the column and the fenced-in planted area at the base of the column. According to the Garden Club scrapbook, "A Committee, headed by Mrs. T. J. Thorne Sr. made a house to house canvas to solicit funds to defray the expense of installation" of gaslights in the entrance columns. (Courtesy of Margaret Thorne Seidler.)

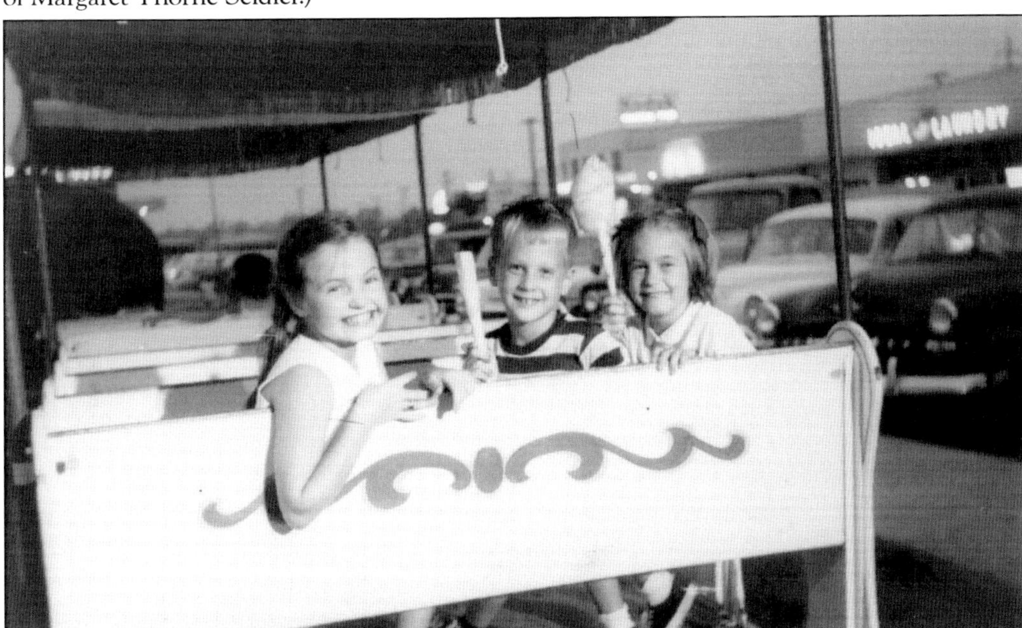

Cotton candy and a ride in a wagon pulled by an elephant put the smiles on the faces of Lynda Thorne (left), Robert Thomas, and Margaret Thorne. South Windermere Shopping Center hosted a fair in the parking lot to promote the center as a fun place for the family. Shopping, of course, was encouraged. (Courtesy of Margaret Thorne Seidler.)

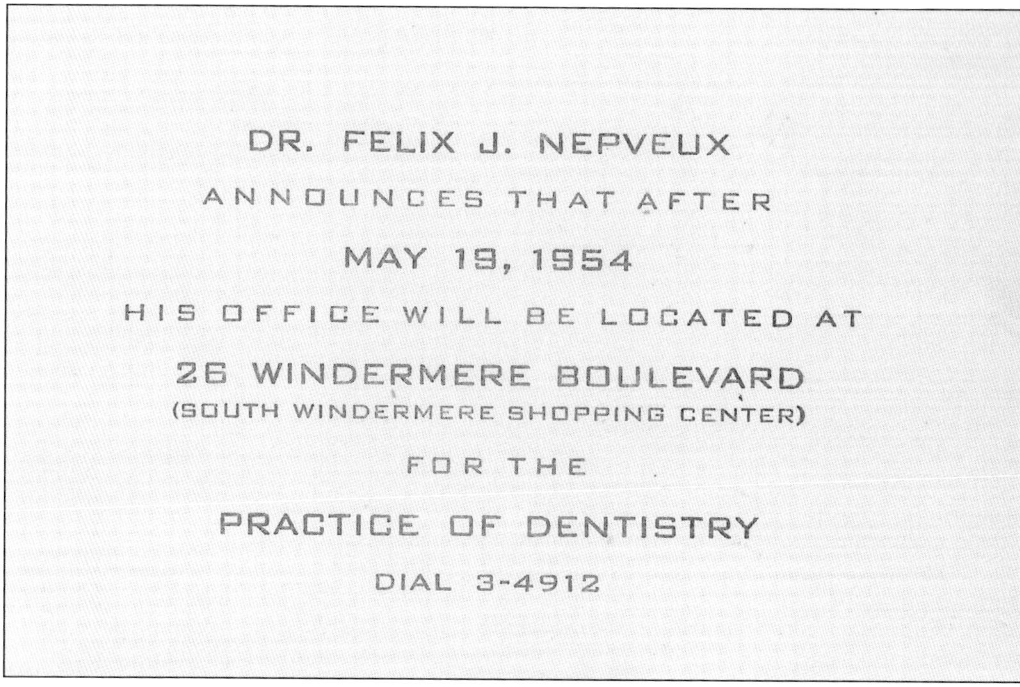

DR. FELIX J. NEPVEUX
ANNOUNCES THAT AFTER
MAY 19, 1954
HIS OFFICE WILL BE LOCATED AT
26 WINDERMERE BOULEVARD
(SOUTH WINDERMERE SHOPPING CENTER)
FOR THE
PRACTICE OF DENTISTRY
DIAL 3-4912

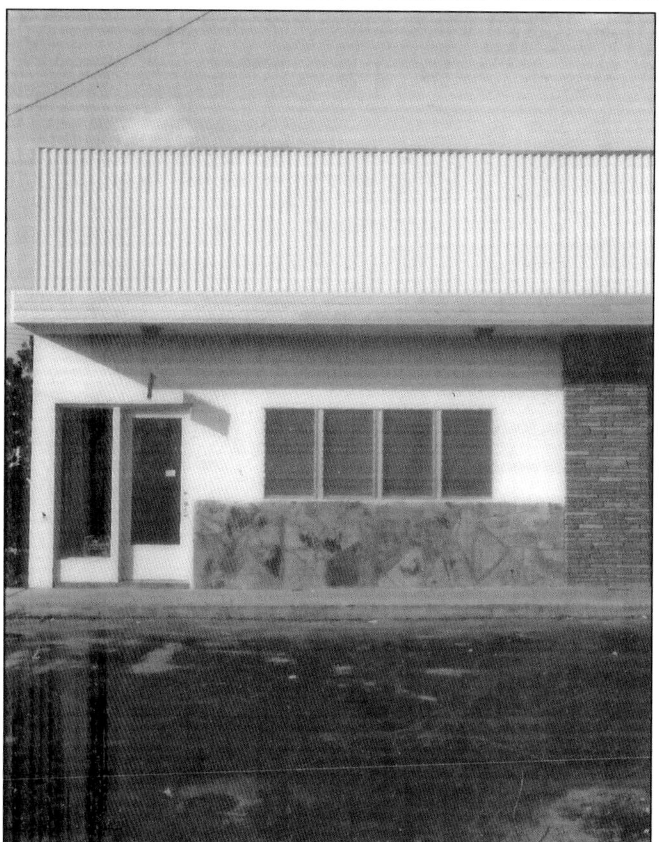

Felix Nepveux served as a dental surgeon in the U.S. Navy for nine years prior to opening his dental practice in the South Windermere Shopping Center on May 22, 1954, as seen in his formal announcement (above). His naval career included serving with the Fleet Marine Force in the Pacific and with the 1st Marine Division, where he participated in the Inchon Landing and battle for the Chosin reservoir. Felix retired from his dental practice in 1982, at which time he turned his attention to volunteer work, winning the Ann D. Edwards Volunteer of the Year award in 2000. His office at 26 South Windermere Boulevard is shown in the photographat left.(Both courtesy of Ethel Nepveux.)

Susan Ann Nepveux, Felix and Ethel's daughter, poses at the front door of her father's new office. At the time, his office was the last building in the section of the shopping center that parallels South Windermere Boulevard. The Nepveuxs lived at 28 Craven Avenue before purchasing their current home on Parish Road in the Moreland subdivision. (Courtesy of Ethel Nepveux.)

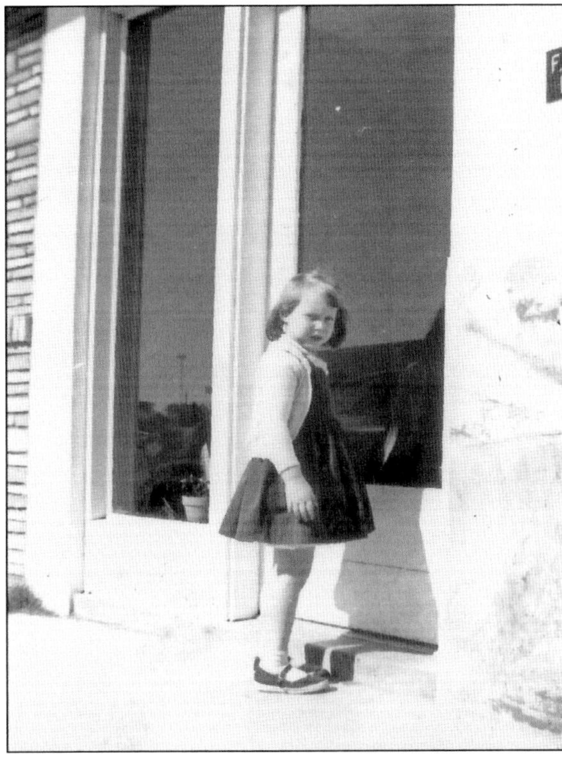

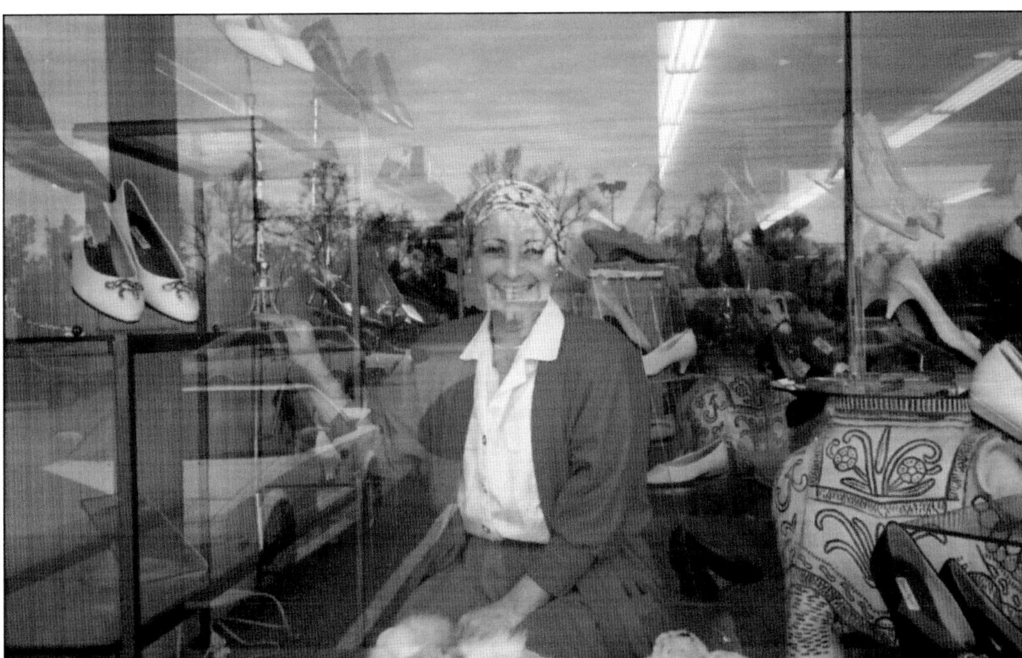

Missy Cohen Gold poses in the window of her father's store—Mr. Don's Shoes. Donald Cohen opened the store in the mid-1970s, and Missy runs the store today. She remembers Bill Ackerman, who developed the shopping center, coming every Saturday, leaning on the mailbox in front of the drugstore, and "holding court." (Courtesy of Missy Cohen Gold.)

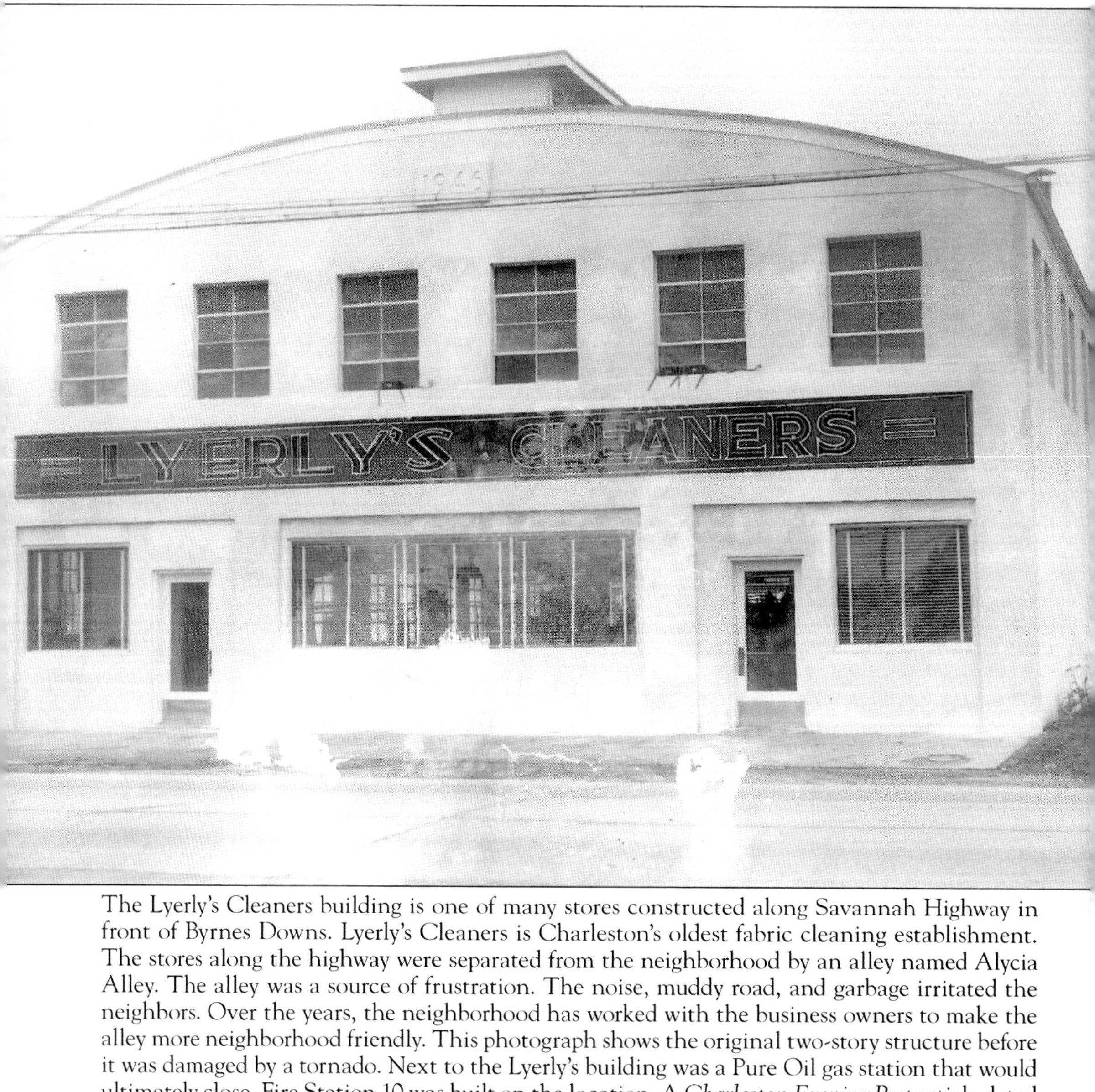

The Lyerly's Cleaners building is one of many stores constructed along Savannah Highway in front of Byrnes Downs. Lyerly's Cleaners is Charleston's oldest fabric cleaning establishment. The stores along the highway were separated from the neighborhood by an alley named Alycia Alley. The alley was a source of frustration. The noise, muddy road, and garbage irritated the neighbors. Over the years, the neighborhood has worked with the business owners to make the alley more neighborhood friendly. This photograph shows the original two-story structure before it was damaged by a tornado. Next to the Lyerly's building was a Pure Oil gas station that would ultimately close. Fire Station 10 was built on the location. A *Charleston Evening Post* article dated May 16, 1974, states that the station was designed to blend with the residential structures of Byrnes Downs. (Courtesy of Michael Rabin.)

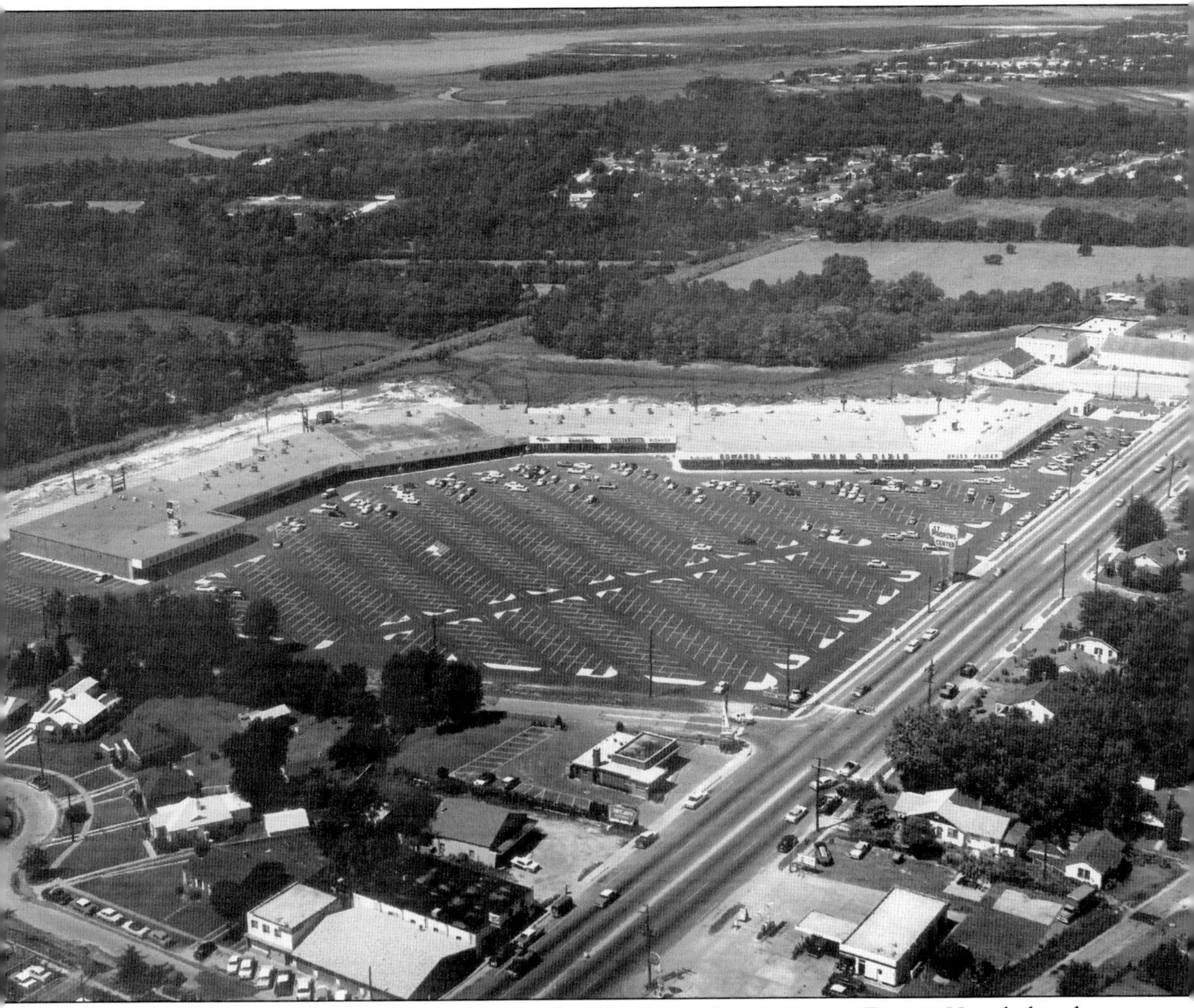

This spectacular aerial photograph highlights the new St. Andrew's Center. Francis Hanckel and Parish Realty Company developed the shopping center that opened in 1959. Grant's, Winn-Dixie, Colonial, Kerrison's Department Store, Lorraine's Children Shop, and Hook Line and Sinker were a few of the 29 establishments originally located in the center. The center also had spaces available for the community, offering meeting rooms and sponsoring Easter sunrise services. Today the center is owned and operated by the Kimco Corporation. Kimco Corporation has plans to give the center not only a face-lift that will include new facades, a landscaped parking lot, and an interior bus stop, but also some new tenants. Some of the storefronts on Daniel Street and a few of the Byrnes Downs homes along Timmerman Drive can be seen in the lower left corner of the photograph. (Courtesy of Frank Hanckel and Charlotte Hanckel Hay.)

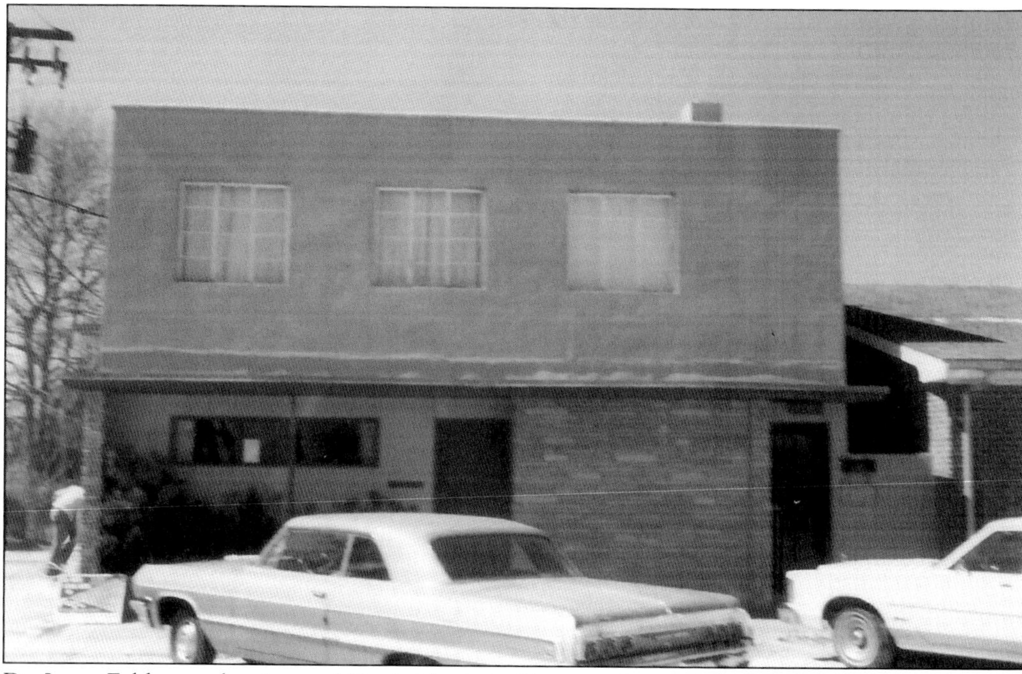

Dr. Leon Feldman, dentist, and Dr. J. Moultrie Townsend, general medicine, converted a store in the Avondale area to a medical office in 1949. J. Moultrie Townsend was known for marrying Joanna Little on June 6, 1944, D-Day. Their story was featured in an article published in the *News and Courier*. In 1953, Dr. Feldman purchased land on Daniel Street in Byrnes Downs from Jack Vane for $7,500. "A good investment," recounts Dr. Feldman. He built this structure to house his dental office and made the claim that his building was the first true dental office built in West Ashley. He practiced dentistry at this location until he retired in 1990. Today the building houses Dr. Chen's Skin Therapy Center. (Both courtesy of Leon Feldman.)

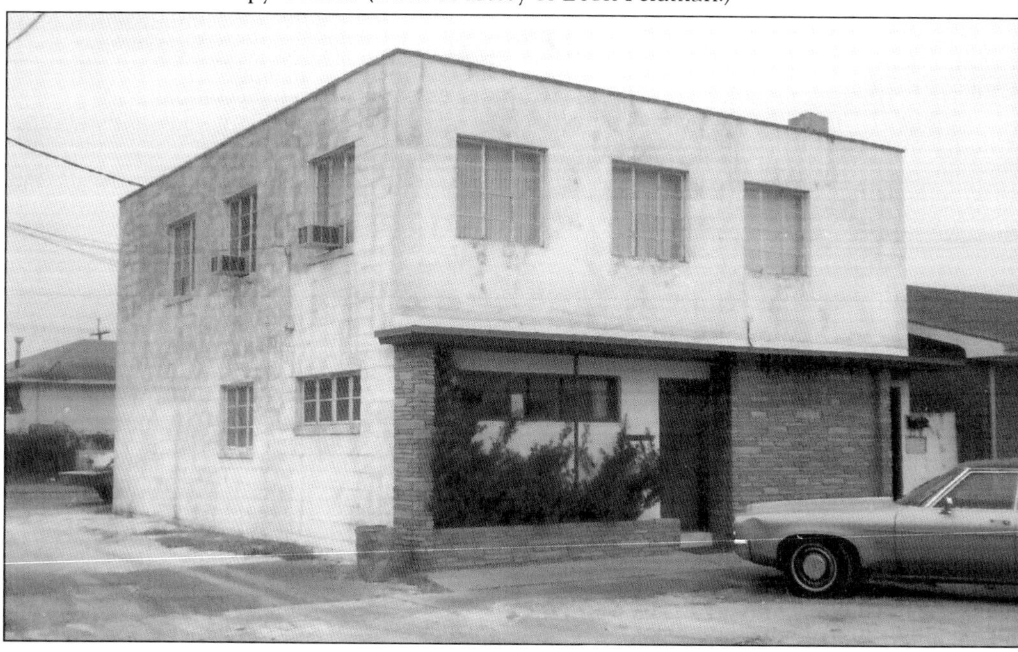

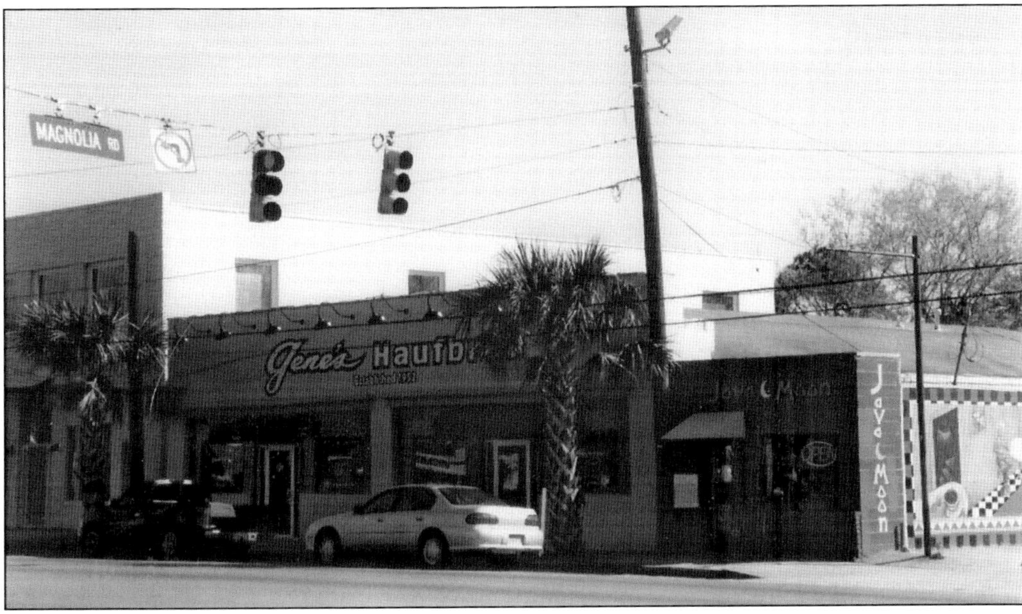

Gene's Haufbrau, established in 1952 and claiming to be Charleston's oldest bar, has long served as a local watering hole. During its history, it was a private club where one paid a membership fee and obtained a membership card and key for entry through the locked front door. The author's 1984–1985 "Member in Good Standing" card is shown here. In 2000, the new owners had the desire to restore Gene's to its original facade and interior. On February 8, 2001, the Byrnes Downs Neighborhood Association held a social event to see the newly restored Gene's Haufbrau. Once again, Gene's is the local watering hole, featuring a wide selection of beers, great wings, pool tables, and darts. In addition, Gene's hosts an annual Oktoberfest.

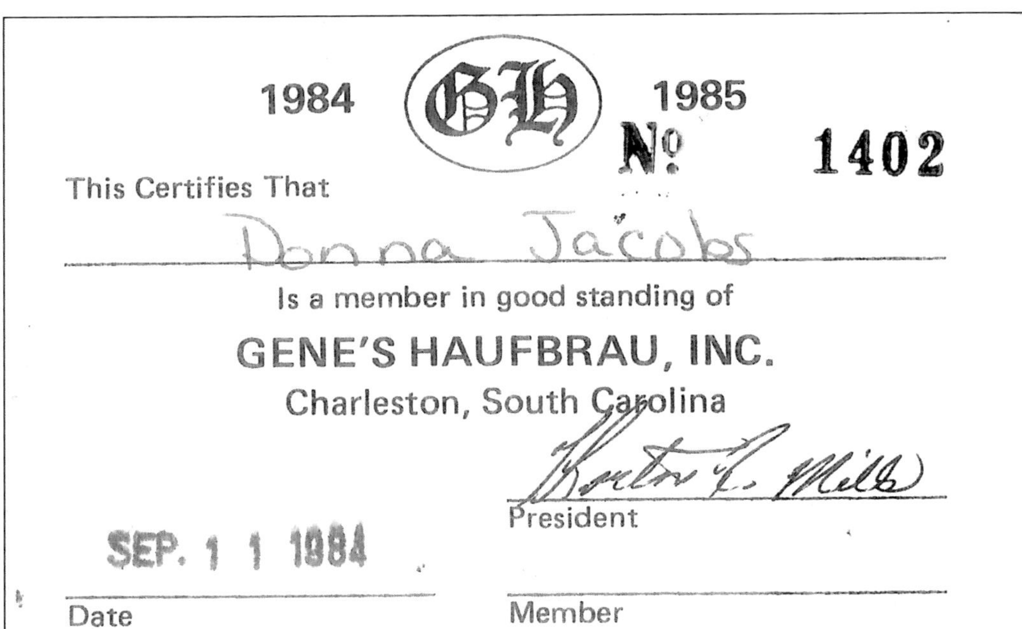

1984 GH 1985

№ 1402

This Certifies That

Donna Jacobs

Is a member in good standing of

GENE'S HAUFBRAU, INC.

Charleston, South Carolina

President

SEP. 1 1 1984

Date

Member

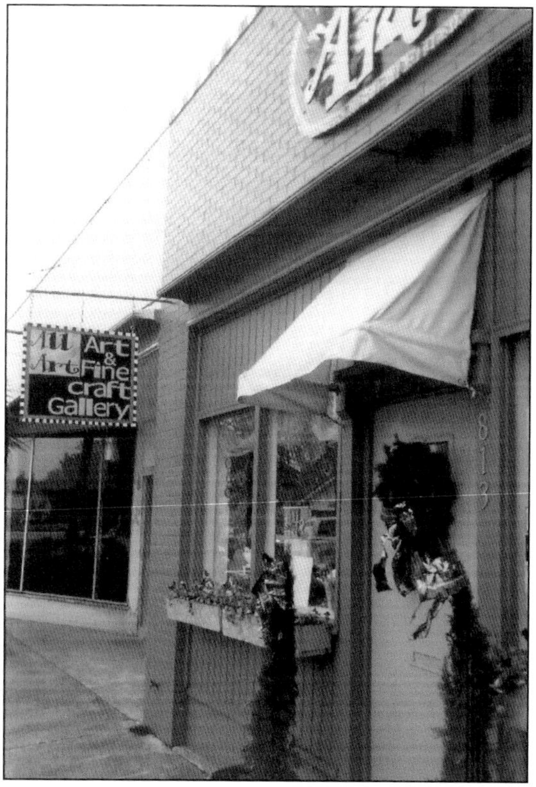

The once-thriving business area immediately adjacent to Byrnes Downs was in a state of decline for a few years in the 1980s and 1990s. Then in 2000, Nicole Elswick took a gamble on one small storefront that had once been a chiropractor's office and opened a funky and fresh store called All Art. The store was a hit, and other trendy establishments like Java Moon and Poe Studio quickly opened. Today Avondale Pointe is still a fun place to shop, taste wine, or dine.

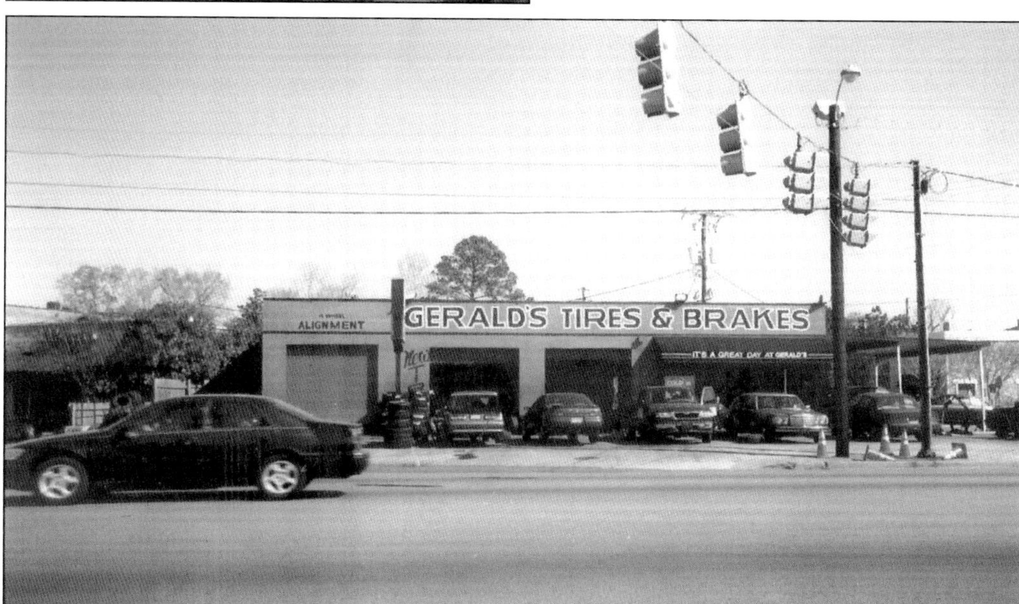

Across Savannah Highway from Byrnes Downs is the famous bright-orange building that houses Gerald's Tires. On May 2, 1986, two hundred photojournalists were commissioned to capture "A Day in the Life of America." The resulting photographs were published in a book with this title. At 6:30 p.m., Aaron Chang captured three workers holding tires in front of this Gerald's on Savannah Highway. The resulting photograph was published in the book.

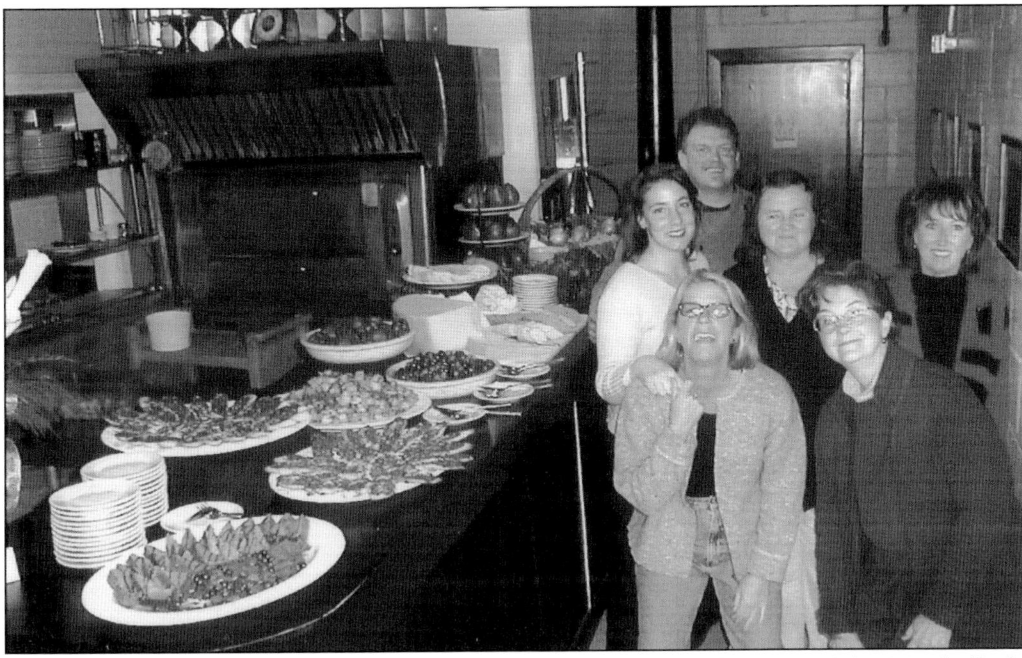

Al Di La, a Northern Italian trattoria, opened on Magnolia Road in 2002. John Marshall, the owner and head chef, invited the Byrnes Downs Neighborhood Association to come and sample his menu. Oh, what a treat it was! Cheeses, fresh-made focaccia bread, and asparagus risotto with grilled shrimp were just a few of the delectable amuses that John prepared for the neighbors. John poses with his food and some of the neighbors (above) while Chris and Lisa Jacobson enjoy a glass of wine and a plate of the delicious treats (below). *Al Di La* is Italian for "beyond." Byrnes Downs continues to look beyond its beginnings as new generations discover the neighborhood and create new pictures with fond memories.

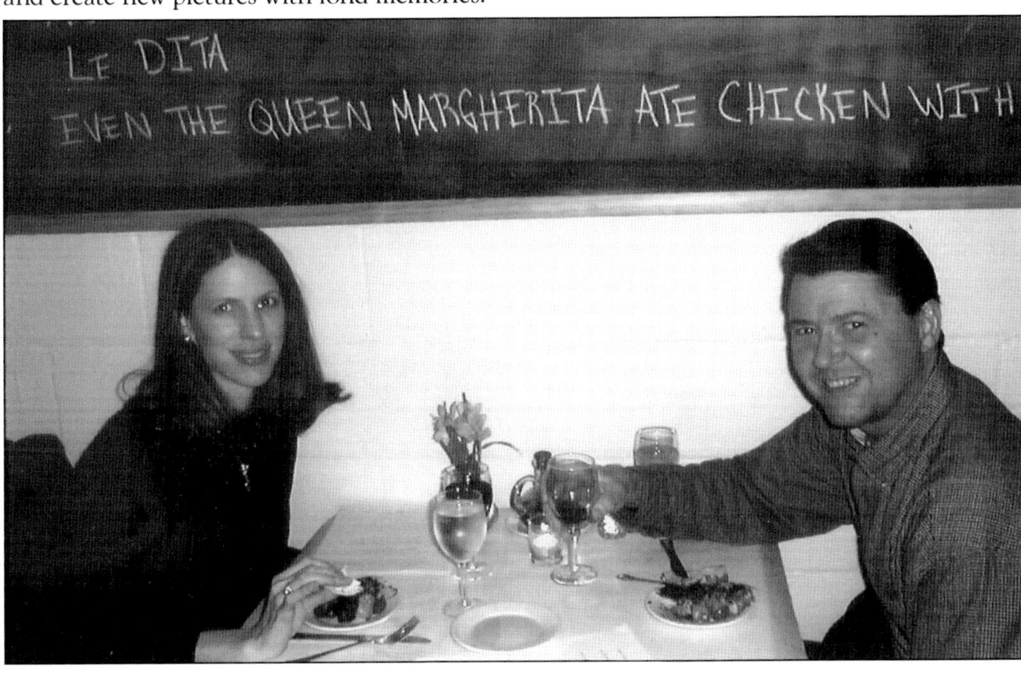

Consistent with our mission to preserve history on a local level, this book was printed in South Carolina on American-made paper and manufactured entirely in the United States. Products carrying the accredited Forest Stewardship Council (FSC) label are printed on 100 percent FSC-certified paper.

MADE IN THE USA